YES! Please enter a subscription to Volume 32-34, 1996 (3 issues) of *Cultural Critique* at the following rate:

Individual Rate: ○ US$38/£25 (Europe)
2-year subscription (1996 and 1997) at 1996 prices:
  ○ US$76/£50 (Europe)

Payment may be made by check, credit card, or money order (made payable to Oxford University Press). ○ Please bill me.
○ Payment enclosed ○ Charge my Amex/MasterCard/Visa

Card no.

Signature   Exp. date

Name

Address

City/State/Zip

Country

CULTURAL CRITIQUE

If card address differs from delivery address, please send details.

Orders must be accompanied by payment. The price includes handling and postage (US only). Subscriptions are entered on a per-volume basis only, and dispatch will commence only after receipt of correct payment. Subscriptions in Canada are now subject to the GST. Please add 7% to quoted prices. Personal subscriptions are available to individuals paying by personal check or credit card, and must not be donated to a library.

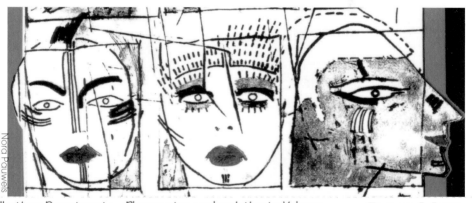

Nora Pauwels

1 8 0 0 8 5 2 7 3 2 3

Collections Department — Please enter a subscription to Volume 32-34, 1996 (3 issues) of *Cultural Critique*. It would be a valued and much used asset to our collection!

Name   Department

Signature

Annual Rate: ○ US$65/£44 (Europe)
2-year subscription (1996 and 1997) at 1996 prices:
  ○ US$130/£88 (Europe)

Library

Librarian

Address

City/State

Zip/Postcode   Country

Does **Y**our **L**ibrary **S**ubscribe**?**

Unfortunately, not all of the libraries that would benefit from a **Cultural Critique** subscription are currently receiving it!

You know how much you value your subscription; wouldn't your students and fellow collegues also benefit by having access to **Cultural Critique** in the library?

Help us reach those libraries who aren't currently subscribing by checking your institution's periodical list. If **Cultural Critique** is not currently included, please use this card to recommend a subscription.

Simply fill out this form and return it to us. We'll send your recommendation along with a free sample issue to your library.

SUBSCRIBE NOW TO CULTURAL CRITIQUE FOR TWO YEARS AT 1996 PRICES!
1-800-852-7323 OR
919-677-0977

Nora Pauwels

Cultural Critique

33

Helen M. Kim   **213**   *Strategic Credulity:* Oz *as Mass Cultural Parable*

Print and cover design: Nora Pauwels

Cultural Critique

Cultural Critique (ISSN 0882-4371) is published three times a year by Oxford University Press, 2001 Evans Road, Cary, NC 27513, in association with the Society for Cultural Critique, a nonprofit, educational organization.

Manuscript submissions. Contributors should submit three copies of their manuscripts to Abdul R. JanMohamed, *Cultural Critique*, c/o African American Studies Program, 305 HTC, University of California, Irvine, Irvine, CA 92717–6850. Manuscripts should conform to the recommendations of *The MLA Style Manual;* authors should use parenthetical documentation with a list of works cited. Contact the editorial office at the address above for further instructions on style. Manuscripts will be returned if accompanied by a stamped, self-addressed envelope. Please allow a minimum of four months for editorial consideration.

Subscriptions. Subscriptions are available on a calendar-year basis. The annual rates (Issues 32–34, 1996) are £25 (UK & Europe), US$38 for individuals, and £44 (UK & Europe), US $65 for institutions. Single issues are available for £10 (UK & Europe), US$15 (USA and elsewhere) for individuals, and £17 (UK & Europe), US$25 (USA and elsewhere) for institutions. All prices include postage.

Personal rates apply only when issues of the journal are sent to a private address and payment is made by personal check or credit card. All subscription, single issue, back issue, changes-of-address, and claims for missing issues should be sent to:

NORTH AMERICA: Oxford University Press, Journals Subscriptions Department, 2001 Evans Road, Cary, NC 27513, USA. Toll-free in the USA and Canada 1-800-852-7323 or 919-677-0977. Fax: 919-677-1714. E-mail: jnlorders @oup-usa.org.

ELSEWHERE: Oxford University Press, Journals Subscriptions Department, Walton St., Oxford OX2 6DP, UK. Tel: +44 1865 267907. Fax: +44 1865 267485. E-mail: jnl.orders @oup.co.uk.

Advertising. Jane Parker, Oxford University Press, Journals Advertising, Walton St., Oxford OX2 6DP, UK. Fax: +44 1865 267835.

Indexing/abstracting. *Cultural Critique* is indexed/abstracted in *The Left Index, Alternative Press Index, Sociological Abstracts* (*SA*), *Social Welfare, Social Planning/Policy and Social Development* (*SOPODA*), *International Political Science Abstracts, MLA Directory of Periodicals, MLA International Bibliography,* and *Periodica Islamica.*

Postmaster. Send address changes to Journals Subscriptions Department, Oxford University Press, 2001 Evans Road, Cary, NC 27513. Postage paid at Cary, NC, and additional post offices. *Cultural Critique* is distributed by Mercury Airfreight International Ltd., 22900-112 Shaw Road, Sterling, VA 20166.

Permission requests and photocopies. All rights reserved; no part of this publication may be reproduced, stored in a retrieval system, or transmitted in any form or by any means, electronic, mechanical, photocopying, recording, or otherwise without either the prior written permission of the publisher (Oxford University Press, Permissions, Journals Subscriptions Department, Walton St., Oxford OX2 6DP, UK. Tel: +44 1865 56767. Fax: +44 1865 267773) or a license permitting restricted copying issued in the UK by the Copyright Licensing Agency Ltd., 90 Tottenham Court Road, London W1P 9HE, or in the USA by the Copyright Clearance Center, 222 Rosewood Drive, Danvers, MA 01923. Fax: 508-750-4744.

⊗ The journal is printed on acid-free paper that meets the minimum requirements of ANSI Standard Z39.48-1984 (Permanence of Paper), beginning with Number 1.

Copyright. It is a condition of publication in the Journal that authors assign copyright to Oxford University Press. This ensures that requests from third parties to reproduce articles are handled efficiently and consistently and will also allow the article to be as widely disseminated as possible. In assigning copyright, authors may use their own material in other publications provided that the journal is acknowledged as the original place of publication and Oxford University Press is notified in writing and in advance.
Copyright © 1996 by *Cultural Critique*. All rights reserved.

The Commodity-Body-Sign: Toward a General Economy of "Commodity Fetishism"

Robert Miklitsch

The following article attempts to formulate what I call a critical affirmative account of, among other things but most especially, commodity fetishism.

The most influential attempt, at least within the Frankfurt School, to come to terms with the problem of affirmation is Herbert Marcuse's "Affirmative Character of Culture." Even though Marcuse performs the, by now familiar, negative critique of commodity culture, he also broaches—in a distinctly pre-post-modernist vein—the question of the body. This attention to the material exorbitance of the body reintroduces one of the master concepts of the discourse of classical Marxism, the *commodity-body*, in which the commodity refers to exchange-value and the body to use-value. I begin there.

After a brief review of Freud and Marx respectively on fetishism and commodity fetishism, I enlist the work of Jean Baudrillard in order to formulate what, after Marx, I call the "perverse," general economy of the commodity-body-sign, where sign-value is the supplement or super-signifier of use-exchange value. The point

© 1996 by *Cultural Critique*. Spring 1996. 0882-4371/96/$5.00.

here is not so much to deconstruct the ostensibly restricted political economy of use-exchange value, as in Baudrillard, as to figure a way to "produce" an alternative conception of consumption as "cultural sign labor." This is not, it is important to emphasize, yet another version of "cultural populism"; in fact, precisely because of the excesses associated with "reception" and "audience studies," I return in the penultimate segment, "Consumption *Redux*," to Marx's programmatic remarks in the *Grundrisse* and *Capital* in order to situate this "affirmative" reading of consumption and commodity fetishism within a determinate, critical context. Further, in the last segment of the essay, I return to the issue of production, reworking sign-value in terms of the still valuable concept of contradiction as well as, equally or more importantly, the "real" of capitalism: the production of surplus-value. This segment on the so-called *rapports de production,* therefore, serves a dual purpose: to punctuate the uncritical drift toward affirmation in contemporary cultural theory and, at the same time, to proffer a more flexible model of the economic than is offered in either classical Marxism or cultural studies. Since a general economy of "commodity fetishism" must, as I see it, be dialectically attentive not only to production and consumption but, in addition to this conventional binary opposition, distribution and circulation, the conclusion to the essay also considers the political implications of the determinate "real"-ization of sign value, in particular the necessity of elaborating a revised concept of commodity fetishism from an emphatically global perspective, what Marx calls the "total circuit of capital."

* * *

The commodity appears, at first sight, a very trivial thing, and easily understood. Its analysis shows that it is, in reality, a very queer thing.

—Marx, *Capital* (1867)

[T]he extraordinarily wide dissemination of the perversions forces us to suppose that the disposition to perversion is of no great rarity but must form a part of what passes as the normal constitution.

—Freud, *Three Essays on the Theory of Sexuality* (1905)

[T]he fetishization of the commodity is the fetishization of a product emptied of its concrete substance of labor and sub-

jected to another type of labor, a labor of signification, that is, of coded abstraction (the production of differences and of sign values).
　　　　　—Baudrillard, *For a Critique of the Political Economy of the Sign* (1972)

From Negation to Affirmation

Whether the logic of negation is understood in its originary, Hegelian form or in that late, nonsynthetic version which goes by the name of "negative dialectics," its history from Hegel to Adorno illustrates the limits of any dialectic that privileges either the false, because teleologically recuperated, positivities of sublation or the superreflexive gyrostatics of negativity "for itself." The play of affirmation associated with the "work" of Nietzsche appears to represent a displacement of, if not an escape from, these negative-driven dialectics, but even Gilles Deleuze's concept of "double-affirmation"—one of the most searching readings of Nietzsche—indicates that this militantly anti-Hegelian practice is subject to the same limits as its Adornian, late Hegelian Other.

Although the above philosophies sometimes suggest that the answer to the aporia of negation/affirmation lies in logic, the classical Marxist position has always been that the solution to any social problem—and the issue of affirmation is ultimately a social rather than philosophical problem—does not lie with what Gayatri Spivak calls "mere philosophical justice" (162).[1] Among other things, the problem of affirmation cannot be divorced from its historical conditions of possibility. Hence, in a now familiar move that explicitly acknowledges its discursive debt, and in the process affirms, *contra* Habermas, the possibility of a materialist dialectic, Fredric Jameson reiterates Marx's "definitive" reconstruction of Hegel's distinction between "individual morality" (*Moralität*) and the "very different realm of collective social values and practices" (*Sittlichkeit*):

> In a well-known passage Marx powerfully urges us to do the impossible, namely, to think [the historical development of capitalism and the development of a specific bourgeois culture] positively *and* negatively all at once; to achieve, in other

words, a type of thinking that would be capable of grasping the demonstrably baleful features of capitalism along with its extraordinary and liberating dynamism simultaneously within a single thought, and without attenuating any of the force of either judgment. (47)

According to Jameson, the Marx (and Engels) of the *Manifesto* (1848) "teach the hard lesson of some more genuinely dialectical way to think historical development as change"—more genuinely dialectical, that is, than either Hegel's or Nietzsche's, Adorno's or Deleuze's way.

The object of this "austere dialectical imperative," however, is not industrial capitalism, as in Marx, but late capitalism, which represents the so-called third, multinational mutation of capitalism, as in Jameson. And yet, if—as Andreas Huyssen observes in "Mapping the Postmodern" (1984)—the culture of postmodernity "must be grasped in its gains as well as in its losses, in its promises as well as in its deprivations," one of the primary effects of postmodernism is that the "relationship between progress and destruction of cultural forces, between tradition and modernity, can no longer be understood today the same way Marx understood it at the dawn of modernist culture" (200). Indeed, for Huyssen, the relation between "culture" and "capitalism" has itself changed, so much so that Jameson's rather orthodox, economistic "logic of late capitalism" must be reconceived in order to account effectively for this changed relation.

Accordingly, Huyssen in the conclusion to his essay advances his critique of both a strictly negative *and* classical-dialectical "postmodernism of resistance":

> [R]esistance cannot be defined simply in terms of negativity or non-identity *à la* Adorno, nor will the litanies of a totalizing, collective project suffice. At the same time, the very notion of resistance may itself be problematic in its simple position to affirmation. After all, there are affirmative forms of resistance and resisting forms of affirmation. (20–21)

Although Huyssen adds that the last may be more of a "semantic problem" than a "problem of practice," his concluding chiasmus— "affirmative forms of resistance and resisting forms of affirmation"—perfectly captures the logical complexity of postmodernism even as it marks the limits of just such an abstract formulation. The latter effect, I think, bears repeating because even Huyssen's "mapping of the postmodern"—still one of the most nuanced and dialectical readings of postmodernism—betrays, it seems to me, a residual modernist politics: a "good" alternative postmodernism *versus* a "bad" affirmative postmodernism. Seemingly despite itself, then—despite, that is, the subtlety of its conclusion—"Mapping the Postmodern" ends up rehearsing the Frankfurt-School critique of affirmation.

Since this critique remains influential, if only as a ghost to be ritually and uncritically exorcized in the recent cultural-populist phase of cultural studies, I want briefly to take up the essay from which, together with Adorno's work, so much of the critique of affirmation derives: Marcuse's "Affirmative Character of Culture" (1937).

Affirmative culture—what is it? What, to be exact, does such a culture *affirm*?

According to Marcuse, affirmative culture is that culture of the bourgeois epoch which led in the course of its own development to the segregation from civilization of the mental and spiritual world as an independent realm of *value*" ("Affirmative" 95, emphasis mine). More specifically, affirmative culture certifies the value of culture as such (*Kultur*)—of, in other words, "spiritual" values such as the Good, the Beautiful, and the True—against those "material" values that define "civilization" (*Zivilisation*). In an epigram: *Geist* is good, body bad. Or, as Marcuse himself puts it: "in affirmative culture, the 'soulless" regions do not belong to culture [but] like every other commodity . . . are openly abandoned to the economic law of value" ("Affirmative" 117).

Marcuse's negative reading of "affirmative culture" is by no means monolithic, though, since the body for him can provide an "anticipatory memory" of nonaffirmative culture. That is, when the body becomes an "instrument of pleasure" rather than an "instrument of labor" (when, in other words, the "production of pleasure" is not in the direct service of profit and reproduction), it counters that systematic commodification of bodies, i.e., wage-labor, from which the affirmative-cultural ideal derives its force.

Of course, if the body can adopt an affirmative role, it also always bears the burden of—as Marcuse's own negative-driven dialectic implies—the surplus-repressive aspects of commodification. For instance, in what I take to be an exemplary text in this regard (since the accent, despite the above negativity, is on the positive position), Marcuse's *Essay on Liberation* (1969) proposes that the "counterrevolution" is rooted in "second nature," in—to be precise—that socially instinctual structure which materializes with the advent of consumer capitalism and its aggressive libidinal politics. If a new culture is, therefore, to emerge, it is necessary to transform not only the "old," exploitative modes of production, but to create new, nondominative modes of consumption and thereby new instinctual needs and satisfactions as well—in a word, a "new Subject."

Marcuse's vision may well be utopian (in the pejorative sense), but for all its limitations, not the least of which is the habitual Frankfurt-School valorization of the aesthetic, it still speaks to us, because spectacular consumption has, in fact, become—at least for many of us in the first world—"second nature" and, more importantly perhaps, because liberatory strategies of the sort essayed in Marcuse's later work constitute an increasingly valuable resource for the "new" New Left.

Given the ineluctably linked critique of "commodity fetishism" and "affirmative culture," it may be useful to turn for a moment to Freud, whose seminal essay on fetishism suggests one way beyond the theoretical impasse of the Frankfurt School position. I should add that this turn represents not only a return to the question or logic of negation, from which, clearly there is no escape, but a turn to a topic that I will argue is central to the problem of affirmation: the commodity-body (*Körper der Ware*).[2]

Turn: Freud, Marx, Baudrillard, or Toward a General Economy of "Commodity Fetishism"

With respect to fetishism, the "model perversion," for Michel Foucault (114),[3] one cannot, I suspect, overestimate the *value* of this particular "aberration" for psychoanalysis. But don't take my word for it, take Freud's: "No other variation of the sexual instinct that borders on the pathological can lay so much claim to our interest as this one, such is the peculiarity of the phenomena to which it gives rise" (*Three Essays* 201).

Insofar as fetishism is itself an instance of "sexual overvaluation," Freud's valorization of it in *The Three Essays on Sexuality* (1905) is worth remarking not simply because it evokes the whole machinery of repression but because it ostensibly "proves" one of the master tropes of the discipline of psychoanalysis: "the existence of the castration complex" (*der Existenz des Kastrationskomplexes* ["Fetishism" 201]). This, the castration complex, can be reduced— without, I think, doing too much violation to Freud's text—to the following negative thesis: "a woman has no penis" (*das Weib [besitzt] keinen Penis* ["Fetishism" 199]). With this strategic reduction, one might say that if fetishism is the "negation" of castration, this negation also always affirms the existence of that which fetishism serves to deny. As Freud himself puts it: "[a]version [*Entfremdung*] from the real female genitals [*wirkliche weibliche Genitale*], . . . remains as an indelible stigma of the repression [*Verdrängung*] that has taken place" ("Fetishism" 200).

Fetishism, then, is not simply a negation of the negation—of, that is, castration—but an affirmation of sexual difference as such (so-called "primary castration").[4] Put another, less orthodox way: the fetish is at once a "substitute for the woman's (mother's) phallus" (*der Ersatz für den Phallus des Weibes [der Mutter]*) and a displaced index of that *complex* of organs which distinguishes the woman's body, where this corporeal complex is not, *pace* Freud, simply the clitoris, "the real little penis" (*der reale kleine Penis*), but the "clitoris *and* vagina, the lips *and* the vulva" (L. Williams 116).[5]

Now, to broach such an antithetical reading of Freud is, I might add, neither to attempt to recuperate classical psychoanalysis and its phallogocentric economy nor to consolidate Foucault's critique of this particular discipline of desire in *The History of Sexuality* (1978). Hence, to expatiate on the latter critique, if it is true— as *The History of Sexuality* argues—that the discourse of Freudianism is itself repressive since it represents yet another moment in the "deployment of sexuality," Foucault's own polemical, productive-affirmative reading of sexuality also *underestimates* the very real force of psychic repression,[6] the material effects of which discourse classical psychoanalysis has historically been at pains to test and contest.

Unlike Foucault, Jean Baudrillard—or at least the Baudrillard of *For a Critique of the Political Economy of the Sign* (1972)—is rather less dismissive of psychoanalysis and, thus, is more sensitive to its still considerable conceptual resources. In, for instance, "Fetishism and Ideology," he submits that among the "social sciences," only psychoanalysis has escaped that "vicious circle" of "magical thinking" (*pensée magique*), which inevitably seems to trap whomever tries to refunction the concept-metaphor of fetishism. More importantly, the psychoanalytic definition of fetishism as a "perverse *structure*" makes possible a general economy[7] of "perversion," which, in turn, helps explains the "generalized 'fetishization' of real life" associated with the emergence of late capitalism.

I will take up Baudrillard's general "theory of perversion" in more detail below, but I want first to review Marx's understanding of commodity fetishism, since this economic concept is not only one of the master-concepts of Marxism but one of the objects of Baudrillard's "critique of the political economy of the sign."

The centerpiece of the Marxian analytic is, of course, the section on the "secret" of "the fetishism of commodities" (*der Fetischcharakter der Ware*) in the first volume of *Capital*. There, Marx contends that the "mystical," "enigmatic character" of commodities originates not in their "use-" but their "exchange-value" (*Gebrauchswert/Tauschwert*). Moreover, precisely because the commodity represents a *perversion* of that article of utility from which it derives its interest or use-value,[8] it is a "very queer thing" (*sehr vertracktes Ding* [*Capital* I 61]).[9] Thus, in an extraordinary passage, Marx writes that if commodities could speak, they would say: "Our use-value may be a thing that interests men. It is no part of us as objects" (*Capital* I 83). And in his almost equally extraordinary reading of Baudelaire, Benjamin adds that when the "commodity whispers to a poor wretch who passes a shop-window containing beautiful and expensive things," these fetish-objects are not interested in the "poor" subject of consumption: "They do not empathize with him" (5).

Thus, for Marx as for Benjamin, commodity fetishism can be said to constitute a "negation" of exploitation—a negation, that is, of the abstract human labor-power incorporated in use-value. As such, this negation not only effects the *erasure of a genesis, the obliteration of a history*" (Goux 33) but is itself an instance of alienation. Humans, like the goods and services they consume, become things: "It is with the human being as with the commodity" (*Capital* I 23).

At the same time (to attempt to problematize what I take to be a residual naturalism in Marx), commodity fetishism also always testifies to the "*detour of exchange.*"[10] Such a "general or elementary logic" of substitution suggests, in turn, that commodities can function as fetishes only because use-value itself is a *thing* that "interests" people. In other words, that "original" article of utility which "subjectively" incarnates use-value is always already an *object* of exchange. From this last, critical perspective, one can say—as Baudrillard does—that the commodity-fetishist metaphor and its restricted economy naturalize rather than historicize utility, since use-value itself is only the "*satellite* and *alibi* of exchange value" (*Critique* 139).

However, from another perspective offered by a sumptuary as opposed to subsistence or exchange economy, the commodity-body assumes a different character or, more to the point, form. To wit: if the "*logic of the commodity and political economy is at the very heart of the sign*" (i.e., the sign-form traverses both the "object-" and "commodity-form") and if the "*structure of the sign is at the very heart of the commodity form*" (i.e., a general sign-code differentially structures the exchange of both utility and commodity [*Critique* 146]),[11] then "sign-value" (*valeur signe*) can be said to reaffirm the "body" of the commodity. In this sense, sign-value is, strictly speaking, a supersignifier of use-exchange value, where—and this is crucial for a political-materialist sense of fetishism—the signifier itself is not without a certain materiality, however residual or "synthetic."

I will return to the problem of sign-value a little later in this essay, a problem that any general theory of fetishism which proposes to retain a critical purchase on capital must engage, but I will only observe here that the concept of sign-value does not wholly negate the concept of use-value. Even though Baudrillard tends to valorize sign-exchange-value (*valeur d'échange signe*) at the expense of use-value in order to argue for the "beyond" of sign-value (symbolic exchange is, for Baudrillard, *au-dela de la valeur*), Spivak has persuasively argued the case for the theoretical "utility" of use-value. As she observes in "Scattered Speculations on the Question of Value" (1985), use-value is simultaneously "outside and inside the system of value determinations" and, as such, "puts the entire chain of Value into question" (123). The result of this tactical deconstruction of use-value and consequent "textualiza-tion" of value in general is what Spivak calls, after Marx *and* Der-rida, the "economic text 'under erasure'" (168). Therefore, where Baudrillard speaks of sign-value, Spivak speaks of ~~use-value~~ (*sous rature*) or "use-value" (in quotations).

Given this *re*-conceptualization of use-value, the value, as it were, of Baudrillard's concept of sign-value is that, unlike the classical-Marxist, not to say classical-economist, sense of the term (use-value derives, of course, from Adam Smith), sign-value articu-lates a new, distinctive "moment" in the history of the commodity-body. This moment is postmodernity or, to accent its "aesthetic" aspect, postmodernism, a period which constitutes, as we have seen, the "cultural logic of late capitalism" (Jameson). At the same time, sign-value—which is linked for Baudrillard to the simula-crum—is "beyond" both use-value and any economic theory, such as Jameson's, which deploys the economic, here "late capitalism," as a "concept of the last resort" (Spivak 168). In fact, if, as Spivak claims, the "logical progression to accumulation can only be oper-ated by its own rupture, releasing the commodity from the circuit of capital production into consumption as a *simulacrum* of use-value" (Spivak 167, emphasis mine), sign-value is, *stricto sensu, the* simulacrum of use-value. In other words, sign-value is a simula-crum of the "body" of use-value, or: the commodity's body-*image*.

The Commodity-Body-Sign

Although Baudrillard's theorization of a general economy of perversion or fetishism represents an overt critique of the "re-stricted economy" of classical Marxism as well as the almost equally restricted economy, derived from Mandel, that underpins Jame-son's understanding of postmodernism as the "cultural logic of late capitalism," the peculiar status of sign-value is that it *represents* both a negation and affirmation of the commodity-body—of, that is to say, use-value (body) and exchange-value (commodity).

This, the supersublative status of sign-value, can perhaps best be seen in the post-Frankfurt School account of commodity fetishism that appears in W. F. Haug's *Critique of Commodity Aesthetics* (1971). For Haug, commodity fetishism—or, more precisely, commodity aesthetics—sublimates the contradiction between the commodity's "use-form" (the commodity-*body*) and its "exchange-form," that "aesthetic promise" or *"appearance* of use-value" which defines the commodity as such. The result is the "aestheticization of commodities" whereby the "skin" of the commodity—true to the increasing abstraction and rationalization characteristic of monopoly capitalism—becomes more and more detached from its "body": "What appears here, reflected in the modification of the commodity's skin and body, is the fetish character of the commodity in its monopolistic peculiarity" (Haug 42).

While the determinate reinscription of the classical theory of commodification in the *Critique of Commodity Aesthetics* retains a more than archival interest, for all its originality and performative brilliance (Haug's "close" readings of individual commodities are wonderfully provocative[12]), the book as a whole evinces the kind of prescriptive negativity that dominates the work of the "classical" Frankfurt School. Even as Haug chastises Adorno and Horkheimer for their precritical Marxism, their "cultural pessimism" and merely "metaphysical interest in the critique of capitalist political economy" (120), his own excoriation of the "illusion industry" and "secondary exploitation" suggests that if he is more "critical" than the authors of "The Culture Industry," he is not necessarily more dialectical.[13]

Still, Haug's explicit emphasis on what he calls the "general sexualization of commodities" (56)—together with Baudrillard's surmise about a general economy of perversion—allows one to begin to think the unthought of classical Marxism: an alternative, critical-*affirmative* concept of commodification or "commodity fetishism" (in quotations).[14] That is, rather than restrict commodification to reification, it makes more sense—or so it seems to me at this "late" date in the history of capitalism—to figure a concept of commodity fetishism that comprises use- and exchange- as well as *sign*-value. It is, perhaps, not beside the point to remark here that the aim of this particular project—which is not without a certain polemic—is to develop a "genuinely more dialectical" description of consumption and commodification in order to generate a more compelling *critique* of the limits and defects of contemporary capi-

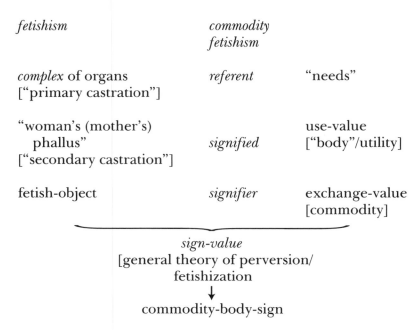

fetishism	*commodity* *fetishism*		
complex of organs ["primary castration"]	*referent*	"needs"	
"woman's (mother's) phallus" ["secondary castration"]	*signified*	use-value ["body"/utility]	
fetish-object	*signifier*	exchange-value [commodity]	

sign-value
[general theory of perversion/
fetishization
↓
commodity-body-sign

Fig. 1.

talism. More specifically yet, the aim of a general-economic account of "commodity fetishism" is to be able to elucidate—to describe *and* explain—the specific allure, produced today via advertising and packaging, marketing and publicity, that is the hallmark of the postmodern (art-) commodity.

To recapitulate (see Fig. 1): if in the language of classical psychoanalysis, fetishism represents a negation of castration (of the penis-phallus) as well as an affirmation of sexual difference as such (i.e., the complex of "real female genitals"), commodity fetishism—in the parlance of classical Marxism—represents a "negation" or effacement of exploitation as well as an affirmation of economic difference as such (i.e., Value).[15] In addition to this logic, though, beyond what Baudrillard calls the restricted economy of ideological reproduction, the "paleo-Marxist dramaturgy" of "projection and capture, alienation and appropriation," there is what I want to call the *commodity-body-sign,*[16] a figure of thought which appreciates commodification as "cultural sign labor" or the "labor of signification" (*travail de signification* [*Critique* 91/93]).

Before I consider the impact of the concept of the commodity-body-sign on the question of consumption, a couple of *caveats*
clearly are in order. First, to take up Baudrillard's critique of Marxist political economy is not—I cannot emphasize enough—to endorse his hyperbolic critique of use-value and consequent "sign
fetishism": use-value, as I indicated earlier, is not simply a mirage
of exchange-value.[17] To reverse tack, it is equally clear that insofar
as Baudrillard's theory of fetishization misprizes the by no means
merely residual efficacy of use-value, the concept of sign-value
must itself be scrupulously *re*-figured, that is to say, re-*worked,* if it
is to bear more than a purely rhetorical burden. I will endeavor to
do just this in the next segment.

These *caveats* registered, it is important to remember that if
the later Baudrillard's depiction of the mass media is even more
monolithic and total-systemic than Adorno-Horkheimer's and,
therefore, even less strategic because even more fatal, his work
from the very beginning—from, to be precise, *Le système des objets*
(1968) and *La société de consommation* (1970)—has always insisted, if
only negatively, on the "primacy" of consumption. Such an emphasis assumes—at least as I read it here—that the subject of consumption[18] is inseparable from the classically privileged problem
of production.

A critical reconception of consumption also involves other,
rather heterodox assumptions, the most important of which, for
me, is a certain, discontinuous history of capital.[19] For instance,
one of the presuppositions of the critical-affirmative notion of commodification proffered here is that late capitalism should be seen
less as a continuation of classical or monopoly capitalism than as a
"different 'order' of commodification," and that this last order is
itself only one among several processes of de-differentiation at
work in postmodernity as a whole (e.g., the deauraticization of culture).[20] In other words, however one reads this general process of
de-differentiation (whether positively or negatively, or both at
once), the emergence of a postmodern mode of commodification,
so-called post-Fordism, suggests that from a "demand" as well as
"supply" side, one would do well to think of the commodity (understood here in the received, pejorative sense associated with classical Marxism) as, *à la* Weber, an "ideal type." Simply put, with the
advent of so-called "specialized" and "positional consumption,"

what Baudrillard calls the "Veblen effect," goods and services should be *read* as being *more* or *less* commodified rather than commodities as such. In this sense, the *work of affirmation,* to recollect and reverse Hegel, demands not only a critical-affirmative understanding of commodification (+/−) but a general (-economic) "rhetoric of commodities" that would better enable us to de-code the *"work of consumption"* (O'Neill 99/102).

In order to accomplish this—that is, to think the work of affirmation as, in part, the work of consumption—it is necessary to rethink the negative, productivist picture of reception that has historically dominated the discourse of Western Marxism, as, for instance, in Haug, as well as the classical position on consumption that grounds this critique. The irony here, albeit one which exacts a certain dialectical imperative, is that in order to fashion a critical-affirmative sense of the commodity-body-sign at *this* particular moment in the history of cultural studies, it is now necessary—after, *inter alia,* Baudrillard—to return to the beginning: to, in other words, the negative.

Consumption Redux: Cultural Populism, Consummativity, and the Consumptive "Beast of Burden"

Jim McGuigan, responding to John Fiske's work on video and popular culture, in particular his work on Madonna,[21] contends that "Fiske's television viewers, unlike Madonna, do not live in the material world" (72). By "material," of course, McGuigan is referring not so much to that ironic or parodic sense invoked by Madonna's "Material Girl" as the "productive," anti-German idealist sense that characterizes the discourse of classical Marxism. McGuigan is referring, that is to say, to *material* production, where production is, as he says, "distinct from productive consumption" (74). Although McGuigan is surprisingly "sympathetic" to the critical charge of "cultural populism" (hence his counterconcept "critical populism" [5]), he is, nevertheless, intent to interrogate the consumptivism associated with the recent, dominant strain of Anglophone cultural studies. Hence, his effort to reopen the question of the "political *economy* of culture" (emphasis mine), which, according to McGuigan, the new, cultural-populist revisionists have relegated to the garbage-dump of history like so much Soviet-style heavy machinery.

However, given McGuigan's critique of "cultural populism" and attendant revalorization of the materiality of production, the question arises: What exactly *is* the economic, with or without quotations?

Without quotations and at least with respect to the problem of consumption, the *locus classicus* remains Marx's "General Introduction" to the *Grundrisse*—in particular, the section on "The General Relation of Production to Distribution, Exchange, and Consumption." In this, the second section of the "General Introduction," Marx distinguishes, like the classical political economists who are the object of his critique (Bastiat, Carey, Proudhon, et al.), between "consumptive production" and "productive consumption" or "production proper" and "consumption proper" respectively (23–24).[22] While not directly identical as in certain Hegelian political economists like Say and the *beaux penseurs socialistes,* there is for Marx a determinate relation, or "intermediary movement," between production and consumption: "Production furthers [*vermittelt*] consumption by creating material for the latter which otherwise would lack its object. But consumption in its turn furthers production, by providing for the products the individual for whom they are products" (24). *Ergo:* "Without production, no consumption; but, on the other hand, without consumption, no production" (24).

Despite the apparent symmetricality of this proposition (which appears to grant a commensurate reciprocity to the sphere of consumption), Marx's understanding of production/consumption appears to fall squarely on the production side of the virgule. In the *Grundrisse,* for instance, Marx submits that consumption "creates the *disposition* [*Anlage*] of the producer by setting him up as an aim and by stimulating wants," but production engenders consumption by (1) "furnishing the latter with *material,*" (2) "determining the *manner* [*Weise*] of consumption," and (3) "creating in consumers a *want* [*Bedürfnis*] for its products as objects of consumption" (26). More simply, production produces the "object, the manner, and the desire [*Trieb*] for consumption" (26).

If the first of Marx's three-fold determination of consumption is straightforward enough—"object"—the latter two—"manner" and "desire" respectively—are not nearly as simple with respect to the current microhistorical mode of production (i.e., "late" or transnational capitalism). That is to say, while the whole point of the "optimistic" cultural-populist movement in cultural studies has been to foreground the active, resistant, even transformative "manner" of consumption, the burden of Frankfurt School critical theory—at least as it has been codified—has been the rather different, "pessmistic" proposition that "desire" or, for Marcuse, "second nature" is itself a product of consumer capitalism. It will, I hope, have become clear in the course of this essay that I do not share either of these general theoretical positions, since neither cultural populism nor its apparent antithetical other, cultural industrialism, offers—at least on its own terms—a sufficiently complex account of consumption.

Still, if the cultural-populist stress on consumption is in part a response, however reactive and extreme, to the Frankfurt School's emphasis on production, this last position derives, in turn, from the canonical, not to say orthodox, Marxist emphasis on the "primacy of production." The critical passage here is the conclusion to the section on consumption in the "General Introduction" to the *Grundrisse,* where Marx lays down what has remained the classical position on "productive consumption"[23]:

> Consumption, as a natural necessity, as a want [*Bedürfnis*], constitutes an internal factor [*Moment*] of productive activity, but the latter is the starting point of realization and, therefore, its predominating factor [*übergreifendes Moment*], the act in which the entire process recapitulates [*verläuft*] itself. The individual produces a certain article and turns it again into himself by consuming it; but he returns as a productive and self-reproducing individual. Consumption thus appears as a factor [*Moment*] of production. (27)

I do not think it is too much to say that if the subject of consumption does not, for Marx, fall completely "outside the scope of economics" (23), his reiteration of consumption as the "finishing touch" of production—"The product receives its last finishing touches in consumption" (24)—tends to unnecessarily delimit the play or agency of what he elsewhere calls the "active subject" (*tätige Subjekt* [25]).

The Marx of the *Grundrisse* is not, of course, the only Marx. For instance, in the chapter on "Simple Reproduction in *Capital*, he differentiates between "productive consumption" and "individual consumption," noting that individual consumption is "totally distinct" from productive consumption (498). While productive consumption has a dual, properly dialectical articulation (the laborer's consumption of the means of production as well as the capitalist's consumption of this labor-power), "individual consumption"—or, in the language of *Capital*, the laborer's "means of subsistence"—refers to "what the laborer consumes for his [sic] own pleasure" *beyond* the surplus-value imperatives of the capitalist. From this last, noneconomic perspective, individual consumption should be understood as "final consumption," in the strict sense that, situated as it is "outside the realm of the circulation of value," it is "no longer defined by the internal logic of capital and its laws" (Fine and Leopold 262).

More precisely, one might say that "final," individual consumption—like use-value (use value/"use value")—is simultaneously inside and outside the circuit of capital, since the "desire" (*Trieb*) that drives individual consumption is itself subject,[24] in however mediated a fashion, to the logic of capital. This is especially the case, it seems to me, in "late," post-industrial as opposed to "early," liberal capitalism where the object of the colonizing logic of capital is not so much the means of (mass) production as the means of (mass) consumption. In fact, in a passage striking for its prescience, Marx himself entertains the idea of a real—that is to say, substantial—increase in individual consumption of the sort now associated with the postwar, Keynesian nation state,[25] but he concludes in classical fashion that, "in reality," individual consumption is "ultimately unproductive" even for the laborer, since it "reproduces nothing but the needy individual" (*Capital* I 499).

In sum, while Marx can certainly be said to have understood "productive consumption," he was not especially interested in the *question* of final consumption, as the following passage from the first volume of *Capital* illustrates:

> The individual consumption of the laborer, whether it proceed within the workshop [*Werkstatt*] or outside it, whether it be part of the process of production or not, forms . . . a factor in the

production and reproduction of capital. . . . The fact that the laborer consumes his means of subsistence for his own purposes, and not to please the capitalist, has no bearing on the matter. The consumption of food by a beast of burden is nonetheless a necessary factor in the process of production, because the beast enjoys what it eats. (498)

One can readily appreciate Marx's point here—that the capitalist need not worry about the sphere of consumption since the laborer's "basic instinct" for self-preservation will insure that she survives for yet another working day—and still wonder at his determination of the proletarian as a "beast of burden" (*Lastvieh*) as well as his categorical disregard of the question of "pleasure" (*Vergnügen*), as if pleasure or enjoyment, not to mention *jouissance,* were only a "factor" or "moment" of production.

In order to complicate the above restricted picture of consumption, one must turn, or return, to the Marx of the *Grundrisse.* Although even in the *Grundrisse,* Marx, it seems to me, ultimately subordinates the sphere of consumption to that of production, his dual perspective there on the latter's effectivity nonetheless suggests a more sophisticated account of consumption, one that does better descriptive and analytical justice to *homo cyberneticus* and the "expanded reproduction of use-value" that is the sign, however invidious (*statuaire*), of the postmodern. In the "General Introduction," Marx argues, first, that consumption itself *produces* production inasmuch as a product—as opposed to a "mere natural object" (*Naturegegestand*)—only *becomes* itself, a product, in consumption (25). As Marx puts it, recollecting Aristotle: "A railroad on which no one rides, which is not consequently used up, is only a potential railroad (or is a railroad on which no one travels) and not a real one" (24). Put another way (to set the Marx of the *Grundrisse* against the Marx of *Capital*): a song—say, the Rolling Stones' "Beast of Burden"—only becomes a "real" song via the act of listening or reception.

Second, consumption, according to Marx, also produces production by "providing the ideal, inward, impelling cause [*Triebenden*] which constitutes the prerequisite of production" (25). In other words, if production supplies the "material object" for consumption, consumption, in turn, furnishes the "ideal" object of production: its "image" (*Bild*), its "want" (*Bedürfnis*), its "impulse" (*Trieb*), and its "purpose" (*Zweck*). Most to the point (at least with respect to a less restricted, more general-economic reading of consumption), consumption offers the objects of production in a "form that is still subjective" (25). In a nutshell: "No needs, no production" (24).

Now, to reaccentuate this Marx, the Marx of the *Grundrisse*, is, it is important to note, neither to reprivilege the sphere of consumption nor, even more regressively, the maximizing "rational choice" individual of microeconomics; rather, it is to maintain that without the "demand" of desire, not to mention "need,"[26] production itself would "be without a purpose" (*Grundrisse* 24). Bluntly put, the consumer is no "beast of burden," though he may, at times, be a cultural dupe or dope, since there is all the difference in the world between animals and that *animal rationale* which is "man." As Marx himself says famously in the *Grundrisse:* "hunger that is satisfied with cooked meat eaten with fork and knife is a different kind of hunger from the one that devours [*verschlingt*] raw meat with the aid of hands, nail, and teeth" (28).

This difference—a "culinary" one, if you will[27]—is the difference between need and desire (or the "raw" and the "cooked"), and if the *Lastvieh* is, therefore, a creature of need, all teeth and cud, *Arbeiter(in)* is an altogether different creature, a "beast" who may well be, as Yeats says, "sick with desire/And fastened to a dying animal" but one who, even as he "wolfs down" (*verschlingen*) cooked meat with fork and knife to satisfy his hunger to stay alive, knows at the very same time that desire itself (*Trieb*) can never really be satisfied.[28]

Marx avec Duchamp: Socialized Consumption and De-Commodification

Although the preceding critique of Marx may suffer from a certain anachronistic character (since a Lacanian reading of consumption is obviously rather less applicable to the relatively "scare" world with which Marx was familiar), recent work in Marxism and critical theory—work that is intimately familiar with postmodernism and poststructuralism—has steadfastly refused the above "culturalist" reading of Marx and has chosen, instead, to pursue a different, "productivist" path. Jameson's work—as his political-economic formulation of postmodernism as the "cultural logic of late capitalism" perhaps suggests—is exemplary in this regard. Specifically, even as Jameson recognizes, if only in passing, the epistemological problems that shadow the classical position on production, he nonetheless argues for the counterhegemonic force of the discourse of productivism: "the affirmation of the 'primacy of production,' (whatever that might mean exactly), offers the most effective and powerful way of defamiliarizing ideologies of the market itself and consumption-oriented models of capitalism" (211). Indeed, for Jameson, the affirmation of consumption as a "vision of capitalism"—projected, for instance, in various "ethnographic" and audience-driven versions of cultural studies—is the sheerest ideology.

Similarly, in a *Primer for Everyday Life* (1991), Susan Willis maintains that the "contradictions of consumption are the contradictions of capitalism" and, consequently, that the "fantastic democracy" proposed by Marxist popular-culture critics like Fiske— what one might call a *commodity democracy*—simply reinforces the fundamental message of capitalism, which is to "say yes to everything" (148). The only way to *trans*form rather than *re*form a culture of the simulacrum is, according to Willis, to confront, head on, the contradictions of capitalism and the commodity-form on which it is predicated. As in Spivak, the key to this social transformation is the concept of use-value, which—unlike, say, the concept of sign-exchange-value in Baudrillard—provides a genuinely alternative, as opposed to merely "resistant," practice of cultural politics.

With the ascension and recent theoretical hegemony of, among other things, a particularly weak strain of cultural politics, it is certainly difficult to deny the conceptual *and* rhetorical value of a non-"facile" notion of use-value as well as the related argument for a nonprescriptive form of "socialized consumption." And to give credit where credit is due, Willis, in particular—unlike all too many cultural critics on the academic Marxist left—recognizes the theoretical interest of both Adorno's and Baudrillard's work, which—in its stress respectively on negative dialectics and symbolic exchange—presents a vision of capitalism as a systemic totality even as it envisions the Other of capitalism as an impossible, utopian "elsewhere."

However, it must, I think, be said that despite her novel, Adornian reading of symbolic exchange, Willis, like Jameson, is unable to resist the lure of an almost strictly negative dialectic, or what I can only call the *seduction of negation*. For instance, while Willis challenges the "reader to resist reading prescriptive models of use value" in the essays collected in *A Primer for Everyday Life*, I challenge the reader to resist reading a palpable rhetoric of—for want of a better word—*dis*pleasure between the lines of the same essays. Perhaps the problem is a rhetorical one (though I dare say rhetoric remains a real, by no means separate, problem in Willis), yet how can one explain—in the wake of Benjamin and Barthes, Lefebvre and de Certeau, Bourdieu and Baudrillard and, yes, Fiske and Hebdige—the following claim: "We all make meanings with the commodities we use and bestow. But the meaning possibilities are already inscribed in the history of production and exchange" (Willis 136). Tell that to R. Mutt and his urinal![29]

Again, it is impossible to dispute the reality of that "spectacle of production" which has pervaded, and continues to pervade, our everyday lives. One has only to stroll down the aisle of any supermarket, as Willis suggests, to see that the display of "exotic" goods today is every bit as theatrical as the latest Madonna video. Still, recent work in social history and anthropology also suggests that the possible meanings of commodities are by no means exhausted by the history of production and that the regimes and "tournaments of value," associated with what Arjun Appadurai calls the "dynamics of exchange," effectively deconstruct the *a priori* invocation of the mode of production. Indeed, for Appadurai, whose work derives from an unexpected convergence between Marx and Simmel, the link between value (Marx) and exchange (Simmel) affords a veritable politics, one that must be sought—at least in part—in the "political logic of consumption" (31).

Against, then, the "excessively positivist conception" of commodification that is entrenched in Marxism, Appadurai insists that a commodity is not simply *"any thing intended for exchange"* (9) but a thing that, "at a certain phase in [its career] and in a particular context, meet[s] the requirements of commodity candidacy" (16). The value of this resolutely temporal, if not properly historical-materialist, approach is that unlike certain classical accounts of commodity fetishism, it can persuasively account for the fact of *de*-commodification. As Appadurai puts it, things "move in *and* out of the commodity state," and "such movements can be slow or fast, reversible or terminal, normative or deviant" (13). More generally, Appadurai's "state"-specific, "career"-oriented conception of commodification goes some way toward constructing a "rhetoric of commodities" that is responsive to the vagaries of value, in particular the hyperreal "body" of sign-value, whose instability and volatility is a direct function of the increasingly rapid flows of information associated with "financial fetishism" or, more specifically yet, the "pure fetish form" (Marx) of the present global credit/debt system.[30]

The point, of course, is not to lose sight of the fact that things *do* become commodities and that to forget about this—that is to say, *surplus-value*—is to abandon in one stroke whatever critical, not to mention ethical, force Marxism commands as a discourse.

Re-Turn: Contradiction, "Real" Surplus Value, and the Production of Sign-Value

If it is imperative to attend to use- and exchange-value—as Willis and Appadurai, respectively, argue—it is equally important—as I have been arguing—to attend to the concept of sign-value. One way to get at the specificity of sign-value is to consider the signification of value per se, as in Fig. 2.

	value-form			
use-*value*	exchange-*value*	sign-*value*		Symbolic Exchange
[signified	signifier]	sign		

Fig. 2.

As the left hand of this diagram illustrates (i.e., non-Symbolic Exchange), the "real movement" of Baudrillard's model—such as it is—derives neither from consumption nor production but *simula*-

tion, the so-called *"monopoly of the code"* (*Mirror* 127).[31] Indeed, the real driving force of the sign, for Baudrillard, is not so much sign-exchange-value as Symbolic Exchange or what he calls the "sacrificial economy" of "true consummation" (not, in other words, *consommativité* but *consumation*), the latter of which is, strictly speaking, "beyond the sign."[32]

If, however, one brackets the question of Symbolic Exchange (as, for example, in the above diagram), the radicality of Baudrillard's "revolution of the object" emerges, as in Fig. 3, where the "fundamental" formula is: "sign-value is to symbolic exchange what exchange-value . . . is to use-value" (*Critique* 126).

| needs | | use-*value* | exchange-*value* | sign-*value* |
| referent | | [signified | signifier] | sign |

Fig. 3.

Here the "referent" or *content* of both classical bourgeois and Marxist political economy ("needs") is decisively bracketed, not unlike Symbolic Exchange, and only its *form*—its structural as opposed to functional character—remains.

Now, this radically non-, not to say anti-, naturalistic conception of political economy poses a number of problems, not the least of which is that it absolutely destroys—as opposed to, say, puts "under erasure"—the notion of need or utility. In fact, just as Baudrillard's emphasis on sign-value obscures the analytic specificity of use-value (which, as we have seen, both Spivak and Willis attempted to highlight), his semiurgic "destruction" of the notion of need—which recollects both Mauss and Bataille, but more Bataille than Mauss—courts the charge of idealism, a *genetic* idealism of which Marxism, whatever its other flaws, cannot be accused due to its insistence on the original, irreducible nature of the material.

Still, to appreciate the force of Baudrillard's reconfiguration of value, it is necessary to understand a further transformation of his model of "political economy," one where not only need but use-value as well as Symbolic Exchange are "expelled from the field of value" (*Critique* 128). The relevant formula here is: "sign-value [is] to exchange-value what symbolic exchange is to use-value" (*Critique* 127).[33] See Fig. 4.

		Symbolic
needs use-value	[exchange/sign-exchange-value]	Exchange

Fig. 4.

The interest of this particular reconfiguration—which involves a double, radical expulsion of "needs" and "use-value" as well as the utopian space of Symbolic Exchange[34]—is that it articulates the internal movement of the Real, that history of rationalization or, for Marx, "real abstraction" which characterizes the logic of modernity or, in this case, postmodernity. What we "see" here, in other words, is the emergence of a "third order" of representation, that phase of political economy when—as Baudrillard glosses Marx—even what is considered "inalienable (love, knowledge, consciousness, etc.) falls into the sphere of exchange-value" (*Mirror* 119). Or, as Julian Pefanis economically puts it, "production produces in order to produce production" (64).

Now, no one, it seems to me, is more articulate or provocative on the topic of simulation than Baudrillard, but the problem with his critique of "use-value fetishism" is that, for all its complexity and ingenuity, it is constitutively unable to explain the *production* of the sign—unless the above formulation ("production produces. . . .") counts as a necessary *and* sufficient explanation. In other words, if a strictly negative conception of consumption and commodification is, as it were, counterproductive, a critical-affirmative account of "commodity fetishism" must—if it is to be effective as *critique*—come to terms with that historical-materialist process which produces the *contradiction* between use-value and value as such (or, for Baudrillard, exchange- and sign-exchange-value), a process I have schematically diagrammed in Fig. 5.

While this diagram is only a *figure* for those "concrete forms" that constitute the contradictory and historically determined process of capitalist production, the force of this particular trope is that it does not simply reduce the *form* of use-*value*, as Baudrillard tends to do, to a "bad" equivalential logic or "simple formal mediation" (Marx). Moreover, there is a "substantial" epistemological stake here, as the dual character of use-value in the final diagram is intended to suggest, inasmuch as use-value (without quotations)

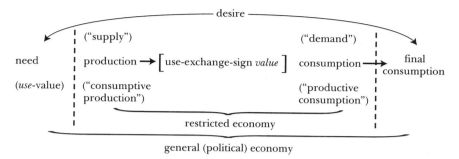

Fig. 5.

can be said to be a figure for "need" (*besoin*) or, more generally, that bio-material referent which is the real.[35] Put another way: if, on one hand, the relative barring (*encadrement*) of final consumption alludes to that which is, in one sense, "beyond" economics (hence its general-economic status), on the other hand, the location of the restricted, classical-Marxist economy of value within a general economy of "commodity fetishism"—one "driven" by *Trieb* (Marx) or *désir* (Lacan)—indicates an additional, critical stake.

I would only add that, with respect to the latter re-installation, the placement of the sign within the restricted political economy of commodity fetishism—a "tactical" gesture that explicitly reverses Baudrillard's strategic "inversion of the logic of value" (Fine and Leopold 266–70)[36]—this "perverse" economy not only accounts for that consumption which is productive (i.e., "productive consumption") but for that site or point from which use-, exchange-, and sign-value can be said to "originate": i.e., production. The "point" of this particular, *political*-economic restriction is, I hope, obvious: in order to retain the concept of *surplus*-value, it is imperative to "remember" the differentially weighted site of production, that *process* where exploitation happens.[37]

Coda: The Total Circuit of Capital

The above reinscription of the relatively dominant role of production may seem like a not-so-subtle return to the classical Marxist position on consumption and commodification or, more generally, political economy, but I would only reiterate the obvious: one doesn't have to subscribe to Baudrillard's anarchist campaign against what he calls the "total dictatorship" of production ("Consumer Society" 28) to realize—*pace* a certain reading of Marx—that the mode of production does not simply determine what Bourdieu calls the "mode of consumption." Neither the concept of alienation nor exploitation negates, to offer a perfectly banal example, "the pleasure obtained from a television set" ("Consumer Society" 40). Not to recognize the little truth of this truism is to risk resurrecting the sort of negative, "Frankenstein image" hidden deep in the heart of classical Marxism and re-"reified" in the concept of reification (Miller 180).

Such a countercritique does not of course mean that we should pursue the "political logic of consumption" at the expense of the mode of production. It is hopelessly regressive, it seems to me, to reproduce endlessly the argument for the "sovereignty" of consumption,[38] a one-dimensional argument that has been enshrined in classical political economy since Adam Smith ("Consumption is the sole end and purpose of all production" [Heilbroner 68]). This sort of consumptivism, liberal or otherwise, is as "unproductive" as the most orthodox forms of productivisim. In order to counter a drift toward a "bad," utopianist sublation of the "cultural contradictions of capitalism," however, one must continually reinscribe not only the concept of production but that of *contradiction*.

Although there are any number of seemingly insuperable contradictions that are at least as "old" as modernity itself (e.g., the conflict between the state and capital), the primary contradiction is not so much between consumption and production—as my concluding graph, admittedly, suggests—as between the forces and relations of production, the latter of which may be rewritten as the antagonism between capital and labor, or most simply: profits/wages. If Ricardo recognized the significance of this opposition (if not its antagonistic character), it was left to Marx to point out that the result of the *contradiction*[39] between the forces and relations of production—or, to adduce the "internal," structural as opposed to "external," historical contrast between concrete labor (relative value form) and abstract labor (equivalent value form)—is *surplus-value* and, in turn, capital formation and expansion, accumulation and reproduction.

While Marx's understanding of that contradiction, which is capitalism, has both a general and particular charge—respectively, class struggle and the proletariat as the historically privileged agent of revolutionary change—the same formulation also invites a rather less orthodox reading. To wit: if the contradiction between capital/labor and the production of surplus-value—especially as it is played out today in the egregious disjunction between "first" and "third world" economies (as various "dependency" and "cultural imperialist" theories attest)[40]—cannot be theorized away, the fact remains that "however opposed capital and labor may appear in the struggle of wage against profit," it is also absolutely necessary— at least for capital to achieve *its* ends—for the laborer "to continue to buy and to continue to desire more goods" (Miller 184). This, the so-called "realization problem," is, one might say, *the* "positive" aspect of the problem of *contradiction*.[41]

Now, it may be entirely too much to hope that an absolute "identity of interests" will ever emerge between capital and labor (where, that is, capital produces only that which its "labor force as consumers demand[s] from it in the way of goods" [Miller 184]); however, the dialectic between profits and wages is, as Marx himself saw, *the* precondition of production. Accordingly, the potential for some real balance, if not identity of interests, between the two—between, that is, capital and labor—is not some mirage of capitalism, the "discreet charm" of bourgeois political economy, but a precondition of politics in general and "affirmative" politics in particular.

I hasten to add that even as the "constant fight for higher wages by members of the work-force cannot be reduced to a demand for the paypacket" but "must always imply a demand for the purchases represented by those wages" (i.e., "wage goods" [Miller 188]), this implicit, structural demand must not be for just *any* goods.[42] In other words, if production for "need" (or, more properly, need and desire *vis-à-vis* profit) means anything today, it must mean the demand for commodities that not only satisfy our desires, however defined,[43] but that do not imperil the planet and its already dwindling resources.

Finally, if it is impossible to comprehend the commodity-body-sign without taking into account use- and exchange- as well as sign-value, it is equally impossible to formulate a critical-affirmative sense of "commodity fetishism" without coming to terms with the concept of *circulation*[44]—with, that is, the various "moments" that constitute the "circuit" of capital: production, distribution, exchange, and consumption. For example (to use my own schema as an object of critique), it is only from the perspective of circulation in the general sense that the binary couple production/consumption appears as the crude opposition that it is. So, in the *Grundrisse*, after explaining the dialectical relation between production and consumption, Marx writes: "Between the producer and the product, *distribution* steps in, determining by social laws his [sic] share in the world of products" (28).[45] Marx himself clearly associates distribution with production, and exchange with consumption here, but he also insists that they are all members "of one entity [*Totalität*], different aspects of one unit" (33).

Even though this sort of theorization may exude a certain expressivist air, its "totalizing" gesture is, it seems to me, something of a necessary risk today, now that theory—even some post-*Marxist* theory—is content to mime those centripetal forces of fragmentation and "schizophrenia," superparticularism and microdifferentiation, that define postmodernity. In just this sense, only a global perspective—one that recognizes not only that every theoretical position is as much an "affirmative as a negative gesture" but that the "little tactics" of theory are always in some sense complicit with the "great," geopolitical strategies of global capitalism[46]—can begin to do social and not merely "philosophical justice" to the very real "fetish character of commodities."

Notes

1. See also the first part of Chow's essay, "The Formalism of Negativity" (3–7).
2. "By means . . . of the value relation expressed in our equation, the bodily form of commodity B becomes the value form of commodity A, or the body of commodity B acts as a mirror to the value of commodity A" (*Capital* I 27). I have—where appropriate—modernized Marx's German (e.g., "Ware" for "Waare").
3. The literature on fetishism is too extensive to begin to cite; however, for a representative sample of current work on the topic, see the collection, *Fetishism as Cultural Discourse*, edited by Apter and Pietz.
4. So, in "A Denial of Difference: Theories of Cinematic Identification" (1982), Friedberg argues that *"fetishism is a relation incurred by the anxiety of sexual difference"* (40). For the Silverman ("primary" and "secondary castration"), see "Lost Objects and Mistaken Subjects: A Prologue," in *The Acoustic Mirror* (1–41).
5. For a provocative argument about, among other things, the "umbilical cord"

as the repressed or suppressed origin of fetishism, see—on, in particular, the conceptual limits of the above signifier—Ian, "Being and Having" (38–39).

6. For a similar sentiment, see the introduction to Butler's *Bodies That Matter* (22).

7. I presuppose here Bataille and Derrida, in particular the latter's "From Restricted to General Economy: A Hegelianism without Reserve." Commenting on Hegel by way of Bataille, Derrida writes: "the phenomenology of the mind . . . corresponds to a restricted economy: restricted to commercial values, . . . limited to the meaning and the established value of objects, and to their *circulation*. The *circularity* of absolute knowledge could dominate . . . only this circulation, only the *circuit of reproductive consumption*" (271). On general economy, see, in general, Plotnitsky's *In the Shadow of Hegel* (10–30) and *Reconfigurations*. For a more detailed discussion of this issue—what I call a "general (political) economy" of "commodity fetishism"—see also the introduction to my *From Hegel to Madonna*.

8. Marx himself explicitly invokes the notion of perversion (in, of course, the pejorative sense): "it is a characteristic feature of labour [that it] posits exchange value in the perverted form of a social relation between things" (*Contribution* 275).

9. My retention of the standard translation here ("queer") is intentional. Thus, one of the effects of the reinscription of commodity fetishism as a general economy of "commodity fetishism" is that it opens onto the question of sexual perversion in particular and, in general, a problematic that articulates both "money" and sexuality. On the last, see, for example, Dollimore's "Sexual Perversion: Pathology to Politics," in *Sexual Dissidence*.

10. I should note that to invoke Goux here is not to accept, without qualification, the structural homologism so insistent in, say, *Freud, Marx: Économie et symbolique* (1973); for a critique, see Spivak (156–57) and D'Amico, "The Economic and Symbolic in Culture," *Marx and Philosophy of Culture* (31–43).

11. Amariglio and Callari put it this way: "The non-determinist view [of commodity fetishism] treats this concept as a sign—a strategically located sign—that the relations between economic and noneconomic processes are neither unproblematic nor unidirectional" (202).

12. See my "Re-Framing the Commodity-Body-Sign: Warhol's *Sticky Fingers, The Fe-Male Gaze, and Ciné-*Psycho Fetishism," in *From Hegel to Madonna*.

13. On the commodity aestheticians—not only Haug but Hans Heinz Holz and Friedrich Tomberg—see Hohendahl, "The Polarization of Aesthetic Theory," in *Reappraisals* (160–70).

14. In order to remark in this essay a revised sense of commodity fetishism, I have—where appropriate—placed it in quotations ("commodity fetishism"). The standard discussion of the former (commodity fetishism) is Cohen's "Fetishism," in *Karl Marx's Theory of History* (115–33). In addition to work cited elsewhere in this essay (as well as the excellent bibliographies in Pietz and Amariglio and Callari), see Mitchell, "The Rhetoric of Iconoclasm: Marxism, Ideology, and Fetishism," *Iconology* (160–208); Keenan, "The Point Is to (Ex)Change It: Reading *Capital*, Rhetorically," in *Fetishism as Discourse* (152–85); Žižek's provocative remarks on the topic in *The Sublime Object of Ideology* (23–27); and, most recently and notably, Derrida, "*apparition of the inapparent*" (*Specters of Marx* 125–76).

15. As I have suggested (see n10 above), there are limits to this sort of homology or, more precisely, metaphor. Which is to say that, from a restricted perspective, the difference between "fetishism" and "commodity fetishism" is irreducible. Thus, where one might argue that the "truth" of fetishism revolves around what I call the complex of (female) organs, the "truth" of commodity fetishism is simply use-value (unless one would want to argue, according to what I take to be a "bad"

homologism, that the proletariat is something like the repressed "body" of woman).

16. See in this context ("commodity-body-sign") Goldman, in particular "Commodity Fetishism" (130–54). I would only add that although I share Goldman's understanding of the *commodity-sign*, my critical-affirmative sense of this term, which also includes the "body" of use-value, differs substantially from his pointed but in many ways classically "negative" critique.

17. See Kellner, "Commodities, Needs, and Consumption in the Consumer Society," *Jean Baudrillard* (37–38).

18. For a very basic introduction to the subject of consumption, see Bocock; for an advanced and absolutely superb discussion, see—among the recent spate of books on the topic—Lee. Consumption is also, of course, a prime philosopheme in Kant and Hegel (e.g., "food for understanding"). For a discussion of this economy of conservation where nothing is discounted, and even "distaste" is a kind of "taste" (*de-gout*), see Plotnitsky, "The Maze of Taste," in *Reconfigurations* (63–112).

19. In addition to Lee, who offers the most nuanced and thorough Marxist discussion of consumption in terms of both Fordism and post-Fordism, see—on the modern history of consumption—Cross and—on the subject of consumption—Shields.

20. See Lash, "Postmodernism: Towards a Sociological Account," in *Sociology of Postmodernism* (5–8).

21. See Fiske, "British Cultural Studies and Television," in *Channels of Discourse: Television and Contemporary Criticism* (270–83) and *Television Culture* (249–54). For a discussion of Fiske's work on, *inter alia*, Madonna, see my "*Corpus Delicti:* The Rise of Madonna Studies," in *From Hegel to Madonna*.

22. I must bracket here the whole question—a tangential one, I believe—of "productive" versus "non-productive consumption." The relevant source here is the section in the second volume of *Capital* (1885), "Exchange within Department II," where Marx divides the "annual production of commodities" into two subdivisions: (1) articles of necessity (those commodities—including so-called "consumer necessities" like tobacco!—consumed by the working class as well as a "portion" of the capitalist class), and (2) "articles of luxury" (those goods which "enter into the consumption of only the capitalist class and can therefore be exchanged only for spent surplus-value, which never falls to the share of the laborer" [*Capital* II 403]).

23. For the most recent, and best, reading of Marx's position on consumption, see Fine and Leopold.

24. I am playing here on the word *Trieb* which can be translated as "desire" or, as in psychoanalysis, as "drive." Although Lacan distinguishes between "desire" (*désir*) and "drive" (*pulsion*), I have strategically conflated Marx's and Lacan's understanding of *Trieb* in order to introduce an analytical distinction into Marx's relatively simple conception of consumption. For Baudrillard, of course, consumption or what he calls "consummativity" mirrors production-as-productivity and, in the process, reduces "need" (*besoin*) to "labor" (*besogne*). On the notion of consummativity, see "The Ideological Genesis of Needs" (*Critique* 83). On the psychoanalytic sense of *Trieb*, see Laplanche's *Life and Death* and Lacan's *Four Fundamentals*. See also n26 below.

25. Marx, echoing Ricardo, writes: "If the accumulation of capital were to cause a rise of wages and an increase in the laborer's consumption, unaccompanied by increase in the consumption of labor-power by capital, the additional capital would be consumed unproductively" (*Capital* I 499).

26. On Lacan's triad—need/demand/desire—see, among other things, "The Signification of the Phallus": "that which is . . . alienated in needs constitutes an *Urverdrängung* (primal repression), an inability . . . to be articulated in demand, but it re-appears in something it gives rise to that presents itself in man as desire" (*Écrits* 286). I should say that my play here on the word "demand"—economic demand as *demande*—is merely meant to underscore the complex "nature" of consumption. See also n34 below.

27. I am alluding here to Brecht's notion of the "culinary" (*kulinarisch*), which—even given its debased status in his aesthetics (i.e., "culinary" *vs.* "epic theatre")—nonetheless plays a critical role. Bluntly, "cooking" can be an art. For the Brecht, see, for example, his notes on *Mahagonny*, "The Modern Theatre Is the Epic Theatre" (1930).

28. For a similar argument about "hunger," which is obviously indebted to Lacan, see Baudrillard, "The Ideological Genesis of Needs" (*Critique* 69n1).

29. I am referring of course to Marcel Duchamp's ready-made, the 1917 *Fountain*. For a history and analysis, see Camfield.

30. According to Pietz, this is where one should look for postmodern commodity fetishism, not in the "extreme development of the commercialization of social appearances" (as in Baudrillard) but in the "full development of financial fetishism" (149). I would only add that if the latter is the most important political economic "expression" of postmodern fetishization, one should attend to the cultural-economic sphere of "social appearances" as well—with the, I think, obvious proviso that one should not do so at the expense of the financial. For a useful discussion of "postmodern" finance and fictitious capital, see Harvey, in particular "Time-Space Compression and the Postmodern Condition" (284–307).

31. The following passage is representative: "In opposition to the competitive system, the monopolistic system institutes *consumption* as control, as the arbiter of the contingency of demand, as planned socialization by the code" (*Mirror* 126).

32. This is how Baudrillard puts it in *The Mirror of Production:* "The real rupture is not between 'abstract' labor and 'concrete' labor, but between symbolic exchange and work (production, economics)" (45). On symbolic exchange, see Gane, "A General Theory," *Baudrillard* (83–85).

33. *Pace* Gane, I want to argue that a "theoretical relation" has in fact been established, if only implicitly, between symbolic exchange and use-value. See Gane (83). For an excellent discussion of these issues (albeit from a rather different, "semiological" perspective, what he calls—with real wit—"bar games," e.g., *exercises à la barre*), see Genosko, in particular "The Table of Conversions" (6–17) where he takes up in detail the "four logics of value" in Baudrillard (*utility* [instrument], *equivalence* [commodity], *difference* [sign], and *ambivalence* [symbol]).

34. Baudrillard: "[N]eed, use-value, and the referent 'do not exist.' They are only concepts produced and projected into a generic dimension by the development of the very system of exchange value" (*Mirror* 30). As Baudrillard notes: "[t]his does not mean *that they have never existed*" (*Mirror* 30n11). Baudrillard's model is not, therefore, without its historical dimension, attenuated as it may be.

35. With respect to the final diagram, the arc from "final consumption" to "need" refers to what one might call the *loop of desire*. It is important to note, however, that although this diagram might seem to imply the existence of some sort of unmediated need which precedes the "moment" or process of production, the above arc or loop is meant to problematize any such naturalism. Put another way: in the late twentieth century, it is virtually impossible—except, perhaps, in infants (hence Lacan's notion of *demande*, where the child is literally dependent

on an external source for physical survival)—to distinguish between need and desire. (See n42 below.) In fact, in the first, post-Fordist world at least, it is pretty clear that desire drives need, and that sign-value in all its phantasmagoric play is, in this sense, all about desire. Rather more to the political point of this essay, while the loop of desire is, as it were, "loopy" (i.e., cannot be reduced to the calculus of restricted economics), this *annulus,* for all its annihilative character (*res nulla*), can also become a manacle of sorts, a silk noose or vicious circle.

36. For this distinction between the tactical and strategic, see Baudrillard: "use-value and the signified do not have the same weight as exchange-value and the signifier respectively. Let us say they have a tactical value—whereas exchange-value and the signifier have strategic value" (*Critique* 137). In this "tactical" context, it is important to add that, *pace* Derrida, the general (political) economy of "commodity fetishism" is *not* merely a "phase within the strategy of general economy" (*Writing and Difference* 337n33). This is, as it were, the difference between Marxism or, more precisely, *post*-Marxism and deconstruction; although the above general (political) economy is not restricted to the classical conception of revolution (i.e., class revolution), it is rather less "sovereign" in its economics than deconstruction since it is still unapologetically invested in the question of the (re-) distribution of (surplus-) value.

I have italicized the word "process" in this sentence in order to remark the dynamic and historical character of the mode of production. As Raymond Williams reminds us: "It is only when we realize that 'the base,' to which it is habitual to refer variations, is itself a dynamic and internally contradictory process—the specific activities and modes of activity, over a range from association to antagonism, of real men and classes of men—that we can begin to free ourselves from the notion of an 'area' or a 'category' with fixed properties" (82).

37. In this sense, it is not enough, for example, to establish fair exchange rates (as neo-classical economics would have it), since such laissez-faire economic justice is strictly after the fact of exploitation, which is a function not of the "individual negotiation of exchange contracts" but of collective, genuinely democratic access to the means of production (Himmelweit 473).

38. For recent, important work on this issue ("sovereignty of consumption") as well, in particular, the relation between consumption and citizenship, see Keat et al.

39. For a *précis* of this concept, see Bhaskar's entry on "Contradiction," in *A Dictionary of Marxist Thought* (93–94).

40. For an excellent critique of reflexive and, all too frequently, "moralizing" theories of consumerism and "cultural imperialism" (which tend to displace the necessity for an *a priori* critique of our own "culture of capitalism"), see Tomlinson, *Cultural Imperialism* (102–39).

41. The "realization problem" refers to the "need to sell that output that is produced in order to convert surplus value from its labour form via its commodity form to profit, its money form" (Desai 495).

42. I am alluding here to the so-called "reproduction schema" developed in the second volume of *Capital,* where Marx distinguishes between the "means of production" (machine goods) and the "means of consumption" (wage goods). See, in particular, the influential and still controversial section on "The Two Departments of Social Production" in the second volume of *Capital* (392–488).

43. I would only cite Veblen here in order to suggest the difficulties of differentiating between "true" and "false needs" (which does not of course excuse us from the task of doing so). Two citations: "In the view of economic theory the

expenditure in question is no more and no less legitimate than any other expenditure"; "It frequently happens that an element of the standard of living which set out with being primarily wasteful, ends with becoming, in the apprehension of the consumer, a necessary of life; and it may in this way become as indispensable as any other item of the consumer's habitual expenditure" (97/99).

44. My sense of circulation is not the restricted one that Marx employs in the *Grundrisse* or the second volume of *Capital*. Thus, in Chapter 5 of the latter text ("Time of Circulation"), Marx not only demarcates the sphere of production from the sphere of circulation but explains that the latter sphere is itself composed of two "processes": (1) the transformation of capital "from the commodity form into that of money" (C-M), and (2) "from the money form into that of commodities" (M-C [124]). My sense of circulation, then, refers less to that "sphere of exchange in which commodities are bought and sold" than to what Marx, in the subtitle to the third volume of *Capital*, calls "The Process of Capitalist Production as a Whole."

On the former, see, however, Chapter 3 in the first volume of *Capital* ("Money, or the Circulation of Commodities" [81–126]); the whole of the second volume of *Capital*, which of course is subtitled "The Process of Circulation of Capital"; and in the third volume of *Capital* (1894), "Medium of Circulation and Capital" (442–60).

45. Given the polemical focus in this essay on a general economy of consumption, it is clear that the issue of distribution—as my citation of Marx here is intended to stress—can hardly be ignored, especially today. As Jameson observes in "The Antinomies of Postmodernity": "[the new developments of post-Fordism blur the distinction betwen the two other categories of the triad, distribution and consumption, in such a way that new modes of distribution (the fundamental trait of Post-Fordism as a concept) can be parlayed into a rhetoric of consumption and of the market as an ideological value" (*Seeds of Time* 41).

46. I am recollecting Spivak here ("putting 'under erasure' is as much an affirmative as a negative gesture" [168]) as well as Foucault: "A whole history remains to be written of *spaces*— . . . from the great strategies of geo-politics to the little tactics of the habitat" (149).

Works Cited

Adorno, Theodor. *Negative Dialectics*. Trans. E. B. Ashton. New York: Seabury P, 1973.

Amariglio, Jack, and Antonio Callari. "Marxian Value Theory and the Problem of the Subject: The Role of Commodity Fetishism." *Fetishism as Cultural Discourse*. Ed. Emily Apter and William Pietz. Ithaca: Cornell UP, 1993. 186–216.

Appadurai, Arjun. "Introduction: Commodities and the Politics of Value." *The Social Life of Things: Commodities in Cultural Perspective*. New York: Cambridge UP, 1986. 3–63.

Baudrillard, Jean. "Consumer Society." Trans. Jacques Mourrain. *Selected Writings*. Ed. Mark Poster. Stanford: Stanford UP, 1988. 29–56.

———. "Fetishism and Ideology." *For a Critique of the Political Economy of the Sign*. Trans. Charles Levin. St. Louis: Telos P, 1981. 88–101.

———. *The Mirror of Production*. Trans. Mark Poster. St. Louis: Telos P, 1975.

———. *La société de consommation*. Paris: Gallimard, 1970.

———. *Les systeme des objects*. Paris: Denoel-Gonthier, 1968.
———. *Pour une critique de l'économie politique du signe*. Paris: Gallimard, 1972. 95–113.
Benjamin, Walter. *Charles Baudelaire: A Lyric Poet in the Era of High Capitalism*. London: New Left Books, 1973.
Bhaskar, Roy. "Contradiction." *A Dictionary of Marxist Thought*. Ed. Tom Bottomore et al. Cambridge: Harvard UP, 1983. 93–94.
Bocock, Robert. *Consumption*. New York: Routledge, 1993.
Bourdieu, Pierre. Introduction. *Distinction: A Social Critique of the Judgment of Taste*. Trans. Richard Nice. Cambridge: Harvard UP, 1984. 1–7.
Brecht, Bertolt. *Brecht on Theatre*. Trans. John Willet. New York: Hill and Wang, 1987.
Butler, Judith. *Bodies That Matter: On the Discursive Limits of "Sex."* New York: Routledge, 1993.
Camfield, William. "Marcel Duchamp's *Fountain:* Aesthetic Object, Icon, or Anti-Art?" *The Definitely Unfinished Marcel Duchamp*. Ed. Thierry de Duve. Cambridge: MIT P, 1991. 133–184.
Chow, Rey. "Ethics after Idealism." *Diacritics* 23.1 (1993): 3–22.
Cohen, G. A. "Fetishism." *Karl Marx's Theory of History: A Defense*. New York: Basic, 1982. 115–33.
Cross, Gary. *Time and Money: The Making of Consumer Culture*. New York: Routledge, 1993.
D'Amico, Robert. "The Economic and Symbolic in Culture." *Marx and Philosophy of Culture*. Gainesville: UP of Florida, 1981. 31–43.
Deleuze, Gilles. *Nietzsche and Philosophy*. Trans. Hugh Tomlinson. Minneapolis: U of Minnesota P, 1983.
Derrida, Jacques. "From Restricted to General Economy: A Hegelianism without Reserve." Trans. Alan Bass. *Writing and Difference*. Chicago: U of Chicago P, 1978. 251–77.
———. *Specters of Marx: The State of Debt, the Work of Mourning, and the New International*. Trans. Peggy Kamuf. New York: Routledge, 1994.
Desai, Meghnad. "Underconsumption." *A Dictionary of Marxist Thought*. Ed. Tom Bottomore et al. Cambridge: Harvard UP, 1983. 495–98.
Dollimore, Jonathan. "Sexual Perversion: Pathology to Politics."*Sexual Dissidence: Augustine to Wilde, Freud to Foucault*. Oxford: Oxford UP, 1991. 169–230.
Fine, Ben, and Ellen Leopold. "Marx's Economics and Consumption." *The World of Consumption*. New York: Routledge, 1993. 254–63.
Fiske, John. "British Cultural Studies and Television." *Channels of Discourse: Television and Contemporary Criticism*. Ed. Robert C. Allen. Chapel Hill: U of North Carolina P, 1987. 270–83.
———. *Television Culture*. New York: Routledge, 1990.
Foucault, Michel. *The History of Sexuality*. Vol. 1. Trans. Robert Hurley. New York: Vintage, 1980.
———. "The Eye of Power." *Power/Knowledge: Selected Interviews and Other Writings, 1972–1977*. Ed. Colin Gordon. New York: Pantheon, 1980. 146–65.
Freud, Sigmund. 1905. "Fetischismus." *Studienausgabe*. Vol. 3. *Psychologie des Unbewusten*. Frankfurt am Main: S. Fischer Verlag, 1975. 381–88.
———. "Fetishism." *Collected Papers*. Vol. 5. Trans. Joan Riviere and ed. James Strachey. London: Hogarth P, 1953. 198–204.
———. *Three Essays on the Theory of Sexuality*. Trans. James Strachey. London: Hogarth P, 1962.

Friedberg, Anne. "A Denial of Difference: Theories of Cinematic Identification." *Psychoanalysis and Cinema*. Ed. E. Ann Kaplan. New York: Routledge, 1990. 36–45.

Gane, Mike. *Baudrillard: Critical and Fatal Theory*. New York: Routledge, 1991.

Genosko, Gary. *Baudrillard and Signs: Signification Ablaze*. New York: Routledge: 1994.

Goldman, Robert. *Reading Ads Socially*. New York: Routledge, 1992.

Goux, Jean-Joseph. *Symbolic Economies: After Marx and Freud*. Trans. Jennifer Curtiss Gage. Ithaca: Cornell UP, 1990.

Haug, W. F. *Critique of Commodity Aesthetics: Appearance, Sexuality and Advertising in Capitalist Society*. Trans. Robert Buck. Minneapolis: U of Minnesota P, 1986.

Harvey, David. *The Condition of Postmodernity*. Canbridge: Blackwell, 1989.

Heilbroner, Robert. *The Worldly Philosophers*. New York: Simon and Schuster, 1986.

Himmelweit, Susan. "Surplus Value." *Dictionary of Marxist Thought*. Ed. Tom Bottomore et al. Cambridge : Harvard UP, 1983. 472–75.

Hohendahl, Peter Uwe. "The Polarization of Aesthetic Theory." *Reappraisals: Shifting Alignments in Postwar Critical Theory*. Ithaca: Cornell UP, 1991. 160–70.

Huyssen, Andreas. *After the Great Divide: Modernism, Mass Culture, Postmodernism*. Bloomington: Indiana UP, 1986.

Ian, Marcia. *Remembering the Phallic Mother: Psychoanalysis, Modernism, and the Fetish*. Ithaca: Cornell UP, 1993.

Jameson, Fredric. *Postmodernism; Or, The Cultural Logic of Late Capitalism*. Durham: Duke UP, 1991.

———. *The Seeds of Time*. New York: Columbia UP, 1994.

Keat, Russell, Nigel Whiteley, and Nicholas Abercrombie, eds. *The Authority of the Consumer*. New York: Routledge, 1994.

Keenan, Thomas. "The Point Is to (Ex)Change It: Reading *Capital*, Rhetorically." *Fetishism as Cultural Discourse*. Ed. Emily Apter and William Pietz. Ithaca: Cornell UP, 1993. 152–85.

Kellner, Douglas. *Jean Baudrillard: From Marxism to Postmodernism and Beyond*. Stanford: Stanford UP, 1989.

Lacan, Jacques. *The Four Fundamental Concepts of Psycho-Analysis*. Trans. Alan Sheridan. New York: Norton, 1978.

———. "The Signification of the Phallus." *Écrits*. Trans. Alan Sheridan. New York: Norton, 1977. 281–91.

Laplanche, Jean. "The Order of Life." *Life and Death in Psychoanalysis*. Trans. Jeffrey Mehlman. Baltimore: Johns Hopkins UP, 1976. 8–18.

Lash, Scott. *Sociology of Postmodernism*. London: Routledge, 1990.

Lee, Martyn J. *Consumer Culture Reborn: The Cultural Politics of Consumption*. New York: Routledge, 1993.

McGuigan, Jim. *Cultural Populism*. New York: Routledge, 1992.

Marcuse, Herbert. "Affirmative Character of Culture." *Negations: Essays in Critical Theory*. Trans. Jeremy J. Shapiro. Boston: Beacon P, 1968. 88–133.

Marx, Karl. *Capital: A Critical Analysis of Capitalist Production*. Ed. Friedrich Engels and trans. Samuel Moore and Edward Aveling. Marx and Engels, *Gesamtausgabe*. MEGA II/9. Berlin: Dietz Verlag, 1990.

———. *Capital* II. Ed. Friedrich Engels. New York: International, 1968.

———. *Capital* III. Ed. Friedrich Engels. New York: International, 1968.

———. *A Contribution to the Critique of Political Economy*. Trans. Salo Ryazanskaya. *Collected Works*. Vol. 29. New York: International, 1987. 257–420.

————. *The Grundrisse.* Ed. and trans. David McLellan. New York: Harper, 1972.

————. *Das Kapital. Kritik der Politischen Ökonomie.* Erster Band. 183. MEGA II/8. Berlin: Dietz Verlag, 1989.

————. *Ökonomische Manuskripte.* 1857/58. MEGA II/1.1. Berlin: Dietz Verlag, 1976.

Miklitsch, Robert. *From Hegel to Madonna: Towards a General Economy of "Commodity Fetishism."* Albany: SUNY P, forthcoming.

Miller, Mark. *Material Culture and Mass Consumption.* Oxford: Oxford UP, 1991.

Mitchell, W. J. T. "The Rhetoric of Iconoclasm: Marxism, Ideology, and Fetishism." *Iconology: Image, Text, Ideology.* Chicago: U of Chicago P, 1980. 160–208.

O'Neill, John. *Five Bodies: The Human Shape of Modern Society.* Ithaca: Cornell UP, 1985.

Pefanis, Julian. *Heterology and the Postmodern: Bataille, Baudrillard, and Lyotard.* Durham: Duke UP, 1991.

Pietz, William. "Fetishism and Materialism: The Limits of Theory in Marx." *Fetishism as Cultural Discourse.* Ed. Emily Apter and William Pietz. Ithaca: Cornell UP, 1993. 119–51.

Plotnitsky, Arkady. *In the Shadow of Hegel: Complementarity, History, and the Unconscious.* Gainesville: UP of Florida, 1993.

————. *Reconfigurations: Critical Theory and General Economy.* Gainesville: UP of Florida, 1993.

Shields, Rob, ed. *Lifestyle Shopping: The Subject of Consumption.* New York: Routledge, 1993.

Silverman, Kaja. "Lost Objects and Mistaken Subjects: A Prologue." *The Acoustic Mirror: The Female Voice in Psychoanalysis and Cinema.* Bloomington: Indiana UP, 1988. 1–41.

Spivak, Gayatri. "Scattered Speculations on the Question of Value." *In Other Worlds: Essays in Cultural Politics.* New York: Methuen, 1987. 154–75.

Terrail, Jean-Pierre. "Commodity Fetishism and the Ideal of Needs." Terrail and Edmund Preteceille. *Capitalism, Consumption and Needs.* Trans. Sarah Mathews. Oxford: Oxford UP, 1985. 6–36.

Tomlinson, John. *Cultural Imperialism: An Introduction.* Baltimore: Johns Hopkins UP, 1991.

Veblen, Thorstein. *The Theory of the Leisure Class: An Economic Study of Institutions.* New York: Viking, 1965.

Williams, Linda. "Fetishism and Hard Core: Marx, Freud, and the 'Money Shot.'" *Hard Core: Power, Pleasure, and the "Frenzy of the Visible."* Berkeley: U of California P, 1989. 93–119.

Williams, Raymond. "From Base to Superstructure." *Marxism and Literature.* New York: Oxford UP, 1977. 75–82.

Willis, Susan. *A Primer for Everyday Life.* New York: Routledge, 1991.

Žižek, Slavoj. *The Sublime Object of Ideology.* London: Routledge, 1989.

The Ideology of Dialogue: The Bakhtin/De Man (Dis)Connection

Tom Cohen

> It is very hard to believe that Bakhtin spilt so much ink just to inform us that we should listen attentively to one another, treat each other as whole persons, be prepared to be corrected and interrupted, realise that life is an endless unfinished process, that too much dogma makes you narrow-minded, that nobody has a monopoly of the truth and that life is so much richer than any of our little ideas about it. He was not, after all, George Eliot or E. M. Forster or a liberal Democrat.
>
> —Terry Eagleton

Following the most popular reception of any theoretical opus into contemporary discourse—what was oddly called Bakhtin's "*re*discovery," as if a quality of repetition were nonetheless interwoven here—there seems to have emerged an impasse in the use of his terms. Not so much a burnout as the gradual awareness, perhaps, of a gap, or flaw, in the dissemination and translation itself, a tension lost, an assumed import receded. Not only has no Bakhtinian criticism clearly emerged (not itself a negative), but highly interpretive decisions by Bakhtin's editors have taken a

subtle toll, particularly as their own roles shift from being translators to defensive priests of ideological turf. This scenario looms
behind two very different recent collections, Gary Saul Morson
and Caryl Emerson's *Rethinking Bakhtin: Extensions and Challenges*,
which loosely represents an American Bakhtin as humanist poet-
ician, and Ken Hirschkop's *Bakhtin and Cultural Theory*, a qua-
simarxist (or British) Bakhtin whose hybrid interventions in "cultural theory" are philosophically sophisticated and diverse. Yet the
battles over the Bakhtin empire (more a multinational corporation
than the "industry" it has been called) show our continuing dependence on readings that avoid questioning the rhetorical strategies
of these writings—too often viewed as straightforward or even "vo-
cal" exposition.[1] If in the Hirschkop volume, cultural theory is expanded through juxtapositions of Bakhtin and reading, Bakhtin
and feminism, etc., the "challenges" and "extensions" of the American school—mostly to and of Michael Holquist's christological
reading in his *Mikhail Bakhtin*—yield a more conservative "Bakhtin," a neo-Kantian moralist and literary typologist suspiciously invested with a rhetoric of the "self" reminiscent of the late-20th-
century American academy.[2]

The politics of Bakhtin's reception was and remains complicated by peculiar alliances, including that between the marxist and
traditional humanist readings brought together to oppose poststructuralism in the 80's, yet—that seemingly accomplished—now
at odds. Thus, Graham Pechey in *Bakhtin and Cultural Theory* attacks Clark and Holquist's reading: "Bakhtin becomes in their
hands a topic in the 'history of ideas'; a shamefaced theologian
who adopts the opportunistic guise of a Philosopher of Freedom,
yet another apostle of sociality as intersubjectivity," arguing instead
for "rescuing Bakhtin from the cold storage of intellectual history
and from the politically compromised liberal academy which pre-
sides over this immobilising exposition" (39–40). Yet if Bakhtin's
somewhat alien constellations were first rendered *familiar* through
analogy to known texts (Buber, Sartre, Benjamin, or Lévi-Strauss),
much was also determined by who "Bakhtin" should not be read
as—specifically, as is familiar, the hypertextualism or "deconstruction" for which Bakthin was to provide a social and historically
grounded alternative.[3] The question remains what problems in
Bakhtin's poetics—the duplicity of his terms, the allegorical role of

signatures—were repressed as a "dialogic imagination" emerged that was later used to legitimate a rhetoric of the self and an ideology of communication? Securing this origin was clearly one aim of Clark and Holquist's book, which united stylistically diverse works under the unitary "Bakhtin" signature and then ascribed a reassuringly christian "transcoding" to the opus. A certain pathos, moreover, was routinely invoked by the narrative of a life and work rescued from the injustice of censorship and returned, supposedly, to its true meaning. Aspects of today's impasse may be traced to demands made on this Bakhtin of the 80's, among them the near total suppression of a permeating presence of Nietzsche throughout the early works (a presence precisely, necessarily, *un*marked in the writings themselves). To point this out is neither to play at "influence" studies nor to attempt another simple homogenization of Bakhtin's text—but rather, since resistance to this reading has itself been constitutive of those that have reigned, to rupture a certain pattern of translation that has framed Bakhtin's reception. Thus, Ken Hirschkop opens by asking the question too often brushed aside: "What is this 'dialogism' that so many celebrate as liberating and democratic: what are its actual cultural forms, its social or political preconditions, its participants, methods and goals?" (*BCT* 3).

If Bakhtin remains a cipher for any attempt to read certain impasses in cultural studies today, it is interesting how the right and elements of the left together constructed a "Bakhtin" who was supposed also to be the antidote of this "formalism." If there now appears a covert specularity between the right and certain left agendas in this appropriation (reflected, say, in Eagleton's early endorsement of Holquist's christological Bakhtin), there also remains a specularity between "Bakhtin" and his textualist others that has often harassed this scene from within. We may remind ourselves, here, of an often overlooked fault or scandal of sorts that haunts the critical scene going into the mid-90's: that, *despite* the "return to history" and the pursuit of the political in the 80's (and the marginalization of supposedly disengaged language-centered criticism), we clearly began the 90's in a *more* neoconservative national environment than before—a fact virtually replayed to the point of parody in Morson and Emerson's "Bakhtin." Moreover, having joined with the right to arrest poststructuralism and return to a foundational subject, the left would be itself linked with deconstruction and turned on by the right (as in the "culture wars"). Other inversions could be traced as well. On the one hand, if the humanist "Bakhtin" was to escape formalism by highlighting an intersubjective "dialogic imagination" of the self and other, it ended by producing a pallidly typological figure (i..e., another formalist); on the other hand, in cultural studies "Bakhtin" became a patron of "new historicism," which, for all of its well-intentioned politics, appears today as a fairly Reaganite phenomenon—one hoarding as capital the presumption of referential "facts." If the name Bakhtin has provided the foil against which a *mimetic* crisis in criticism dissimulates itself, one could say that "theory" was abjected in the 80's not because it was apolitical, or ahistorical, but because it represented a political problem that demanded other terms to be resolved. Despite the real critical opposition between the left and right versions of Bakhtin I began by noting, a troubling specularity resides at times in their projects.

My pretext for reexamining this scene involves a sort of katabasis then—a return to a curiously encrypted "past" scene, one of (non)reading between De Man and Bakhtin that suggests an alternate history to the official one outlined above. While much has occurred in and to the itineraries of both names in the intervening decade, my intent in returning to this site is also practical. I will ask not only why the *descriptive* poetics of "Bakhtin" seem to have led to an impasse in practical criticism, but what iconic role this repressed exchange has in the genealogy of the present scene. Specifically, if a tendency toward representational, historicist, or mimetic interpretation determined much in Bakhtin's construction, ignoring the rhetorical side of Bakhtin's performance has been costly. After surveying the terms of this exchange as staged by De Man, I will suggest that "dialogue" as used by Bakhtin may be an intentionally misleading figure. Rather than implying hermeneutic exchange or communication, Bakhtinian "dialogue" may be read as a wildly agonistic scene of power, positioning, deception, seduction, and defacement in the structural absence of "communication" as we tend to define it—and that containing this problem motivated Bakhtin's official guardians from the first. Moreover, if Bakhtin's project from this perspective seems to participate in a fundamentally posthumanist agenda (or postmarxist and postdeconstructive), I am finally less interested in the repressed presence of "Nietzsche" in Bakhtin's text than in the articulation of a certain *MarxNietzsche* (or *NietzscheMarx*) it today gives rise to. I suspect, accordingly, that beneath the story of Bakhtin's construction lies a politically relevant contest over how *referentiality* itself is to be conceived—and hence how politics, history, the "literary," formalism, and so on, are defined. If so, then any revision of the Bakhtin of the 80's we are still stuck in involves the possibility of moving leftist cultural studies from a mimetic model that frequently echoes the foundationalism of the right toward a linguistic materialism that sees the problematic of language less as formalistic play than as an agent of cultural intervention. My initial purpose in the following, then, is both to make more apparent to readers today how a decision was made early on about how Bakhtin should be installed and marketed, and to see where this event still haunts the uses of Bakhtin. That decision has to do not only with the way that linguistic theory (poststructuralism) had been "otherated" to favor certain interpretations of history and the social, but how the turn toward the political may have been in ways compromised by an implicit *re*turn to conservative representational models. A subsidiary consequence of reading this exchange is one to which I can give only brief attention: the question of the role today of De Man—let us even specify, "late De Man"—in the contemporary rearticulation of the political.

1. Making Bakhtin Prosaic (And Why It Wasn't That Hard)

While Hirschkop's collection has a philosophic range and depth nowhere matched in the American approach, the latter project is more interesting for what it tells us of the malaise of today's Bakhtin—particularly as the editors (Morson and Emerson) lay out the interpretive agenda followed in their subsequent *Mikhail Bakhtin: The Creation of a Prosaics*, where three totalizing "global concepts" (Prosaics, Unfinalizability, and Dialogue—the first the authors' *own* "neologism" to indicate Bakhtin's interest in prose and the everyday) are used to interpret and hierarchize Bakhtin's concerns. The collection is also interesting for containing (or, literally, trying to contain) the dense, tricky, and largely ignored essay by Paul De Man, "Dialogue and Dialogism," which has the unique status of speaking back, as it were, from within one specular méconnaissance that defined Bakhtin in the 80's. De Man's short essay, first given as a talk before an MLA audience on "Fiction and Its Referents" in 1981, then published in *Poetics Today* (1983) before appearing in *The Resistance to Theory* (1986), was an appropriately dialogic choice, since on its surface it dismantles the hermeneutic conception of "dialogue" or Bakhtin most celebrated by the editors—exposing it, essentially, as dependent on a false claim of immediate access to alterity. Interestingly, the collection immediately inserts a counterpiece designed exclusively to contain and negate this, Mathew Roberts' "Poetics Hermeneutics Dialogic: Bakhtin and Paul De Man." What is odd and suggestive is that, rather than analyzing or debating De Man's apparent thesis—that Bakhtin promises an access to alterity he nowhere delivers—he suspends any possibility of this "dialogue," and this by arguing that the two critics could not possibly understand one another anyway (he notes their "mutual unintelligibility" [134]), since they supposedly have different concepts of the "self" ("the most fundamental differences between Bakhtin and De Man lie in their respective conceptions of the self or subject" [116]). He generally opposes De Man's "rigorous, unending effort to dis-close and distinguish an ontological self" (120) to Bakhtin's embrace of "the world in general" (134).

This critical tack further raises suspicion as to what is at stake in De Man's piece—or what drew the editors, with a certain intuitive doom, to include it? Whatever must be isolated in De Man's piece seems nonetheless to subtly contaminate the collection by the emergence of the last essay, which, oddly yet tellingly in Nietzsche's name, turns against "dialogism" itself. While one could read "Dialogue and Dialogism" as a brief and minor discrimination in De Man's late work, his recurrent self-references in it give the piece a weirdly trenchant and uniquely autobiographical tone. One might speculate that a certain doubling, present in the title, was imposed on De Man for this occasion—a sort of contract to address a "Bakhtin" set against deconstruction, found in that audience's construction—that required him to fend off the invariable other Bakhtin engendered by the encounter, one too proximate or even irritatingly susceptible to a De Manian reading, and that this fundamental duplicity and doubling pervades the simulacrum of "dialogue" in the essay (with Bakhtin, with the audience, with a reader of Bakhtin to come).

I will examine this exchange, then, by keeping in mind the manner in which the stakes of the outcome—who wins, who loses; who is read, who isn't; who is misread, and how—remain a cipher for the contemporary critical landscape in certain ways. Thus, while De Man repeatedly exempts himself from the critical community then engaging and celebrating Bakhtin, his sweeping erasure of almost every available reading in the final line addresses the current impasse of Bakhtin's terms. Against the hermeneutic understandings of dialogue, then, De Man early on notes that we may translate the term as "double-talk" ("[i]t can, first of all, simply mean double-talk, the necessary obliqueness of any persecuted speech that cannot, at the risk of survival, openly say what it means to say" [*RB* 106]), thus raising the specter of a Bakhtin whose own text dissimulates substantially more than his fondest readers—or strategically, "De Man" himself—assumes.

We cannot ignore, moreover, that this *dialogue* as if between "dialogue" and "dialogism" (if this even is a binary) is foreclosed by and within the collection itself. In another sense, *Rethinking Bakhtin* conceals a family affair that is later played out in the editors' subsequent *Prosaics* (like *Mikhail Bakhtin,* a jointly authored effort). *Rethinking Bakhtin*'s programmatic introduction is designed to revise the American "Bakhtin" as long managed by a small rotating group of brilliant and energetic slavicists (Holquist and his slightly Oedipal successors, Morson and Emerson). If it attempts to reverse and refine—"challenge" and "extend"—the ideological investment of Holquist's biography, what is worrisome is that the collection produces a Bakhtin refined into an oddly reduced neoformalist or right-wing practical critic subtly at odds with the Bakhtin familiar through tropes like the carnivalesque. As elsewhere, the rhetoric of self and other oversees a manageable economy of "difference" while asserting and defending an ideology of authorial intent and meaning. Thus, the *Prosaics* distances the entire import of the carnivalesque, which involves the transvaluative import of the priority of the reversible ("like Janus") material sign in Bakhtin: "From an ethical perspective as well, the role of the 'public square word'"—that is, the word as sheer exteriority, the very import of Bakhtin—"is somewhat inconsistent with Bakhtin's other formulations. . . . This separation of the word from any grounding in the ethical speaking person is said to be one of the privileges of the people's laughter" (447).[4] Where Hirschkop would expand Bakhtin through diverse cultural juxtapositions, Morson and Emerson (henceforth ME, keeping in mind the projected ideology of the self) respond by further paring Bakhtin's territorial canon, stripping it first of the critical "pseudonymous" production signed Voloshinov and Medvedev.[5] Such decisions seem designed primarily to control interpretive or ideological options. If in *Rethinking Bakhtin* any American school to emerge appears both occasional and parochial, the volume's culminating section on "The Dangers of Dialogue" unveils its own anxieties. This is most explicit in Michael Andre Bernstein's interesting and finally open assault on dialogism as a figure of Nietzschean *ressentiment* that stands opposed to the rhetoric of the speaker's authenticity and pathos ("The Poetics of *Ressentiment*"). Billed as the critical revision of a master who has evinced too much "hero-worship," the move in fact exudes a discrete hostility toward an unassimilable aspect of the text for this group of Bakhtinians (no wonder that, in the *Prosaics*, ME will have to go on and excise from the scene, virtually, the carnivalesque and the *Rabelais* book itself). Here the early 80's attempts to appropriate "dialogism" for the ideology of the self, from Todorov's Buberesque redaction to Holquist's communicationist ideology, *come full circle*. In one sense, the editors' strategy to create a Bakhtin for the neocon 90's is, in part, another response to the "dangers of dialogue."

The move is not uninteresting for what it says of American cultural appropriation in the 80's and the legitimating aura the academy attaches to the act of translation—as though proximity to the "original" (language) guaranteed reading skills. One problem is that the editors' new Bakhtin cannot quite get out of being the unhappy specular double of Holquist's. A retreat from the latter's religious and biographical reductions (an untranslated christian urtext, "transcoding," the production unified under one name) ends by creating a sort of neoconservative antimarxist and antitheorist who, however timely for contemporary politics, is divorced even from "cultural theory." If ME's methodology both repeats and reverses Holquist's most problematic simplifications through revising the question of authorship, this American Bakhtin of the 90's appears divested not only of poststructuralist errancy but marxism, and without old-time religion.[6] If one of the naïvetés of Clark and Holquist's *Mikhail Bakhtin* was the claim that an uncirculated early sketch, the "Architectonics of Responsibility," might be paraphrased to interpret the entirety of the later work as a "transcoded" christian text (which shows an allegorical awareness, however flatfooted), ME—or, we might say, ME's duplex "I"—almost comically repeats the move with a newly uncovered counter urtext of their own, "Toward a Philosophy of the Act."[7] This text is cited not for its unifying christian message, but (more timely still) for its polemic value, when properly paraphrased, in positioning Bakhtin as a user-friendly antitheoretical theorist. The result is engaging, since the once carnivalesque Bakhtin appears here ever meaner and more repressive ("Ethics for Bakhtin is a matter not of norms but of 'oughtness'" [8]). The irrascibly critical Bakhtin to emerge gets to dismiss, in the name of clear "beliefs" attributed to him, not only marxism and relativism, but sociology and "theoretism" (which becomes a kind of code-word for contemporary theory): "Hostility to all forms of 'theoretism,' evident in 'The Philosophy of the Act,' was one constant of Bakhtin's long career" (29). Bakhtin's ethos of dissemination is supplanted by the dissemination of ethics (though, as Hirschkop notes, "Bakhtin's appeal to the concrete, and his hope that 'responsibility' would follow from attention to one's immediate situation, sounds rather hollow" [*BBC* 17]). The entirely remarkable and pivotal early theoretical works on the performative exigency of language are thus exiled anew, returned to their "real" signatories, Voloshinov and Medvedev, with the antimarxist Bakhtin "dialogically" learning from them ("[w]e believe that the relations among Bakhtin, Voloshinov, and Medvedev were genuinely dialogic. Their readers can only be the poorer for losing the chance to choose among them" [48]). Yet if Holquist unified the works under Bakhtin's name so that his beliefs could be asserted, here a similar purification happens in reverse by purging the pseudonymous/nonpseudonymous texts. In both instances, the object is to establish a Bakhtinian author whose neoconservative "beliefs" can be ideologically asserted.

There is, of course, a hitch. If the question of *signature* is usually probed as one of literal attribution, we erase where its intentional irresolvability functions as a complex marking that permeates and (perpetually) alters the production and its textuality, transversely dislocating (and here is the threat) the import of the signature "Bakhtin." At no point has the use (or erasure) of Voloshinov's *signature* been a matter of indifference to the ideology of commentators. Rather than being celebrated as a trickster, as was once popular, a puritanical figure emerges for whom any "pseudonymous" strategy is rejected, which would contradict "Bakhtin's key belief (stated in 'Toward a Philosophy of the Act') that action must be ethical and 'responsible.' It will be recalled that for Bakhtin 'signature' was a fundamental ethical act" (40). While a general claim for unity reassuringly domesticates "polyphony" ("Bakhtin offers us the image of a world . . . still possessing its own unity" [21]), the considerable contradictions in Bakhtin's rhetorical use of "relativity" appear unilaterally vanquished by ME's edict ("[i]ndeed, if anything, relativism is the worst form of theoretism— worse than ethical and cognitive systematization" [9]). As becomes yet clearer in the *Prosaics,* ME produces an excluded middle version of "relativism" to enroll their Bakhtin against contemporary theory: "If, as some have recently concluded, all disputes ultimately reduce to questions of power and interest, then 'authentic dialogue' about values and meanings is pointless" (233). The new Bakhtin's greatest sin may be to be all too prosaic, stripped of almost all that made him interesting, become an existential apparatchik and somewhat embarrassing *moraliste.* In place of the carnivalesque or, for that matter, the problem of the social, we find emphasis on ethics, "parody," genre applications: "Bakhtin's early writings were emphatically *not* sociological, except in the trivial sense in which every meditation on selves and others is sociological" (48). The cost of this gambit is transparent. The remarkable rhetorical strategies of Voloshinov and Medvedev's works are occluded, since, by the formula, they must be simplified as "sincerely Marxist" and systematic ("[t]hey appear to have taken some of Bakhtin's specific concepts and shown that they could be integrated into systems" [47]). It is not incidental that the very early "Act," as the new key to the work, precedes Bakhtin's revolutionary turn toward the materiality of language. Insisting on the rhetoric of existential humanism to eclipse the priority of language, ME will assert in *Prosaics* against Todorov's supposed concern with "the autotelic text" that "the developing person and the dialogic voice . . . were Bakhtin's main concerns" (6) or that unfinalizability is positively defined "to specify its nature and function in our lives" (38). That ME's views remain, in the end, extensions of rather than challenges to Holquist's theologic traces becomes apparent at many points in the *Prosaics* ("Bakhtin's ultimate image of such dialogic faith is, characteristically, a conversation with Christ" [62]). My point, of course, is that rather than an aberration, this Bakhtin only realizes that begun with Holquist—and, as we will return to, contaminates that of cultural studies as well.

Thus, Bernstein's rejection of "dialogism" as a techne of *ressentiment* merely articulates a more profound resentment in the collection. Here that seems to be against the implications of a "crisis of citation" in dialogism that threatens the authenticity of the self or a voice that is its own—a direct, if unseen, resentment at the principle of material otherness as such. Bakhtin, who clearly had been enrolled as an unthreatening figure to help manage a restricted economy of difference, is here castigated for resisting: he has all along been a time-bomb. The inversion is familiar yet done in Nietzsche's name: the rhetoric of the other's word empties the autonomy of the speaker or self and is that of the reactive slave, rather than the master, though it is the delusion of mastery whose blindness is expressed, here, as Bernstein's resentment at the supposed implications of *ressentiment:* "what Bakhtin understands by the 'dialogic imagination' is uncomfortably similar to Nietzsche's account of the slave's reactive, dependent, and fettered consciousness. Every word the Nietzschean slave utters, every value he posits, is purely reactive, impregnated by the words and values of others and formulated entirely in response to and as an anticipation of the responses he will elicit" (201). The attempt to bring Nietzsche into play remains insightful, if almost upside-down, since it focuses on the relation between the "other's word" as such and memory, repetition, or sheer anteriority.[8] For Bernstein speaks in the name of a restored immediacy ("[t]he dialogic status of their words, ideas, and sentiments is experienced as pure entrapment, triggering only rage and *ressentiment*" [208]), echoing Morson's assumption of "Bakhtin's unquestioned valuation of the new, the original, the authentic" (60), as if unaware that the "living word" may only be a necessary trope for a particular recirculation of the "dead," the material, the *alien word*. It is not accidental that Menippea's "dialogue of the dead" should be a model of antigenre, since the most alive word metaphorically is not that spoken immediately but that, as in the polyphonic novel, suffused with the most antithetical (scriptive) traces or "intonations." For Bernstein the antidote for Bakhtin's "dialogism," or, one might add with all sorts of conditions and in *a* positive sense I will return to, *nihilism*, turns out familiarly to be Habermas ("a salutory correction to the abstractions of Bakhtin" [291 fn]), though the "dialogism" Bernstein attacks is the most comfortably affirmative redaction to begin with, the intersubjective version of Holquist or Wayne Booth, with whom his own allegiances clearly lie.[9] The entire gameboard seems to depart from some original unmarked reversal, a specularization of Bakhtin which would indeed be less in evidence if "dialogism" were first grasped not as an ethos of communication (from Buber to Habermas) but an agonistic battle for mastery. Much seems to turn on the suppression of a Nietzschean reading to begin with.

Bernstein's allusion to Nietzsche could be developed differently. For one thing, the Bakhtinian word is repeatedly depicted as anticipating in the other's word an anticipation of one's own (anticipation), with the intent of overpowering and incorporating the counterreading of an always verbal other. What is infrequently noted is that the all important trope of the "other's word [*chuzoe slovo*]" merges figuratively with other categories in Voloshinov's mythographic history in *Marxism and the Philosophy of Language*—that is, genealogy of what precedes the permanent contemporaneity of the text—specifically with the "alien word" ("coalesce(d) in the depths of the historical consciousness of nations with the idea of authority, the idea of power" [*MPL* 75]), philologism ("the inevitable distinguishing mark of the whole of linguistic thinking" [*MPL* 71]), the "priest's word," descriptions of writing that recall passages from the *Genealogy of Morals*, and with the "dead word" of formalism—pure anteriority at the point that becomes another figure for materiality, exteriority, or trace as such. In each of these categories a variation on the idea of the memory trace, repetition, and materiality is at work, since any "crisis of citation" has to do more with the anteriority of a word that itself generates "consciousness" ("*consciousness itself can arise and become a viable fact only in the material embodiment of signs*" [*MPL* 11]).[10] The American critics' obsession with the explanatory pretense of biographic "fact"—particularly in one who pointedly, biographically, erases just this—and talk of "authoring a self" indicates an anxiety about authority and origin that Bakhtin provokes. As an allegorical figure, *formalism* itself appears less a concrete school or epoch—as it is in Medvedev's *The Formal Method*—than a problem posed by the permanent *anteriority* of cited, inhabited, incorporated, or repeated words. The entire configuration might illuminate a duplicity within the word or concept of formalism itself: specifically, that "formalism" may be, figuratively, what *always has just been the case* and *what will return* as the aesthetic moment of language's phenomenality: that is, one ambivalent cipher for the materiality in language itself. Despite the loud insistence of the hermeneutic reading of Bakhtinian dialogue, it is nowhere clear that Bakhtin deploys the concept of "self" that American commentators so prize.[11] Quite the contrary, this particular conceit seems interdicted openly and repeatedly in Voloshinov's antisubjectivist *Marxism,* where personality itself is the effect of a self-differing and material word (*"a word is not an expression of inner personality; rather, inner personality is an expressed or inwardly impelled word,"* MPL 153).

As the *Prosaics* makes clear, the deletion of Voloshinov's essay from the Bakhtin canon has everything to do with enforcing a conventional enough ideology: "Presenting a picture of Bakhtin's views of the self entails special difficulties, because so many earlier accounts—including our own—have been based on the belief that Voloshinov's book on Freud and his comments on psychology in *Marxism and the Philosophy of Language* belong to Bakhtin" (172). Bakhtin may even be said to practice a covert yet systematic Nietzschean reversal of values in undermining the too familiar concepts he empties and recirculates (sign, dialogue, value, ideology, genre), terms that negatively and anamorphically trope their "official" or philosophic meanings by moving "in between" and undoing the binaries that upheld the terms themselves. This "interindividual" linguistic and material space on which visibility, publicness, and materiality hinges is sometimes called, simply, the "social." However belated a Nietzschean Bakhtin might seem, the *Genealogy of Morals* and *The Birth of Tragedy* would be the texts to begin it and are omnipresent, if uncited, in the work of the 20's. Returning now to the one piece in this collection that is out of place, Paul De Man's strategy appears odder still, since in dismantling the hermeneutic appropriation of dialogue, he seems to set aside a very different interpretation that he shows no interest in developing—what allows us to address a second or effaced "dialogue" in this scene. With this, it seems, we open onto a crypt—or a cryptic exchange—within recent critical history or the archaeology of the present itself.

2. Doubles of "Dialogue"

If the problem of assessing cultural criticism's investment in a certain (mis)reading of Bakhtin is a practical one—and if the impasse in today's Bakhtin is traceable to such a move—the point of returning to this site must be itself practical. Since rewriting this (hi)story involves projecting, as it must, a different present as well, underlying questions must include: What *other* ways of reading "dialogue" exist? If the 90's has succeeded in creating a retrohumanist ethos mirrored in the rights to (or exploitation of) "Bakhtin," what direction will dismantling this investment take? Moreover, does the mere invocation of Nietzsche not simply call up the supposed aporia of poststructuralist "politics" as such?[12]

An address originally before an MLA audience, De Man's "Dialogue and Dialogism" evinces an odd tendency toward autobiographical inscription. Among other things, it covertly marks the framework of the performance, in which the sociological "Bakhtin" of De Man's audience is potentially doubled, if not overtly against the textualist De Man, at all events against "deconstruction." In asking whether "dialogue" cannot first be translated as "doubletalk," De Man marks that as the performative premise for any reading of (which is and is not to say dialogue with) "Bakhtin," which he demonstrates by solemnly referring to Bakhtin's "highly competent and clear-sighted introducers," Holquist and Todorov. When the postscript later replaces the hermeneutic model of dialogue with Rousseau's model of "parrying, feinting and setting traps in a sequence of attacks and defenses somewhat like a fencing match" (106), De Man implicitly exposes his own strategy of calculated entrapment at a moment it cannot be openly responded to or countered—thus tactically derealizing the potential to name that duplicity. While the performance occurs before its MLA audience in the mock-dialogic manner of inscribing "I" and "you" repeatedly, De Man doubles dialogue itself (already "double-talk"), as the two words of the title suggest. If there are also two Bakhtins in the address, one who seems marked by "double-talk" and who, unread, is set aside, and the other of the hermeneutic reading of the audience, there is also a "De Man" clearly represented by the self-references, disqualifications, and mock-exclusions in the reading (as when De Man excludes himself from those having anything to take from Bakhtin). Thus, De Man maneuvers not only to dismantle Bakhtin and deny the specular relation he inherits from outside, but to repeatedly block the reverse moment of that specularity from emerging—the generally unconsidered possibility of a "De Manian" Bakhtin. For in opposing the hermeneutic reading of Bakhtin to an agonistic and dissimulative (that is, truly social, material, and pragmatic) notion of "dialogism," De Man seems to mark another Bakhtin "betrayed" by his readership.

De Man's critique of Bakhtin's *dialogism* involves splitting the same term first into two moments: "Bakhtin at times conveys the impression that one can accede from dialogism as a metalinguistic (i.e., formal) structure to dialogism as a recognition of exotopy. . . . the passage, in other words, from dialogism to dialogue" (111), or from poetics to hermeneutics.[13] The argument may also be read as a sequence of traps:

> Very summarily put, it is possible to think of dialogism as a still formal method by which to conquer or sublate formalism itself . . . The self-reflexive, autotelic or, if you wish, narcissistic structure of form, as a definitional description enclosed within specific borderlines, is hereby replaced by an assertion of the otherness of the other, preliminary to even the possibility of a recognition of his otherness . . . Whether the passage from otherness to the recognition of the other, the passage, in other words, from dialogism to dialogue, can be said to take place in Bakhtin as more than a desire, remains a question for Bakhtin interpretation to consider in the proper critical spirit. This renders premature any more specific consideration of how this recognition is to occur: as a religious transcendentalism which would allow one to read "God" wherever Bakhtin says "society," as a Heideggerian disclosure of ontological truth in the

otherness of language or as a secular but messianic ideologism that would bear a superficial, and perhaps misleading, resemblance to the position attributed to Walter Benjamin. (109–10)

De Man's intervention will momentarily focus on three moments: Bakhtin's aberrant exclusion of trope, his misleading binarization of lyric and dialogue, and his subsequent collapse into a precritical phenomenology. His argument also moves through a series of tactical asides that obliquely revise the text's figural import, as when he notes that polyphony involves less the Greek *phone* than differential musical notation ("as in a musical score" [109]). At the heart of the critique, however, De Man determines that in Bakhtin "trope" is itself deemed undialogic or unsocial, and this moment—related to Bakhtin's notorious exile of the lyric from his concerns—opens a contradiction:

> One would have to point out (1) that, for Bakhtin, the trope is an intentional structure directed toward an object and, as such, a pure episteme and not a fact of language; this in fact excludes tropes from literary discourse, poetic as well as prosaic and locates them, perhaps surprisingly, in the field of epistemology; (2) that the opposition between trope as object-directed and dialogism as social-oriented discourse sets up a binary opposition between object and society that is itself tropological in the worst sense, namely as a reification; (3) and more revealing for us, that as the analysis of dialogical refraction develops, Bakhtin has to reintroduce the categorical foundations of a precritical phenomenalism in which there is no room for exotopy, for otherness, in any shape or degree. When it is said, for example, that "the heteroglot voices . . . create the background necessary for (the author's) own voice" (1981: 278), we recognize the foreground-background model derived from Husserl's theories of perception and here uncritically assimilating the structure of language to the structure of a secure perception: from that moment on, the figure of refraction and of the light ray becomes coercive as the only possible trope for trope, and we are within a reflective system of mise en abyme that is anything but dialogical. It is therefore not surprising that, still in the same passage, Bakhtin modulates irrevocably from dialogism to a conception of dialogue as question and answer of which it can then be said that "the speaker breaks through the alien territory against his, the lis-

tener's, apperceptive background" (282). Again, there is no
trace of dialogism left in such a gesture of dialectical imperialism that is an inevitable part of any hermeneutic system of
question and answer. The ideologies of otherness and of hermeneutic understanding are not compatible, and therefore
their relationship is not a dialogical but simply a contradictory
one. It is not a foregone conclusion whether Bakhtin's discourse is itself dialogical or simply contradictory. (112)

When De Man first excuses himself from "taking part" in a
critical activity that has, he adds, "barely begun," that is given an
active form: "since I ignore the Russian language, it is not an enterprise in which I can responsibly hope to take part" (107). This self-
removal might be doubly read, if "the Russian" actively ignored is
also an *other* or untranslated Bakhtin, one rhetorically set aside for
the duration of the critique. The term "ignore" recurs in describing the novelists' supposed otherness ("they simply ignore such
strongly suggestive oppositions as those between author and character" [108]). The nonrelation that obtains between De Man and
his characters, "De Man" and "Bakhtin," will not be easily ex-
pounded. In fact, De Man stages the address within the question
of "fact and fiction" (107), shifting the borders of these two continually. If the reading of Bakhtinian dialogue as communication of
self and other was a fiction, it nonetheless behaves like a fact of
the critical community that reifies and uses it. After extending the
preliminary definition of dialogue as "double-talk" to the Russian
("there is ample evidence . . . this meaning is entirely relevant in
his case" [107]), he brackets its import as his critique proceeds.
Later, in citing the text to be taken apart, a brief piece from "Discourse in the Novel" on "tropes," De Man notes another suspension: "if one is willing to suspend for a moment the potential dialogic otherness of these statements, he seems, on the whole, to
consider that the discourse of tropes is not dialogical" (110). If
De Man puts aside a certain Bakhtin—he who speaks in effaced
"double-talk," whose statements subsequently can be read in a "potential dialogic otherness," whose passages are "appropriate(d)"
(111)—it is not clear whether De Man stages a reading (as a "battle
for mastery") with the audience's Bakhtin, or whether the refusal
of such an engagement is not itself strategic.
    This dialogic model of fencing or entrapment further in-

scribes the reader in the text: "the smart reader always outwits an author who depends on him from the moment he has opened a dialogue that is never entirely gratuitous, that is always a battle for mastery" (113). De Man appears at times to perform a reading of "Bakhtin" that acts as the novelist does to the poet: "the novelist does not set out to take the place of his master, the epic poet, but to set him free from the restricting coercions of his single-minded, monological vision" (108), yet this is also blocked by his refusal to adopt a usurpative relation to Bakhtin. Thus, De Man makes himself the negative pivot of the "odd list" of Bakhtin's "admirers" he at first excludes himself from, only then to (pretend to) reverse: "at the moment I appropriate these passages as the ground of my own admiration . . . , I have included myself in the odd list of Bakhtin admirers from which I first pretended to be excluded" (111–12). For what these *admirers* "have in common, at least negatively" would be the one critic who alone cannot be inscribed in Bakhtin's methodology: "a literary theoretician or critic concerned with tropological displacements of logic, with a rhetoric of cognition as well as of persuasion" (111)—that is, De Man. De Man, after exempting himself from partaking of the dialogue on Bakhtin's work because he ignores Russian, points to himself as what "negatively" binds Bakhtin's readers by his own exclusion. I, "De Man," am not a reader of Bakhtin or an admirer—the text says—though (another?) "De Man" later seems to anamorphically invert this parenthesis. What must be established to follow this doubling is where dialogue itself is doubled into two versions (dialogue and dialogism), and whether they are fact or fiction. But if De Man recognizes his negative inscription in the "hermeneutic" Bakhtin, at least in that represented by his audience, he cannot wholly control the specular relation he so steadfastly refuses (and thus accelerates). He seems less concerned with the opposition to Bakhtin he uses to attack the hermeneutic reading than with the figure of "substitution" the latter implies. As was clear above, one of the problems of the American Bakhtin is that it always suppressed the performative dimension of the text. Like the author "Rousseau" invoked in the postscript ("it would be naive to ask who wins the match since in this model, Rousseau, as author, controls the moves of each of the antagonists," 111) our attention is drawn to "how one fights"—dialogics, I might add, as sheer will to power, the site not of shared understanding but the fight over who will install and mnemonically control a (no doubt political, yet also) interpretive or aesthetic regime.

De Man's strategy is to repeatedly double back over a figure he has just critiqued, assuming its reversed position while exposing his own violation of the reader's presumed contract. Thus, after denouncing binaries ("to the extent that they allow or invite synthesis . . . the most misleading of differential structures," 103), De Man can pass unseen into producing what might be called the binary of binaries, announced in his title, by indicting "the passage, in other words, from dialogism to dialogue." This passage occurs "in other words" because two forms of the same word, *dialogism,* are at stake: a passage from "dialogism as a metalinguistic (i.e., formal) structure to dialogism as a recognition of exotopy." Since the distinction does not belong to Bakhtin, this dialogism covertly cites the expectation of the audience (an "author and a concept— dialogism—that can be made to accommodate" various critical models). Moreover, the narrative movement toward the *promise of alterity* itself appears to almost invert the normal narrative direction in Bakhtin (one equally suspect) from monologue to dialogism. This now appears, however, as the "passage" from dialogism to (hermeneutic) "dialogue," the latter being, nonetheless, "not necessarily monologic." Yet the binary that results in the doubling of dialogism appears as if already suspended in De Man's title, "Dialogue and Dialogism," where the order is reversed in advance and the "and" declares no necessary direction. Thus, the two *D*'s in the title and De Man's refused doubling against this Bakhtin suggest another subtext. Rather than "De Man" substituting for Derrida in the public opposition of Bakhtin to deconstruction, Derrida can inhabit, momentarily, the specular position of "Bakhtin" in relation to "De Man" within the article's staged agon—a position criticized, by contrast, for its hermeneutic shortcuts. The two D's of (the) "dialogue" (or deconstruction) appear in a fractured specular model that De Man simultaneously refuses, as he does all doubling between himself and Bakhtin. The text focuses not only on fact and fiction but on otherness as such and rewrites dialogue as who is inscribed (or not) in whose text—that is, dialogue *as* usurpative inscription. (There are certain moments in De Man's Bakhtin connection, so to speak, in which the imaginary "dialogue" is, simply, cut-off, hung up on, disconnected from either (ventriloquized) side, to be resumed over that interruption.)

Behind this ostensible "dialogue," however, there is another scene of reading. At the center of the critique Bakhtin is excluded from the ranks of critics "concerned with tropological displacements" through a bracketing of "the potential dialogical otherness of these statements." Bypassing De Man's tongue-in-cheek treatment of the chosen text ("among the richest in the canon") and his planting there of a "conception of dialogue as question and answer" that facilitates the polemic, two moments stand out. Bakhtin's segregation of lyric from dialogic prose that "excludes tropes from literary discourse, poetic as well as prosaic," and a return to a "precritical phenomenalism" void of otherness that is indicted as "assimilating the structure of language to the structure of a secure perception: from that moment on, the figure of refraction and of the light ray becomes coercive as the only possible trope for trope, and we are within a reflective system of mise en abyme that is anything but dialogical" (105). What is acknowledged by De Man's language is the possibility nonetheless of a *tropological* reading of Bakhtin. In fact, in playing against the Russian's own fictive binary—that of lyric and prose, epic and novel—De Man calls him "tropological in the worst possible sense, namely as a reification." Another way to say this would be that he is *indeed* tropological, only in another or even bad "sense," or indeed, the worst, since Bakhtin unforgivably muddles important distinctions by his typological strategies and general imprecision. Moreover, it is in the site of a *trope for trope* that De Man fingers the collapse of "the tropological" into "a reflective system of mise en abyme." What is entailed, though, by a return to "precritical phenomenalism," particularly if we know that Voloshinov's dismantling of phenomenology through the primacy of the material "sign" over perception renders that regression impossible to read literally, that is, as other than a strategy itself?

Here De Man's move illuminates Bakhtin's own cultural entrapment. The closing examination of Rousseau's "Dialogue on the Novel" as a countertext presents "Rousseau" as an alternate signature of De Man. As in the case of "Rousseau," the author "controls the moves of each of the antagonists," and what appears at first as a session of question and answer (a hermeneutic exchange) comments on the preceding performance itself. Thus, De Man rewrites the exchange between Rousseau's author and reader as that between a poetics and a hermeneutics: "The relationship between poetics and hermeneutics, like that between R the author and N the reader, is dialogical to the precise extent that one cannot be substituted for the other, despite the fact that the non-dialogical discourse of question and answer (the mode of the cited text) fully justifies the substitution" (113). The author now in question, Rousseau–De Man, guards against any slippage toward the "smart reader" ("the smart reader always outwits an author who depends on him"). De Man ends with the surprising erasure not of Bakhtin, but of those readers who imitate or apply his criticism or hold dialogue with him, that is, almost all familiar strategies of reading: "To imitate or to apply Bakhtin, to read him by engaging him in a dialogue, betrays what is most valid in his work" (114). Yet there is an equivocation in the cited Rousseau text or its commentary, where it seems that the ignored or excluded Russian—that is, the Bakhtin whose text is "betrayed" by his readership—threatens to reenter the text as a potential reader of De Man. In the Rousseau text, De Man says, it is N (the reader) who is identified as the straight-man to the continuing irony and control of R (the author): "The character designated by R and who is the author, refuses the substitution offered to him," which is "the refusal, in terms of poetics, to grant the substitutive symmetry implied by a hermeneutics" (114). Yet in the text, it is in fact N the reader who *both* proposes *and* dismisses the prospect of this exchange, and not R:

> **N:** . . . I advise you, however, to switch parts. Pretend that I am the one who urges you on to publish this collection of letters and that you are the one who resists. You give yourself the objections and I'll rebut them. It will sound more humble and make a better impression. **R:** Will it also be in conformity with what you find to be praiseworthy in my character? **N:** No, I was setting you a trap. Leave things as they are. (114)

Why does De Man give the priority to the author, since the refusal—the controlling gesture—is not that of R, as De Man explicitly says ("R . . . refuses the substitution offered to him"), but the reader N? If the text's own dialogue is inevitably a form of double-talk—the only honest approach to poetics—what is represented as a "hermeneutics" in Bakhtin (likened to the reader, N) appears here to be marked as yet another poetics of writing and reading anyway. A new material conception of dialogue as dissimulation is opposed to the familiar icon of Bakhtinian dialogue, the hermeneutic one, only to find that this "false" reading itself may have been a calculated trap or moment in Bakhtin's own double-dissimulation (or dia-logos).

The specularity that a certain De Man here refuses yet differently enacts might be addressed in the use of "admire" or "admiration." The term is used to organize the intervention throughout, down through the late double reversal that feigns to "include" De Man on this list he exempted himself from at first: "What one has to admire Bakhtin for (that is, want to be in his place in having written what he wrote), as all his present readers, including myself, do, is his hope that, by starting out, as he does, in a poetics of novelistic discourse one may gain access to the power of a hermeneutics" (114). Here admiration exists outside the possibility of any "switching" of places, as a desire to be in the place of when writing, yet De Man's admiration is ironically effaced as for the "hope" evinced for what is never realizable, and becomes a weakness. What does it mean to admire or not to admire Bakhtin—to imitate, to mirror, to deface, to envy, to appropriate, to desire to substitute for? With whom is De Man conducting his battle of entrapment, the reader, the simulacrum "Bakhtin," another Bakhtin? What may be rewritten as a(d)mir(ror)ation suspends or defaces the mock-specularity that Bakhtin seductively solicits from numerous readers. We may well understand why Roberts wished only to neutralize this essay, which literally defaces Bakhtin (before being caught in this move). Yet it also has no obvious exit. The obstacle presented to any subsequent reader is how to apply Rousseau's conception of "dialogue" to Bakhtin's own writing, yet in doing so to evade the appearance of merely "saving" Bakhtin from De Man (an ironic nontask). But why the catastrophe? Why can we not "imitate or apply" Bakhtin—outside of a more critical reading of his text—without *betraying* (a harsh word) what may seem most valid in his project?

3. The Transvaluation(s) of Bakhtin

In a distinct sense, De Man creates his text as a trap that cannot be gotten out of, but only broken with—yet it is also imbricated in the critical politics of the 80's in a way with distinct resonance still. If anything, then, it seems one knife by which to force an exit from the enclosure of the American Bakhtin without providing another. It is what is not in De Man's text, or the blindness and aggression that sustain its controlled vituperation and inscription in the general text of its audience that remain of interest here. I want to proceed, then, with the beginning of a reading which, decidedly not De Manian, nonetheless helps situate De Man's notion of aesthetic ideology today and could be called with all sorts of clarifications "Nietzschean" in a distinct and obvious sense. My suspicion is that since, it seems, just this reading was (and remains?) excluded or repressed, it may currently be a necessary detour.

If De Man's reading of "dialogism" is the pragmatic or, indeed, materialist one—that dependent on a materialist conception of language—ME and Holquist's readings remain "subjective expressionist" in that sense dismantled by *Marxism*'s critique of phenomenology, the text that may be most crucial to rereading Bakhtin today. The ideology of dialogue is a prototype of ideological anamorphosis itself as defined by Slavoj Žižek: the site where a piece of radical exteriority is enfolded as the dispossessing kernel for a discourse of interiority.[14] Yet De Man–Rousseau's model of dialogue as an agonistic encounter of inscription, seduction, and counterentrapment may have all along been Bakhtin's own, mysteriously unread as such, as numerous textual analyses from the *Dostoyevsky* book rather explicitly testify—for example, in the penultimate analysis of Stavrogin's maneuvering with Tikhon over the inert (and unread) text of his "confession," a duplicitous battle for reverse empowerment said to represent "the functions of the other person in dialogue, the other person as such, deprived of any social or pragmatic real-life concretization" (*PDP* 264).[15] While an interpretation of Bakhtin's writing as a duplicitous strategy was outlined by Holquist, if only to appropriate the whole for a christian model, it is at least interesting to ask not where Bakhtin provides us with new critical terms—which has all along been uncer-

tain, since so many of them are either very old (sign, ideology) or
clunky neologisms (chronotope, heteroglossia)—but where a little
remarked Nietzschean component makes the writing itself appear
transitional, destructive (ruinous, in Kristeva's sense), or more specifically *trans*valuative.[16]

Some directions for this reading might be indicated. It would,
for example, regard the "pseudonyms" as markers of author functions that reflect the textual nature of the projects they adhere to,
indicating, for instance, the necessity of reading Voloshinov's
Marxism not only as a performative but at once ironic and allegorical text. One would want to account, elsewhere, for where in Bakhtin an anamorphic logic is frequently projected through a temporal narrative, as when carnival or dialogue is said to follow in some
genealogical sequence a monologic or epochal period. In each
case, the "prior" terms appear preceded or framed by categories
that, like carnival, have no "before or after." It would also examine
the construction of pseudo-terms or pseudo-concepts (dialogue,
genre, ideology, the social) that, strategically unmarked in their
difference, systematically empty the "official" meanings they cite,
relocating them "in between" the binaries that defined them as
such.

What is this *other* Bakhtin, then, produced through and despite De Man's reading? What has been called De Man's a(d)mir-
(ror)ation of Bakhtin would not simply promote an *ironic* Bakhtin,
·though that would be plausible in a writer who uses "a still formal
method by which to conquer or sublate formalism itself." The Bakhtin first depicted as void of tropes (who "excludes trope from literary discourse") appears now reversed and overtly tropological. It
is possible, then, to read Voloshinov's *Marxism and the Philosophy of
Language* not as a treatise on the "philosophy of language" but as
a performative work whose title would undermine each concept it
named ("Marxism," "Philosophy," "Language" as linguistics). The
text properly appears as a duplex writing strategy that covertly
consumes a literary subtext it means to subvert, that being none
other than Hegel's *Phenomenology*—after which it is almost parod-
ically modeled. It may seem nearly parodic since the work presents
itself as a "phenomenology" of precisely what renders any phenomenology impossible, the materiality of what is given the name
sign. What comprises this "materiality" remains a central heuristic

question in the contemporary use of these works. The prospect shifts cultural criticism itself from "descriptively" using Bakhtin ("imitate or apply") to exploring where his conception of the social results less in a new set of academic typologies than a technological shift in the signifying order itself, within the material structure of mimesis—one of the consequences of which is the closure of all models of interiority, including any theological use of the word "social" itself. *Marxism* might best be read as a (fictional or literary) text that projects across a narrative axis a movement—from sign (a covert reversal of Saussure's figure) or inner speech outward to reported speech—that is in fact simultaneous. Thus, Voloshinov contrives a "materialist" semiotics that dismantles all semiotic models as such. Pivotal figures like the "dead word" of formalism or the "alien word" ("this role of the alien word led to . . . the idea of authority, the idea of power, the idea of holiness, the idea of truth" [*MPL* 75]) similarly return as historical allegories for the perpetual anteriority of citational language. Moreover, its conception of an "outer word" that constitutes "inner speech" ("nowhere is there a break in the chain, nowhere does the chain plunge into inner being" (*MPL* 11) puts into question the trope of exteriority that it relies on as well. It is clearly such a reading of Voloshinov that the *Prosaics'* strategic exile of it from Bakhtin's own canon is designed to preempt. If the so-called American school aims to return Bakhtin to a category of interiority or "the self," this resubjectivization seems apparent in the chapter of the *Prosaics* on "Psychology: Authoring a Self," where Voloshinov's "outer word"—what, strictly, suspends any theory of psychology as such—is familiarized, simply, as "the fundamental tenets of Voloshinov's theory of psychology" (203).

Bakhtin's unconvincing exclusion of the lyric may be a clue here, since what it technically represses may be the apostrophic model of utterance that appears in the only detailed sketch of the dialogic utterance we have, Voloshinov's "Discourse in Life and Discourse in Art." Analyzed in the example of the utterance "Well!" made at the sight of a snowfall in May, the social scenario of dialogue turns out to be neither social nor dialogic in the usual sense of each. It is not the unmediated interaction of two persons talking, but *triadic* and even narcissistic in structure. Moreover, the second person or listener (called a "reader" [105]) is not even ad-

dressed, but seems to merely *over*hear a closed address to a third
participant, one that is not necessarily human ("[w]ho is this third
participant? Who is the recipient of the reproach? The snow? Nature? Fate, perhaps?" [103]). This triadic model rarely receives
comment yet is the foundation of "the social" as such, which in
Bakhtin always begins with three and not two. When the third participant is brought into speech through personification or apostrophe, the second person must be antithetically positioned or seduced—hence inscribed—as "witness and ally" (103). Finally, the
first person can be said at his own point of emergence into language to be representationally murdered or disfigured by instantly
becoming a third person. In this agonistic model the listener or
"reader" must usurp in retort the specular position of the first person as the system itself invariably rotates. While I cannot analyze
it at length here, the specular scenario of "dialogue" in this model
appears almost self-cancelling as a mobile system, erasing and sup-
planting as it proceeds. If Bakhtin's "dialogism" involves, as both
De Man and Holquist note, dissimulation before a disfiguring
power, that might as readily be called the "discourse scenario" or
even official language as Stalin. Finally, as remarked, such double-
talk extends to the most familiar and assumed words that are de-
ployed, like the word "social" itself. In Voloshinov's work, for example, the "social" appears to name an "*inter*individual" site that
is primarily linguistic and itself "in between" binary concepts it
undoes, among which would be the term "social" it cites. Bakhtin's
"social" may at times appear to close out that concept, at least as
what we too quickly translate as a familiar referential of history—
and in this he surprisingly recalls what Baudrillard announces as
the "end of the social" through the acceleration of media (at least
as the metaphysical reserve it is taken for). The "social" seems to
operate at times as a term of linguistic exteriority, transindividual,
that eviscerates what Pechey termed mere "sociality as intersubjectivity." If Bakhtin and Voloshinov practice an unmarked or
Nietzschean desemanticization and reversal of familiar values
within both official or philosophic terms, and these are systematically unmarked in the words themselves, it recalls how Henry
Louis Gates, Jr. describes black discourse troping white terms without outwardly altering them, in the process usurping all rhetorical

properties while depleting the official term ("Signification") in a political "guerrilla" action within the signifier.

It is interesting that for Bakhtin, or in "his" text, dialogue is *not dialogic*—and it is interesting that this seems almost *never* noted, as if it were a scandal unassimilable to most agendas. *It* can only exist or be mobilized by the Listener's (or Reader's) attempted usurping of an always *imaginary* position of a first speaker, in which the latter (who, personifying his addressee, can only simulate retrospectively the first person's position) is representationally always as if *murdered* by the act of speech, becoming in turn a third person. Apostrophe or prosopopeia in this way is applied not to the third person (impersonal, voiceless, dead) but the first itself (impersonal, otherwise voiceless). Rather than being static or nurturingly dialogical, Voloshinov's model appears to *rotate, displace, and erase as it advances*—a threshing machine in which *I*'s are routinely harvested. It is a model that one may not like or wish on one's friends, being violent, usurpative, and without repose—yet it is Bakhtin's.[17] Yet to read Bakhtin through De Man raises other questions. In the text cited, "Well!" appears as the general type of any utterance, yet as "a word virtually empty semantically" ["Discourse" 102]) it is also "of a kind verging on *apostrophe*" (103), and one with a "tendency toward personification." That Voloshinov locates the origin of the utterance in the premimetic trope of apostrophe places Bakhtin's conception of language in working contact with De Man's persistent analyses of prosopopeia or hypogram in his late work—a site that precedes "voice."[18] It is this that is recognized in the early and in ways still relevant work of Kristeva as well, where "dialogue" is first read as an intertextual scenario in which the rules for the emergence of the speaker are sought.

If dialogue is actually a trialogue dependent on a "third" figure, it is also a highly unstable scene of multiply shifting positions that are less constituted than performatively assumed. Moreover, the "third" figure that may not even be human (or must not) can also appear like a text or *inscription* over the reading and management of which the disputants clash. But aside from opening the figure of dialogue to a site in which the exteriority of an inscription, another's or dead word, is conceived as a personified site (and hence unhuman), we see why this has all along been dangerous. As with De Man's late use of prosopopeia as a trope for what precedes figuration (or representation), a rupture haunts the verbal scenario that both perpetually opens a possibility of freedom or historical intervention—the suspension of causal historical chains in carnival, with the potential, preceding "face" itself, to rewrite those—and closes that by producing the speaker as the aftereffect of a sort of threshing machine model. Something within Voloshinov's use of apostrophe here announces a posthumanist model of material discourse that includes in its logic what Walter Benjamin theorizes as a "shock" effect—that site at which the historical materialist engaged in an active historiography of the present intervenes in the nihilism of historicism and, potentially, rewrites the past and the future.

Aside from asserting an agonistic model of dialogue less as "communication" than usurpation and defacement, any Nietzschean reading of Bakhtin today might ask where the very logic of Voloshinov's two-faced sign compels an implicit transvaluation of sorts ("each living ideological sign has two faces, like Janus" [23]). Voloshinov strategically uses terms like ideology, or value, or intonation, or theme, or emotion—terms that appear nearly intersubstitutible—as the markers of dialogic difference (utterances "are joined with one another and alternate with one another not according to the laws of grammar or logic but according to the laws of *evaluative* (emotive) *correspondence, dialogic deployment,* etc." (38), *"the psyche effaces itself, or is obliterated, in the process of becoming ideology, and ideology effaces itself in the process of becoming the psyche"* [39] emphasis added). While *Marxism* subscribes to the linguistic analysis of value or ideology under the name of translinguistics, at the same time it seems to performatively suspend the initial import of "value," itself reversible or two-sided, thus placing the value of *value* momentarily—albeit, it is a long, carnivalesque moment—into question. It is this way that we might read what Bakhtin called Dostoyevsky's "criterion" of evaluation ("The possibility of simultaneous coexistence, the possibility of being side by side or one against the other, is for Dostoyevsky almost a criterion for distinguishing the essential from the nonessential" [*PDP* 29]). Yet insofar as carnival logic cannot escape itself, is a "theatre without outside," Bakhtin appears to suffer from that representational closure often hastily used to attack a loosely defined "deconstruction" as such, since the carnivalesque begins not as a historical or medieval experience but as the mock-semiotic logic of permanent reversibility. The generally unremarked presence of Nietzsche's *Genealogy* in Voloshinov differs from the inverse use of Nietzsche, made to defend the authenticity of the self, that Bernstein pretends to when castigating dialogue as reflecting the slave's resentment for not having a voice or word of his own. Voloshinov and Bakhtin not only situate *aesthetics* socially, as is generally and now somewhat banally noted, but situate the social as an aesthetic, that is, material and linguistic, event. They render the materiality of "word"— which is also to say the "dead word," formalism, or writing—the prototype of experience (*"expression organizes experience"* [*MPL* 85]). De Man's definition of allegory in *The Rhetoric of Temporality* as the commentary of a sign on a sign defines "consciousness" itself in *Marxism,* where sign "reflects and refracts another reality" (9) that is always another material sign. Where the *materiality of the word*— or another's word, anteriority as such, or *inscription*—is the prototype of aesthetic phenomenality or perception (*aisthanumai*), as it is in Voloshinov, ideology itself can be rewritten as an aesthetic or linguistic effect: "Language, so viewed, is analogous to other ideological phenomena, in particular, to art—to aesthetic activity" (*MPL* 48).

While I want to return to what this means for contemporary cultural criticism still invested in Bakhtin, one may note, briefly, where the above account leads (as De Man was no doubt aware and wished to avoid), that is, to viewing Voloshinov's proposed science of ideologies as a dissimulative project essentially allied to De Man's proposed analysis of aesthetic ideology (which has the secondary benefit of reading De Man as "marxist"). Aesthetic ideology for De Man, of course, means several things, including the ideology of what is (or is not) dismissed by us as the aesthetic, and the manner in which the formalization of linguistic properties generates our own ideology. It is entirely possible to view *Marxism,* then, as a strong and covertly Nietzschean reading of the *German Ideology,* with the latter's address of language as "practical consciousness."[19] That such a nihilist Bakhtin returns as the domesticated neo-Kantian crank or the apostle of benign communication theory today is only one irony (albeit a particularly bitter one). While a critical rereading of Bakhtin may be under way, as it seems

at times in *Bakhtin and Cultural Theory,* one could excuse a call along
the lines of Baudrillard's *Oublier Foucault* to "forget Bakhtin," or at
least the Bakhtin that has saturated the critical horizon with compromised formulations. It may be that Bakhtin's text has practiced
a mode of rhetorical entrapment against its fondest readers all
along.

A last aside on De Man's reading. If Bakhtin's metaphor of
intentionality as verbal "light-ray" is a trope of trope concealing "a
reflective system of *mise en abyme*" anything but dialogical, the Bakhtin who is betrayed or who does the betraying of others (or "the
other") appears more problematic still. Thus, we read in "Discourse in Life" the following passage, which links the figure of
"light" not to cognition but to *value:* "They (social evaluations)
have entered the flesh and blood of all representatives of the
group. . . . We seem to perceive the value of a thing together with
its being as one of its qualities, we seem, for instance, to sense,
along with its warmth and light, the sun's value for us, as well. All
the phenomena that surround us are similarly merged with value
judgments" (101). Bakhtin's text appears to evoke a mock-solar
poetics which precedes phenomenality itself, producing sense or
nature as an effect of material signs and placing "value" side by
side with sense impressions or phenomena ("along with its warmth
and light"). The only possible "trope for trope" proceeds, then, as
a figure in which the "sun" has no priority, value no claim. The
logic indicates a certain nihilism in a constructive sense obvious
in carnivalesque laughter, one which Bakhtin's interpreters back-
pedal from furiously—not because it is irrecoverably tragic, but
because it casually empties out the vocabulary (sign, ideology, consciousness) and claims to identity or *interiority* they remain mimeti-
cally dependent on. When, pages later, Voloshinov discusses the
"hero" of his triadic discourse scenario (the addressee), the "sun"
appears not as a center but merely one personified object on a list
of equal possibilities including "thought" itself: "How often we
shake our fist at 'someone' in a fit of temper or simply scowl at
empty space, and there is literally nothing we cannot smile at—the
sun, trees, thoughts" (104). Rather than locating discourse in a
new referential sociology, Bakhtin here at least situates the materiality of language as what precedes mimesis and the human. We
might now read "carnival" less as a figure bursting with life and

the rule of immediacy than as a formalistic or mimetic trope that, difficult to leave, in the end evades the *transvaluation* Voloshinov's text began with its radical modification of inherited terms. If so, it would be in the essay on chronotopes that Bakhtin attempts, and fails, to move beyond this site—by imposing a differential typology on types of "carnival" and presenting them as a narrative history leading beyond Bakhtin's own text.[20]

The point of juxtaposing De Man and Bakhtin in this way is not to recuperate "De Manian reading," whatever that now would be, but to use the one encounter that has proven indigestible to the Bakhtin industry to help us intervene in that genealogy and impasse to produce another "Bakhtin" in the wake of the American figure that has proven perhaps too serviceable. What emerges from surveying this juxtaposition, however, is that the axis (or apostrophic monster?) "De Man/Bakhtin" itself could appear antidotal for a misleading binary that has mobilized much historical and cultural criticism—the scapegoating of the problem of the materiality of language, its cold war otheration, during a "return to history" that has not been unilaterially successful (the academy feels, if anything, even more conservative than in the early 80's). It may turn out, that is, that the fall/rise of Bakhtin tells the story of an appropriation of the figure of history by a still regressively humanist and mimetic ideology seeking an exclusionary *interior* reserve for which the idea of the materiality of language remains a dispossessing corrective to be rethought. Even if that means asking where the problem of *in*scription remains at the heart of what Bakhtin has called "dialogue" (which we might redub *ex*scription), and with that a more involved conception of history than that immediacy which, ever mourning, many sought in the (once) most popular—and now often inert—appropriations of Bakhtin.

I return to my first question: what does *this* genealogy of the American Bakhtin say to a cultural studies still invested in productive uses of his text—and why does a return to a question of "materiality" (one earlier considered formalist) point to a different pragmatics? One, that is, different from either the humanist typologies of ME or the frequently descriptive poetics of British cultural studies—one I would tentatively call less "Nietzschean" than that of a certain *NietzscheMarx*. This opens a series of questions I can hardly address in full. To begin this, though, I will return to the seemingly monstrous or discomfiting hybrid outlined before—"De Man/Bakhtin"—to suggest at least some perspectives.

4. Dialogue as Inscription; or, The Mnemotechnics of Cultural Transformation

The prospect of a postmarxist, postdeconstructive "Bakhtin" raises questions about where Bakhtin might be located now in cultural studies, or if the latter itself stands to undergo a fundamental reorientation in its project. Such a shift would be away from representational and context-centered "studies" that remain determined by a mimetic logic and toward a transvaluative or transfigural agenda that rethinks different forms of mimesis and their dependence on the materiality of language: the element most suppressed in the "Bakhtin" of the 80's.

The question returns to why there has been a neoconservative consolidation going into the 90's. The apparent error of both the retrohumanist right and certain leftist agendas in the 80's seems reflected in the general scapegoating of theory, or language centered analysis (the same gesture, say, that ME turns against "marxism" itself in the final move on this gameboard). What certain left agendas participated in might be called a mimetic ideology: that is, a regressive desire for the immediacy or transparency of reference which, among other things, "dialogue" seemed to proffer, a desire that satisfied itself that poststructuralist discourse (by now, a codename) represented the aestheticizing obstacle to the more serious mission of engaging history or recontracting the "subject's" political agency. Under the aegis of a certain definition of the political (already inscribed in this self-enforcing mimetic logic) the leftist agenda could be assimilated to the right's requirement for a new foundationalism. It could then be disciplined through official institutional organs when necessary, something made relatively easy when global marxism was seemingly discredited. What may have been less obvious was that the sacrificial logic applied against the linguistic model (the case of deconstruction) was not only in ways self-mutilating but one that echoed, by inversion, the binary gesture of a cold war epoch—an inverting, perversely nostalgic gesture for the left. The partial result was the spectacle of leftist itineraries that depended not only on historicizing logics but the covert effort to restitute interiorist economies of meaning (*Meinung*[21] the formation of the "me" as interior economy dependent on the abjection of an other). What the "story" of Bakhtin's production now suggests is that aspects of the politically progressive trends of the 80's had in fact been regressive—as various identity politics and new historicism now suggest—and must return to problematics of figuration and linguistic materiality to recalibrate the tasks of cultural criticism as intervention. Among other things, that cultural critique dependent upon installed habits of thinking mimesis, referentiality, or action stands to be reterritorialized if it is to exceed merely forming another archive within the greater field of a largely nihilistic humanism itself.

For cultural criticism, one may anticipate a "Bakhtin" who does not lend himself to the further production of historicist narratives but to the alteration of signifying orders and systems of mimesis as such. What may be at stake is a fundamental shift from a mimetic (restorative, referential, foundationalist) to a transformative and transvaluative model.

We may selectively review (or caricature) several phases in the genealogy or translation of "Bakhtin" to make this point. First, the appropriation of the trope of "dialogue" dependent on an ideology of self and other helped open a controlled and unthreatening discourse of difference in hermeneutic exchange whose primary use was to counter "deconstruction." Second, the deployment of Bakhtin's myriad typologies were used to promote a new *descriptive* poetics with the unexamined promise of alterity and historicality (despite the absence of all historicism in Bakhtin's work). Third, focus on a more extended definition of the "dialogic," viewed against the context of "official language," yielded the Foucauldian Bakhtin of new historicism and cultural studies. It is at this point that the concealed ressentiment of ME's agenda at once returns to the ideological closure of the first move and, involuntarily, exposes the dependence of the other Bakhtins on this initial (mis)translation as well. The great value of ME's study, in short, may be to have exposed and imploded this narrative construction by displaying the inner logic of this Bakhtin all along as neoconservative, as absurdly shorn and curtailed—a figure that even the leftist "Bakhtin," immeasurably more valuable, intricate, and sophisticated, could not quite escape the determination of. Yet if ME's study dialectically exposes (that is, produces) the underlying meconnaissance as the primal scene of translation here, what, if anything, supersedes these phases?

The shift out of descriptive historicism, in fact, gives to cultural studies a more interventionist and less archival trajectory— for as long as the latter is fundamentally oriented toward a descriptive or mimetic analysis, it can be said to reproduce or even enforce a conservative representational machine. Only this overriding fact—present in the nostalgia either for the subject, or for an overliteral "social" real before which linguistic or textual theory appears an aestheticized detour—explains the collusion mapped in the promoters and appropriators of Bakhtin between the right and, in obscurer but consequent ways, social pragmatists of the left.

Several possibilities emerge which would no longer be possible to unify as a specific agenda (or narrative). The consequences of foregrounding a certain "materiality" to which we have given the chimerical yet transmorphic label NietzscheMarx might include the following:

• The dyadic or hermeneutic reading of Bakhtinian "dialogue"— a model installed and defended by the American slavicists—is supplanted by the triadic, disruptive model which involves an overtly agonistic arena of usurpation and defacement. Here the projected and never realized identity of the speaker is dispersed among a series of effects and agencies. In this model—much more historical, yet abandoning the desired return of the subject—the situation of the personified "third" figure (Thing, inscription, hero, *speaker* by turn) opens a previously closed scenario of meaning to nonhuman or material site as well. This scene of perpetual power plays in which no "one" ever unifies the speaker's position literally suspends the reinstallation of any merely descriptive model.
• The "materiality" of language that is again foregrounded in this Bakhtin has certain consequences associated with a reconceptualization of the "social," a figure that itself now passes through memory, inscription, technology, visibility. For the social, the public, the visible are here linked not to a mimetic reference (the *old names* dismantled by Voloshinov), but to a linguistic site of sheer exteriority from which no interiorist model can return (interindividual,

"in between"). Perhaps oddly, the materiality of language here represents less a retreat to aesthetic preoccupations divorced from history (though even the "aesthetic" must be redefined) than a rethinking of historical agency. If if is useful to shift from the name "Bakhtin" to positing, for heuristic purposes, the more chimerical "Bakhtin/De Man," it is also to examine a few consequences of the system MarxNietzsche. Specifically, the trace of the material in Bakhtin is known through an always implicit temporal disruption (carnival) that confutes all descriptive historicism—a mode which, as in Benjamin's *Theses on the Philosophy of History*, is implicitly conceived as an unwitting collaboration with "fascist" (that is, mimetic) ideology. "Historical materialism" for Benjamin is not only what resists that topography or mapping, of course, but what opens the possibility of intervention, rewriting the past, saving the future. The *material* is thought through the other's word not as immediately present but as mediated ("dialogically") by pure anteriority, another's or dead word, that is derived from *memory*—or, more literally, the anteriority of inscription. Rather than being at the heart of some interior model of textuality, inscription ("the materiality of inscription" in De Man) appears itself the site of publicness, of "the social," of consciousness, or of the aesthetic. This chain of associations is already present in Bakhtin/Voloshinov. Inscription or, more accurately, *ex*scription resides at the anterior site of authority to be maneuvered about, publicly seduced, or usurped by the stakes for power of "dialogue"—not between a speaker and a listener, but between (at least) two speakers positioning one another as listeners, impersonating the "speaker's" position itself as *strategic* reader of a "hero" (text or inscription) who, in turn, anticipates a rhetorical countermove by the simulated, usurping listener: no one ever quite occupies the first person's position as such (I, the King, Being). In a sense, *action* as historical intervention occurs through memory, through a mnemotechnic altering the model or power of a signifying cluster: historical intervention, in Bakhtin, does not occur in an always allegorical street scene, but in the mnemonic systems (genres) out of which values, discourse, and ideology proceed. Each possible or projected future involves the loop of a katabasis, a visit to the underworld bent on altering an inscription, and the "present" itself is only the absent site of this negotiation. Yet like Benjaminian *Jetztzeit*, the structure of "dialogue" (always already carnivalized) represents a potential disruption in the historical continuum itself. It is a potential—present, too, in the prefigural trope of personification or prosopopeia at its core (Voloshinov)—that is interventionist, that evokes Benjamin's opposition of the "historical materialist" to the "historicist" in actively rewriting the text of the present.[22] Thus, Donna Haraway has spoken of one task of the posthumanist landscape as "resetting the stage for possible pasts and futures"—and, in her case, one of the tools of this is leveling speciesist discriminations between animal, human, and machine.[23] The merely descriptive use of Bakhtinian categories gives way, here, to a different sense in which his postbook, linguistic models represent less an effort to return to the voice (it does *not*), than an initial disclosure of the cyberspace of discursive traces and power—which may also be claimed for De Man.[24] Indeed, the strongest use of Bakhtin's categories may not be one that pretended to a descriptive access to history. While such uses have proven fertile, we may well want to ask from now on how active participation in Bakhtin's project—that which we may now read across Bakhtin's dispersed writings and signatures—involves a sacrifice as well: that, perhaps, of the descriptive model itself. This is itself already undertaken in anamorphic terms like chronotope, dialogue, carnival, or laughter that actively dissolve familiar concepts and the borders of representational logic—terms that must, as we saw with ME's monograph, be hysterically *policed*, edited, and excluded by certain interests.

• One of the implications of the phrase "aesthetic" ideology is that the very manner in which the *aesthetic* is defined—itself the cipher of historical materiality conceived as text (or semiotic effect)—underlies various political systems. (Another way to say this is that there is a frequently unexamined politics to how referentiality itself is constructed and processed as knowledge, information, power, and how perception (*aisthanumai*) derives from this.) For the postmarxist "De Man/Bakhtin," the term ideology seems removed from any field of "false consciousness" or utopian narrative, while orienting itself toward a radical materiality impossible to divorce from signification. In this regard, we might say there are two De Man's, in the same way that Slavoj Žižek partitions a middle from a late Lacan, a Lacan who moves from concerns for the metonymic slide of the signifier and the symbolic order to the unnarrativizable encounters with *the real*. De Man's "late" text—with its move toward the prefigural, prosopopeia, and inscription—may have been misread on the whole through his protracted focus on systems of tropes and undecidability.[25] For where the "sublime object of ideology" is presented as Lacanian "Thing," as Thing "beyond the wall of language" (Lacan), this for Žižek can only result in a regression from metonymy (mere "post-structuralism") to metaphor of sorts (identifying with the protrusion of the "real," the Lacanian *sinthom*).[26] Žižek errs, we might say, by conceiving his rather gothic Thing within a rhetoric of immediacy that can only be restaged again and again as the obliteration of the symbolic mode, while in fact the *materiality* in question always passes through representation, memory, anteriority, inscription. There is no "beyond" the wall of language, but that wall may be differently inscribed, refigured, defaced with mnemo-graffiti. Bakhtin/De Man—particularly where the latter turns toward the premimetic figures of hypogram and prosopopeia—supersedes Žižek by designating the real not as an ineluctable *Ding-an-sich* but as a facticity of inscription *preceding* face or figure. This conception of the power, materiality, and anteriority of inscription—at once De Manian and Bakhtinian—does not only suggest the format of Althusserian ideology (or the ISA). If intervention in such an apparatus can only be thought of as interrupting or disinstalling a certain memory grid or system of relay—if contesting these historical implants is one broader implication of "dialogue"—both De Man's use of prosopopeia and Bakhtin's trope of dialogue harbor technologies of reading that are, in the last analysis, pragmatic and interventionist rather than "descriptive." The Lacanian "Thing"—Žižek's "sublime object of ideology"—may be defined not as a gothic prosopopeia of the inanimate (perpetually "uncanny" for recalling where the human is itself such), but as the facticity of public inscriptions around and against which discursive eddies coagulate in inverting, anamorphic clusters.[27] The pragmatic consequences of this revision seem apparent in the shift from a mimetic pretense to immediacy (in fact reproducing a past signifying order) toward a conception of mimesis without models (carnivalized) working through the density of signifying clusters—such as generate any "present." For De Man, the labor of a figure like prosopopeia (Voloshinov's "apostrophe") appears less that of a trope to be identified here and there than a *technique* for preceding representation, and this to interrupt and intervene in an always already situated (representational) history, suspending the presumption that a "human" face was ever assured or in place in a specific way. That is to say, in the very figure that may seem most irredeemably *aesthetic*—yet which lies at the very core of Voloshinov-Bakhtin's model of "dialogue"—there lies a technology intended to intervene in historical sedimentation, and, like Benjaminian "shock" or what Haraway calls figuration itself, produce new pasts or futures. It is a tool for dissolving supposed "facts," a technology of responsibility (ME, who abject carnival as a "dead end" and extol the moralism of responsibility, have it, of course, precisely inverted). There is even a way in which a new humanism lies in the path of this posthumanism—though in any case, what "Bakhtin/De Man" here presents seems an active rather than mimetic approach to representational memory itself. And hence to a conception of the social, the material, the mnemonic, and the public that dissociates the idea of the political from being exclusively determined by a regressive mimeticism which, in some extent, arrested critical culture within the specular detour of the late 80's. Once this mnemotechnics is more fully explored, the postmarxist and postdeconstructive De Man/Bakhtin of this essay may appear, in name, secondary or irrelevant. If reading appears one viable metaphor for the production of the future based on the retroprojection of others' words or legacies passing through reading's supposed "present," then the technologies that intervene in this scene remain—together with others—viable and pragmatic tools.

In a recent attack on "Pun(k)deconstruction," Mas'ud Zavarzadeh assaults the way that the aestheticizing project of reading covertly ensures the reign of humanism: "humanism is the traditional mode of producing an acquiescing labor force through reading texts of culture as embodiments of transcendental moral and ethical values and as the site of sophisticated aesthetic pleasures" (8). Yet in fact he collapses two *antithetical* projects (moral transcendentalism and the "sophisticated aesthetic" pleasure of linguistic materialism), and in the process obscures where his own position replicates the mimetic ideology that is the perpetual stronghold of that "humanism" itself. Today, pursuing a posthumanist trajectory that is based upon rethinking "materiality" (always also linguistic) remains a necessary itinerary of cultural criticism, one much more decisive and consequent than fiddling with the perpetually specular side-show of opposing modernism and postmodernism (itself a stalling tactic before the difficult demands of the former, which is the site I here call NietzscheMarx). Politically inspired rhetoric may no longer serve itself well by bracketing "postmodernism" (poststructuralism, deconstruction, the linguistic moment) as a nonhistorical parenthesis: that episode was, it now seems obvious, part of an ongoing historical intervention. What seems more likely is that "humanism" functions most insidiously and nihilistically—on the right and certain factions of the left—by being bound to long familiar habits of referentiality, to a desire controlled and produced by a *mimetic ideology* that continues to govern numerous apparatuses of consumption, economy, culture, and commodification. This mimetic ideology—through whatever loops it passes (the subject, god, history, advertisement, "revolution")—only pretends to guarantee a certain promised return, while picking the pocket of its own agents. It is particularly dangerous at a time when leftist thought seems tempted by various nostalgias—not to mention the aesthetic pleasures of scapegoating (poststructuralism, "theory") that weirdly invert familiar cold war emotional logic. Increasingly, today, different, more practical, less ideologically preset questions arise—and they increasingly demand a response removed from the specular labeling of the right and a certain left. Who is to say, now, how much certain institutionalized habits of representation effect or order, produce and participate in how critical situations in society (homelessness, the environment, population, joblessness) cannot enter representational space? If Zavarzadeh's move actually repeats the humanism he wants to displace, it is less because of the position he takes than the mimetic and sacrificial logic he adheres to. The entire narrative of this recent episode in critical culture can be read in the genealogy of today's "Bakhtin"—which displays a certain left in an uneasy specular relation with the right. One which, as occurs around the cipher presented by the critical genealogy of today's "Bakhtin," brings a certain left and the right into an uneasy specular relation, while distracting cultural critique from what appears more and more its task: to devise new conceptions of posthumanist materialism, and to shift from a mimetic paradigm to one that is altered and altering in its approach to language and history.

Notes

1. Caryl Emerson, in her editor's preface to *Problems in Dostoyevsky's Poetics,* by Bakhtin, suggests that Bakhtin's "works seem designed less to be read than to be overheard, in a sort of transcribed speech" (xxxiii), encouraging an assumption of transparency and "communication." As I will detail below, this approach seems echoed in the ideological need to purify the voice of the author, "Bakhtin," either by returning all the "pseudonymous" texts to him, as in Katerina Clark and Michael Holquist's *Mikhail Bakhtin,* or segregating them definitively, as in Morson and Emerson's *Mikhail Bakhtin: The Creation of a Prosaics,* where the "Voloshinov" texts are discarded (and even the *Rabelais* side-lined). There is a corresponding need to appeal to the biographical "facts" in order to assert Bakhtin's "beliefs"— part of a conservative theologicohumanist vein that I will scrutinize below. By naming an "American" Bakhtin school, I am of course identifying, primarily, the group of slavicists who have presided almost exclusively over his translation, dissemination, and commentary (Holquist, Emerson, Morson), and not the numerous trends, uses, and debates he has otherwise spawned, particularly in cultural studies. That this particular Bakhtin gets conceived of almost nationalistically is apparent in the pivotal exclusion of poststructuralist and marxist readings from its conceptual domain, as when *Prosaics* ejects without discussion Julia Kristeva's important early essays as "appropriations" that offer "a French 'Bachtine' alien in spirit" (4). *Creation of a Prosaics* interestingly reverses, in its title, the critical valence of Kristeva's interrogation of Bakhtin's *destructive* rhetorical strategies, "The Ruin of a Poetics," by making it positive (creation) and familiar (prosaic). There is an interesting study that remains to be done here on how the academic (and un-Benjaminian) presumption of authority to a work's *translators* has negatively impacted on contemporary critical history.

2. Of "dialogism" Hirschkop notes that "this is a case in which the careful analysis of a concept is required, for otherwise dialogism seems to appear as simply a new word for justifying established literary and cultural preferences" (*BCT* 200). One example is its use in the Michael Holquist's recent *Dialogism: Bakhtin and His World,* where the term appears in every chapter heading as a kind of differential if conceptually vague theology of "self and other." While we are told "that for (Bakhtin) 'self' is dialogic, a relation," and that the "key to understanding . . . is the dialogue between self and other" (19), the "event of being a self" (21) is hypostasized as a unity ("The gate of the 'I' is located at the center not only of one's own existence, but of language as well" [23]), and Holquist's early Buberisms seem merely revamped. This is apparent, for instance, when Bakhtin's "principle of simultaneity" (*PDP* 27) is misread as a transcendental ("self/other is a relation of simultaneity" [19]) rather than material and linguistic problem. Extending Holquist's iconography in this regard, Morson and Emerson consecrate a chapter of *Prosaics* to what they term "Psychology: Authoring a Self," oddly with special reference to Voloshinov. In writing on "Bakhtin's Imaginary Utopia," Lahcen Haddad critiques the American appropriation of Bakhtin, mostly for its "antihistoricist" character, yet appropriates from this site a precritical notion of

"history" itself for Bakhtin that seems to replicate the American slavicists' anxious dismissal from Bakhtin of theory ("theoreticism") itself. By contrast, Anthony Wall and Clive Thomson's "Cleaning Up Bakhtin's Carnival Act" indicts Morson and Emerson for their editorial mutilation of Bakhtin's canon in order to produce a neoconservative figure (noting their work's determining "moralizing tone" [58]). After remarking on the explosion of recent publications on Bakhtin and the resulting "mess" of variously politicized "Bakhtins," they complain of the authors' calculated dismissal of the *Rabelais*, and with it the entire problematic of carnival itself (which Morson decrees, simply, a "dead end"), implying that Morson and Emerson exclude editorially what they cannot incorporate (anti-)theoretically. The "debate" between the cultural critic "Bakhtin" of the British left and the American retrohumanists (Morson) flared again in a letter exchange in *PMLA*, where Ken Hirschkop and David Shepherd (yet again) note that Morson's "'prosaic' Bakhtin is a political creature in disguise" (117). While there can be little doubt that the left wins this argument intellectually—the "prosaic" Bakhtin of Morson and Emerson is, finally, reduced, pared, typological, pious, *diminished in interest altogether*—a larger question looms as to, in what particulars, the two have not been locked in a certain specularity (left-right, ostensibly) that effectively diverts attention from a more important turn in the materiality of Bakhtin's text.

3. For a reading of Bakhtin as promulgating the "return to history" of the early 80's by his theoretical access to the "others of the text," see David Carroll.

4. By neoformalist I mean a figure whose strategies of displacement have become typologies, as evidenced in two different yet complementary pieces by Morson and Linda Hutcheon on Bakhtin and "parody." In each case, the writers fail to ask where they use the term (at best, minor to Bakhtin) as an ideological tool of centering and control reasserting the originary (or parodied) text—a strategy barred within Bakhtin's broader deconstruction by ambivalent laughter. Similarly, when Caryl Emerson in "The Tolstoy Connection" interrogates and reverses Bakhtin's category of the monologic as applied to Tolstoy, yet another so-called "extension" entails merely refining and literalizing an arguably dissimulative binary utilized by Bakhtin (like his generally enigmatic dismissal of the lyric).

5. The problem of signature in the Bakhtin Circle has habitually been probed as a matter of literal attribution, rather than as a complex system of marking that permeates and (perpetually) alters the production and its reading from within, rewriting *in particular* the signature "Bakhtin." Without reviewing this history, at no point has the use or deletion of Voloshinov's *signature* been a matter of indifference to the interpretive/political aims of commentators/editors. It has never been *simply* a case of historical evidence, of fact versus fiction, since the parameters of that dyad have been (rather systematically) erased by the inability to restore anything outside the need to compulsively renarrativize this (hi)story—a situation even given the "historical" Bakhtin's apparent imprimatur (by his refusing to sign an acknowledgment of the pseudonymous scheme late in life). What remains is how the "story" is (re)produced and why—a production that still awaits being critically read through the problematic of *signature* that places his text in a group of critical writings including Plato, Kierkegaard, and Nietzsche.

6. In fact, this hostility to marxism is not only restated, but made the basis for the only motivated attribution of irony to a Bakhtin text by Ann Shukman—the "marxist" introduction to Tolstoy's *Resurrection*.

7. In an aside directed at Holquist, De Man ruminates on the "symptomatic" narrative by which the legacies of "oppressed thinkers" are appropriated through "the rumored (and often confirmed) existence of unpublished manuscripts made

available only to an enterprising or privileged researcher and which will decisively seal one mode of interpretation at the expense of all rival modes—at least
until one of the rivals will, in his turn, discover the real or imaginary counter-
manuscript on which to base his counterclaim" (*RB* 107)—the latter, in fact, being
ME's own strategy. As Neil Hertz has observed to me, the entire passage on persecuted writing and doubling casts an interesting light on the debate surrounding
De Man's wartime writings and his later production.

8. It is a mark of how consistently the performative parameters of Bakhtin's
text remain unread that Caryl Emerson, in her Editor's Preface to *Problems,* simply pronounces: "His entire understanding of the word, and of the specificity of
the utterance, invalidates the very concept of repetition. Nothing 'recurs' . . . The
phenomenon is perhaps better understood in the linguistic category of 'redun-
dancy,' that is, as the surplus necessary for a certain mode, or force, of communication" (xxxv).

9. For Nietzsche, of course, there are two antithetical *nihilisms:* the first, which
is that fostered by a kind of moralism of reference (including historicism, various
ascetic or Christo-Judaic rhetorics, humanism, the rhetoric of paternal meaning)
and a second that exists in its (positive) negation of the terms of the first.

10. The reading of Bakhtin as actually, all along, theorizing an intervention in
the real through *memory* rather than through some model of dialogic or historical
immediacy—including what is called genre memory—is raised by Wall and
Thomson. In a section titled *Memory* in their discussion, they bypass the metonymic chain that leads from "other's word" and the "alien word" to the "dead
word" (and "absolute past"), wherein the trope of materiality itself is inscribed:
"Memory becomes a complex space where new communities and relationships
can be forged through such inscription. It seems entirely appropriate to recall
Walter Benjamin's 'Theses on the Philosophy of History'" ("Cleaning Up" 62).
Dismissing Morson's *faux* bid for immediacy and transparency through the pretense of purging "theory," they note that: "on the contrary, the everyday is, for
Bakhtin, a theoretical concept of the first order" (63). They further wonder over
the cold war anachronisms of ME's study: "Not only does their study seem to set
up a traditionally nationalist opposition between the free enterprise, individualist
Bakhtin and the evil, collectivist Bakhtin. In a further twist, Marxism is made to
encompass everything dialectical, utopian, and collect" (67)—or theoretical. Yet
this "cold war" pattern had haunted the left-right scapegoating or otherating of
"theory" itself (poststructuralism) throughout the late 80's, as is particularly evident in the nationalist rhetoric of American "neo-pragmatism."

11. It is telling that some of the terms most publicly attached to Bakhtin's work
are the inventions of his commentators and never occur in his text, such as Holquist's "dialogic *imagination*" (a distinctly humanizing label), Todorov's "dialogic
principle" (borrowed from Buber), and ME's "prosaics," their own "neologism"
yet called one of his three "global concepts."

12. A deft rearticulation of this familiar position can be found in Mas'ud Zavarzadeh's "Pun(k)deconstruction and the Postmodern Political Imaginary."

13. The "two distinct senses" of dialogue that ME distinguishes—that applying
to "all language" ("it orients itself toward a listener, whose active response shapes
the utterance") and that opposed to a figural monologism that attempts "to 'forget' the multiple dialogizing qualifications" (*RB* 52)—have no correspondence to
De Man's strategic binarization.

14. The dynamic of "ideological anamorphosis" is outlined in Slavoj Žižek's
The Sublime Object of Ideology (98–100). One import of Žižek's ideology critique is

disinvestment: "the contours of a postmodern critique of ideology . . . , whereby the ideological anamorphosis loses its power of fascination and changes into a disgusting protuberance" (*Enjoy Your Symptom!* 140).

15. In the following example of Zosima and the "mysterious visitor" that comments on this one, the relation to the other is called "pure hatred toward 'the other' as such" (264). Bakhtinian "dialogue" here is precisely an engine of power, erasure, dislocation, and representational murder implicitly, even as the figure of the "social" depends upon just that fact. For an application of this "agonistic" reading of dialogue in multiculturalist terms, see Wlad Godzich.

16. It should be recalled that the term "value" does not operate like a content or a motivating figure: it is always also a retroprojection, coextensive semantically with "ideology" in Voloshinov's work: both, moreover, are two-sided inflections carrying what alone matters semantically (as intonation), yet which doubleness is also reversibly put in play in carnival, menippea, ambivalent laughter, and so on. "Value," as a term or effect, is a trace being emptied in Bakhtin's text by its own double structure, being *trans*valued.

17. If the position of the second person (Listener) is in fact that of being outside the utterance, a "reader" of it who must usurp the imaginative site of power to appear in turn to speak, he is always a strategic "listener" and the first person is automatically placed in a posture of dissimulation before this prospective violence.

18. For varying treatments of Voloshinov's text on the utterance "Well!," see Juliet Flower MacCannell's "The Temporality of Textuality: Bakhtin and Derrida," Michael Holquist's "The Surd Heard: Bakhtin and Derrida," and my "'Well!': Voloshinov's Double-Talk" in *Sub-Stance*. For a treatment of how this model might effect reading the materiality of language, see my "Bakhtin, *Othello*, and the Death(s) of Dialogue," chapter one of *Anti-Mimesis from Plato to Hitchcock*.

19. For a consideration relating Voloshinov's use of sign to Nietzsche's in *The Gay Science*, see Samuel Weber; otherwise, see James M. Curtis and my "Reading a Blind Parataxis: Dostoyevsky (Nietzsche) Bakhtin," where the argument is made that Dostoyevsky is, in part, a signature for Nietzsche in Bakhtin's text. It should go without saying that the argument, here, has nothing to do with some study of "influence" (Nietzsche "on" Bakhtin, say). On the contrary, the whole issue is rife with implications for how we process Bakhtin's writings and represents, in itself, a major and fairly conscious repression during the 80's construction of "Bakhtin." The resistance to select "Nietzschean" implications of Bakhtin's linguistic materialism has been quietly relentless—and reducing the question to one of influence represents, it seems, another way to forestall this issue.

20. One subtext of the essay on chronotopes would seem to be this: under the pretext of narrating a differential typology for the chronotope itself, Bakhtin attempts implicitly to break out of the problematic of carnival itself, determining a series of different versions that deflect its totalizing tendency and project an (entirely contradictory) "beyond" to the narrative itself. It can be read, that is, as an attempt to give narrative form to the transvaluation that would get beyond the representational dilemma of "carnival." If so, it fails because it returns precisely, and always, to the old or cancelled narrative format to perform this task (typology, narrative progression). The chronotope itself remains one of the most tempting and confusing conceits to put into circulation.

21. I am here playing off the punning resonance between ME (and the interiorist-humanist concept of meaning that lies behind it) and the German *Meinung*, in which "meaning" can be paleonymically heard as what is *mine*.

22. Clearly, ME's rigorous suppression of everything linked in Bakhtin to "carnival" as a "dead end" (including the *Rabelais* book) is not only linked to his/her/their abjection of "Marxism" *and* "theory." "Carnival" remains a limit term for Bakhtin not because it describes some medieval ritual, but because it names a moment in which historical narratives are dissolved, not as merely formal semiotic play, but to reach the moment of responsibility (ME's favorite misused term) where new pasts and futures can be written—of the decision on the far side of undecidability out of which alternate trajectories emerge: it is a term of intervention.

23. The quote I have in mind occurs in "Ecce Homo, Ain't (Ar'n't) I a Woman, and Inappropriate/d Others: the Human in a Post-Humanist Landscape": "These are moments when something powerful—and dangerous—is happening. Figuration is about resetting the stage for possible pasts and futures. Figuration is the mode of theory when the more 'normal' rhetorics of systemic critical analysis seem only to repeat and sustain our entrapment in the stories of the established disorders. Humanity is a modernist figure; and this humanity has a generic face, a universal shape" (9).

24. Bakhtin's actual model of "voice" may be less reminiscent of Buber's I and Thou than of Avital Ronell's conception of the telephonic switchboard in *The Telephone Book*. One could, indeed, easily read the trajectory of De Man's focus on "reading" as a dissolution of the monumental age of the book rather than its refetishization.

25. In time, it will certainly be worth asking whether *one* component of the way the "scandal" of De Man's wartime writings was publicly handled—no matter what the interpretation—was implicitly to displace or occlude this last, and most pragmatic, challenge to the mimetic order.

26. This is the opposite of De Man, for whom metaphor, like symbol, involves a mystifying and totalizing function. Žižek's modification is to posit that "metaphor" as itself over an empty site: "The 'original metaphor' is not a substitution of 'something for something-else' but a substitution of something for nothing: . . . which is why *metonymy is a species of metaphor*" (*They Know Not What They Do* 50). Žižek's notion of the Real also precludes descriptive historicism: "the ultimate mistake of *historicism* in which all historical content is 'relativized', made dependent on 'historical circumstances',—that is to say, of historicism as opposed to *historicity*—is that it evades the encounter with the Real" (101).

27. The figure of inscription is, accordingly, adopted by those working to efface a self-mutilating binary between the political and theory. An example occurs in Judith Butler's *Gender Trouble:*

> [T]he question of agency is not to be answered through recourse to an 'I' that preexists signification. In other words, the enabling conditions for an assertion of the 'I" are provided by the structure of signification, the rules that regulate the legitimate and illegitimate invocation of that pronoun, the practices that establish the terms of intelligibility by which the pronoun can circulate. . . . What constitutes a subversive repetition within signifying practices of gender? I have argued ('I' deploy the grammar that governs the genre of the philosophical conclusion, but note that it is the grammar itself that deploys and enables this 'I,' even as the 'I' that insists itself here repeats, redeploys, and—as the critics will determine—contests the

philosophical grammar by which it is both enabled and restricted) that, for instance, within the sex/gender distinction, sex poses as 'the real' and the 'factic,' the material or corporeal ground upon which gender operates as an act of cultural *inscription* . . . The question is not: what meaning does that inscription carry within it, but what cultural apparatus arranges this meeting between instrument and body, what interventions into this ritualistic repetition are possible? (143–46)

Works Cited

Bakhtin, M. M. *Problems in Dostoyevsky's Poetics.* Trans. C. Emerson. Minneapolis: U of Minnesota P, 1984.

Butler, Judith. *Gender Trouble.* New York: Routledge, 1990.

Carroll, David. "The Alterity of Discourse: Form, History and the Question of the Political in M. M. Bakhtin." *diacritics* 13.2 (1983): 65–83.

Clark, Katerina, and Michael Holquist. *Mikhail Bakhtin.* Cambridge: Harvard UP, 1984.

Cohen, Tom. *Anti-Mimesis from Plato to Hitchcock.* Cambridge: Cambridge UP, 1994.

———. "Well! Voloshinov's Double Talk." *Sub-Stance* 21.2 (1992): 91–102.

———. "Reading a Blind Parataxis: Dostoyevsky (Nietzsche) Bakhtin." *boundary* 2 (1988): 45–71.

Curtis, James M. "Michael Bakhtin, Nietzsche, and Russian Pre-Revolutionary Thought." *Nietzsche in Russia.* Ed. B. Rosenthal. Princeton: Princeton UP, 1986.

Gates, Henry Louis, Jr. *The Signifying Monkey: A Theory of Afro-American Literary Criticism.* New York: Oxford UP, 1988.

Godzich, Wlad. "Correcting Kant: Bakhtin and Intercultural Interactions." *boundary* 2 (1991): 17–35.

Haddad, Lahcen. "Bakhtin's Imaginary Utopia." *Cultural Critique* 22 (1992): 143–64.

Haraway, Donna. "Ecce Homo, Ain't (Ar'n't) I a Woman, and Inappropriate/d Others: The Human in a Post-Humanist Landscape." *Feminists Theorize the Political.* Ed. J. Butler and J. Scott. New York: Routledge, 1992. 86–105.

Hirschkop, Ken, and David Shepherd, eds. *Bakhtin and Cultural Theory.* London: Manchester UP, 1989.

———. Letter to the Editor. *PMLA* Jan. 1994.

Holquist, Michael. *Dialogism: Bakhtin and his World.* New York: Routledge, 1990.

———. "The Surd Heard: Bakhtin and Derrida." *Russian Formalism: Theoretical Problems and Russian Case Studies.* Ed. G. S. Morson. Stanford: Stanford UP, 1986.

Kristeva, Julia. "*Une poétique ruinée.*" *La poétique de Dostoievski.* Ed. M. M. Bakhtin. Trans. I. Kolitcheff. Paris: Seuil, 1970.

MacCannell, Juliet Flower. "The Temporality of Textuality: Bakhtin and Derrida." *MLN* 100.5 (1985): 968–88.

Morson, Gary Saul, and Caryl Emerson. *Mikhail Bakhtin: Creation of a Prosaics.* Stanford: Stanford UP, 1990.

———, eds. *Rethinking Bakhtin: Extensions and Challenges.* Evanston: Northwestern UP, 1989.

Ronell, Avita. *The Telephone Book.* Lincoln: U of Nebraska P, 1988.

Voloshinov, V. N. "Discourse in Life and Discourse in Art." *Freudianism.* Trans. I. R. Titunik. Bloomington: Indiana UP, 1987. 93–117.

———. *Marxism and the Philosophy of Language.* Trans. I. R. Titunik and L. Matejka. New York: Seminar P, 1973.

Wall, Anthony, and Clive Thomson. "Cleaning Up Bakhtin's Carnival Act." *diacritics* 23.2 (1993): 47–70.

Weber, Samuel. "The Intersection: Marxism and the Philosophy of Language." *diacritics* 15.4 (1985): 86–105.

Zavarzadeh, Mas'ud. "Pun(k)deconstruction and the Postmodern Political Imaginary." *Cultural Critique* 22 (1992): 5–46.

Žižek, Slavoj. *They Know Not What They Do: Enjoyment as a Political Factor.* New York: Verso, 1991.

———. *The Sublime Object of Ideology.* New York: Verso, 1989.

———. *Enjoy Your Symptom!* New York: Routledge, 1992.

The Practical Theorizing of Michel Foucault: Politics and Counter-Discourse

Mario Moussa and Ron Scapp

Introduction: Hand Grenades

Michel Foucault has often been criticized for producing radical political analyses with little practical value. So many writers have assailed him on this score that Foucault now seems distinctive for what he *lacks*. He has, for example, been criticized for lacking a theory of "agency," a theory that would somehow encourage revolutionary political action; for lacking a normative justification of the exercise of power, an alternative to the liberal framework; for lacking a sense of history as progressive, as more than an endless story of oppression; and for lacking a notion of freedom, a notion that might inspire other radical theorists.[1] From our point of view, however, these criticisms ignore a continuous practical and positive thrust in his work, from the early history of madness to the studies of ancient sexual practices (see Moussa "Foucault"). Admittedly, the characterization of Foucault as a practical philosopher—rather than the nihilistic, dizzyingly abstract theorist he is typically ac-

© 1996 by *Cultural Critique*. Spring 1996. 0882-4371/96/$5.00.

cused of being—requires an argument. Our goal in the following essay is to provide one.

Contrary to his critics on the left, we think Foucault can actually serve to encourage "radical agency." For us, *how* he does so, much more so than his distinctive claims about power, knowledge, subjectivity, and even politics, is what makes him a philosopher worth reading. Foucault himself repeatedly declared he never wanted to establish timeless, acontextual truths. Instead, he hoped that his books would have the effect of hand grenades, scattering the accepted theoretical ideas about madness, social order, and sexuality (see Foucault, "Questions of Method" 101). We argue that this disruption of received wisdom constitutes Foucault's practical engagement, as a *theorist,* with real-world politics. What he did as an activist, significant as it was, falls outside the boundaries of our argument; we want to show the specific way in which Foucault's theoretical work—his theorizing—was practical, hence our term "practical theorizing."

We begin our argument, in the first section, by clarifying what Foucault calls "counter-discourse." We contend his work aims at clearing a space in which the formerly voiceless might begin to articulate their desires—to *counter* the domination of prevailing authoritative discourses. In the second section, we answer those critics who accuse Foucault of creating theoretical systems that provide no means or guidelines for political action. Driven by various concerns, these critics have all focused on the much-discussed "problem of agency." In the third section, through a discussion of bell hooks' work, we offer a definition of what might be called "Foucauldian activism": a way of undermining oppressive discourse and even keeping one's own theoretical discourse as "counter" as possible. Moreover, the example of hooks' work suggests a way to be simultaneously a theorist and a producer of counterdiscourses. We conclude, in the fourth section, with some brief remarks concerning the academic left's desire to find an ultimate metaphysical foundation for political action and, consequently, to overlook the practical value of Foucault's political analyses.

1. Counter-Discourse: The Indignity of Speaking for Others

In 1972 Gilles Deleuze paid Michel Foucault the following well-known compliment: "In my opinion, you were the first—in your books and in the practical sphere—to teach us something absolutely fundamental: the indignity of speaking for others" (Deleuze and Foucault 209). Foucault responds by saying that when those usually spoken for and about by others begin to speak for themselves, they produce a "counter-discourse." This counterdiscourse, he says, is not another theory, but rather a practical engagement in political struggles (Deleuze and Foucault 209). When, in other words, the formerly voiceless begin to speak a language of their own making—a counterdiscourse—they have begun to resist the power seeking to oppress them. In this narrow sense, the very act of speaking is political, and Foucault's *writing* is political to the extent that it helps clear a space in which the formerly voiceless might begin to speak.

The narrow sense of "political" as it applies to Foucault's written work has been misunderstood by his critics, many of whom have argued that Foucault merely reduces politics to language. Neil Lazarus, for example, claims that Foucault transforms social life into an "infinite text" and, like other postmodernists, dissolves "everything into discourse" (127–28). According to Lazarus, Foucault's genealogies, therefore, have a "suffocating and tentacular" quality as though there were no "way out" of them (126). Lazarus and other critics like Barbara Ehrenreich (to whom we will return in the final section) have argued that the "way out" can be illuminated only by Truth, with a capital "T," which the discourse-loving postmodern theorists like Foucault, Jacques Derrida, Richard Rorty, and Stanley Fish have supposedly rejected.[2] This common criticism of postmodern political theory relies on an often-repeated idea: radical politics itself will collapse when Truth vanishes and only discourse remains, since there will no longer be any quarter from which to challenge the status quo and, moreover, any autonomous actors who might raise a challenge in the first place. As Anthony Appiah puts it, Foucault assumes a "structural determinism," which leads to a "conception of the subject which is purely epiphenomenal" (67).

Yet, this point about determinism stems from a basic misunderstanding of the Foucauldian genealogies. By no means are they meant to be treated like traditional philosophical theories, evaluated as true or not true to "reality." In the genre of pure theory, or what could loosely be called philosophy, Foucault attempted to write "the history of the games of truth and error" within which, for example, claims to objectivity and normality had force (see Foucault, *The Uses of Pleasure* 8). In a strict Foucauldian sense, these so-called "games" produce philosophy; much as Lyotard and Wittgenstein have argued in their own distinctive ways, "language games" establish the boundaries within which philosophers carry on their debates about morality, politics, and other perennial topics. As we emphasize in the next section, Foucault never understood himself, in his analysis of subjectivity, to be discussing the nature of actual people—people trapped like helpless dupes within the grip of discipline. He never claimed to be offering theories about subjectivity, its power, or powerlessness, to bring about social change. Rather, in the later works especially, his focus was rather on how particular theories served to buttress particular practices—and vice versa—and how their combined effects produced totalitarian institutions and efficient workers. Foucault called these effects "power/knowledge," about which he offered, unapologetically, a theory (see Foucault, *The History of Sexuality* 92–102). At the same time, he should be taken seriously when he expresses a desire to assist in the emergence of counterdiscourses and when he says a counterdiscourse is not a *theory* at all. But what, then, is a counterdiscourse? Why isn't it swallowed up by the tentacular institutions posited by Foucault's theory?

In our terms, a counterdiscourse is the hoped-for result of *practical theorizing*—an activity with, as we understand it, comparatively modest goals. The practical theorist hopes only to clear a discursive space in which those who were previously silenced might speak up or, as bell hooks says, "talk back"—that is, produce their own counterdiscourse. Yet Foucault's critics, because they have not understood how to read his genealogical work or how to understand the notion of a counterdiscourse, credit him with too much and too little. On the one hand, they credit Foucault with having produced a theoretical "system" that has the effect of "politically paralyzing" his readership (see Lazarus 126). Even though no reader-response studies have been published that support such a claim, it continues to be a staple of Foucault's critics. If they did somehow attempt to substantiate the claim, they would probably discover it to be empty or perhaps a comment on their own reaction to Foucault's work: perhaps *they* feel paralyzed prior to reading Foucault and, thus, project their feeling onto the theoretically naive people they imagine reading Foucault's work. Ironically, the theorists themselves have evaded the paralyzing effects. On the other hand, Foucault's critics fail to credit him with any real-world political sensitivity. Thus deficient, he cannot see that, despite his literary avant-gardism, he plays into the hands of the bourgeois world-system. When he claims theory is always "local" and "particular," for example, he is merely being parochial and supporting the bourgeois stay-at-home attitude that assumes "everybody else is just like us" (see Spivak, "Criticism" 6). Foucault, therefore, appears to be, at the same time, a political Godzilla and a political dope: he has blasted the radicals' political will and settled into a mushy, slightly disguised universalism.

In fact, both characterizations—Foucault as Godzilla, Foucault as dope—misconstrue what he was attempting through his practical theorizing. Deleuze, again, puts it aptly: "We [philosophical radicals] ridiculed representation and said it was finished, but we failed to draw the consequences of this 'theoretical' conversion—to appreciate the theoretical fact that only those directly concerned [with a political struggle] can speak in a practical way on their own behalf" (Deleuze and Foucault 209). If Deleuze is right, then Foucault offers more than a philosophical critique of representation, along the lines suggested by many American deconstructionists: Foucault's critique is practical. Foucault's critics, however, have muddled the specific meaning that "practical" should be given in this context. Put simply, the word means that Foucault's theorizing explicitly *ends* where real-world politics begins. Foucault does not, that is, first construct a theory and then apply it. It, rather, emerges in the midst of the "struggle against the forms of power . . . in the sphere of 'knowledge,' 'truth,' 'consciousness,' and 'discourse'" (Deleuze and Foucault 208). Because he sees his writing as linked in this way to political struggles—as an engagement in a particular sphere, namely theory—Foucault dismisses the time-worn problem of the relationship between theory and practice. In one of those gnomic pronouncements that strike his critics as empty word-play, Foucault says: "[T]heory does not express, translate, or serve to apply practice: it is practice" (Deleuze and Foucault 208).

Foucault makes good on the pronouncement by, among other things, recognizing that traditional theory alone falls short of being political and, in turn, that politics often relies on theory. He shows that "theory"—by which he means not theory in general, but rather theory as he *practices* it—arises from the impulse to provide a clearing for political action. In the realm of theory, for example, he "allows" prisoners to speak by disrupting common assumptions about the French penal system with *Discipline and Punish;* likewise, the *History of Sexuality* is originally intended to release bodies from the grip of the so-called experts on sexuality who seek to replace pleasures with pathologies. Of course, neither Foucault the theorist nor Foucault the activist is literally capable of allowing or disallowing prisoners to speak. In the same way, *he* is not capable of allowing or disallowing bodies to seek their pleasures. Rather, in the case of both prisoners and bodies, Foucault the theorist provides a political clearing in which others, including himself as an activist, might then speak—might form counterdiscourses. Foucault's *practical theorizing* is the act of creating spaces, within a discourse, where a counterdiscourse can emerge.

Foucault says the idea that "writing is necessarily" (and the qualification is significant) "a subversive activity" deserves to be "severely denounced" (Deleuze and Foucault 214). The point is that writing or theory must somehow be linked with activism in order to be subversive. At the same time, we recognize that theory can pose a challenge to the *status quo* and, as such, *can* have profound political importance: Theory is political to the extent that it *can* blast apart totalizing hegemonic discourses which, at their most insidious, manage to include revolutionary viewpoints. A counterdiscourse, however, is *always* political—political, we are suggesting, by definition—*though not necessarily progressive or liberating.* In his own case, Foucault was careful to distinguish between his theoretical writing in the narrowest sense—"bookish acts of participation," as he put it in another interview—and his activism. "One is not radical because one pronounces a few words," he said. "The essence of being radical is physical; the essence of being radical is the radicalness of existence itself" (*Foucault Live* 190–91). In the end, one must, in the most uncomplicated sense, *act.*

Foucault's remark about bookishness should be enough to answer the wide-spread complaint that he suffered from an obsession with the power of "discourse"—or, as the cultural critic Robert Hughes put it, with the idea that "repression is inscribed in all language" (46; see Appiah 67–68 and Lazarus 126–27). In fact, Foucault maintained that the politics of language is only part—and not the most significant part—of politics in general. Moreover, he never contended that *all* language is oppressive. What he said, as we have been arguing in this section, is that repression works *through* language and that the struggle to overturn repression includes speaking out against it. Language *can* be oppressive. Speaking out, not theorizing, constitutes a counterdiscourse, and it is produced by those involved "radically" and "physically" with existence. Hughes and others have, therefore, made a basic mistake: Foucault, as a theorist, did not produce counterdiscourses, and he would say, in general, the theorist does not typically do so. Foucault had too much respect for real-world acts of political participation to claim otherwise.

The critics who lump Foucault together with other French "textualists" have failed to see that a counterdiscourse is not just another theory, no matter how philosophically "radical"—whether archaeological, genealogical, or even deconstructive—a theory might be. Just as only those who hold political power can meaningfully discriminate against stigmatized groups, so only those who have been oppressed by a discourse can form a counterdiscourse. In metaphoric terms, it is a voice that rises directly from below; it is, for this reason, not a theory or discourse that bears a merely uncertain relationship to practice. Prisoners, madpeople, gays, lesbians, and other "non-normals"—Foucault hoped to clear a space in which they might speak up and begin defining themselves through their counterdiscourses. The act of clearing away oppressive discourses is itself practical or, in Foucault's limited sense, political. *Madness and Civilization, Discipline and Punish, The History of Sexuality*—in this sense, they are all "political" works.

What happens once a space is cleared, however, depends not on theorists, but rather on those who have begun to speak up. As Deleuze put it in conversation with Foucault:

> Practice is a set of relays from one theoretical point to another, and theory is a relay from one practice to another. No theory

can develop without eventually encountering a wall, and practice is necessary for piercing this wall. For example, your work began in the theoretical analysis of the context of confinement, specifically with respect to the psychiatric asylum within a capitalist society in the nineteenth century. Then you became aware of the necessity for confined individuals to speak for themselves, to create a relay. . . . [T]his group is found in prisons—these individuals are imprisoned. (Deleuze and Foucault 206)

Foucault did not set discursive guidelines for these prisoners. As he declared, "The intellectual's role is no longer to place himself 'somewhat ahead and to the side' in order to express the stifled truth of the collectivity." Theory, says Foucault, is an "activity conducted alongside those who struggle" (Deleuze and Foucault 208). And what they say—their counterdiscourse—*might disappoint and even horrify* the very intellectual who produced the theory that made space for the counterdiscourse. Intellectuals never know exactly where political actors and events will lead, even those events that they have tried to influence or celebrate with their theories. Consider Foucault's eventual reaction to the Iranian revolution, which he had initially cheered as an attack on Western power: he was saddened. Nothing in theory can protect the theorist from such a reaction.

Unlike recent deconstructionists, Foucault never agonized over how to make his writing political, or how to apply it, because he acknowledged that theory purely as theory is never political. The question of application—inevitably a pseudo-mechanical problem involving conceptual pieces that do not quite fit together—should not even arise. Foucault dissolved the question: theory always needs a "relay." In contrast, deconstructionists like Gayatri Spivak and Bill Readings, and at times even Jacques Derrida, have tried to make theory itself somehow politically engaged. They understand the theorist's role as an interpreter of meanings—as a reader of the social text—to be essential to politics.

Spivak, for example, admires Derrida for his work on the "*mechanics* of the constitution of the Other," because "we"—apparently a reference to other theorists—"can use it to much greater analytic and interventionist advantage than invocations of the *authenticity* of the Other" ("Can the Subaltern Speak?" 294). The implied in-voker of authenticity, in this context, is Foucault, while Spivak's interventionist theorist mounts an attack on "discursive practices" that, she claims, is more directly political ("Can the Subaltern Speak?" 305). This political intervention would and does appar-ently take place in scholarly circles, just as Spivak's does, and this *can* be politically important. Readings offers a similar account of deconstructive engagement as he wants to "extend the operation of deconstruction to the manner in which the sphere of the politi-cal is conventionally thought" (225). In this case, the very *conception* of politics can be radical or conservative, and so the effort to change minds about political theory—mostly those in literature and philosophy departments—qualifies as political action. Der-rida, for his part, characterizes deconstruction as the "tireless anal-ysis (both theoretical and practical) of adherences" to the logic of racism, Nazism, totalitarianism, and other pernicious doctrines (648). The audience for such analysis would, again, have to be mostly academics. Who else has the freedom to scrutinize, philo-sophically, "tireless" and "rigorous" analyses of political logics?[3] All three writers, then, share a desire to view typically theoretical activ-ities—interpretation, categorization, analysis—as inherently po-litical.

For better or worse, Foucault was not motivated by this desire. Where politics begins, the production of high theory inevitably stops. And vice versa. Spivak, Readings, and Derrida seek to "dis-close political relationships where they were unsuspected," what the *engaged* intellectual has traditionally done (Readings 207). Fou-cault, however, believes the oppressed are "capable of expressing themselves"—outside the strictures of theory. No doubt this point has caused some confusion: contrary to Spivak and others, Fou-cault never claimed that those who speak for themselves are *trans-parent* or *authentic*. Spivak accuses Foucault of crudely assuming that workers, for example, know themselves and their political aims with perfect transparency. But Foucault was trying to disen-tangle politics from just such epistemological claims. What he says is that, as activists, workers lack nothing that theory can give them. To put it differently: the academic intellectual, even one who writes as an engaged theorist, has no *privileged* knowledge of politics, no justification for being a representative of the oppressed. This is the reason why Deleuze, subtle enough to understand all the nuances of a tradition-rich term like "representation," characterized speaking for others as a fundamental indignity.

2. Discourse Misunderstood: Neither a Relativism Nor a Determinism

Since the 1960s, Foucault has been saddled with two basic charges about his seemingly intertwined theory and practice: on the one hand, he is accused of being a linguistic relativist and, therefore, intellectually irresponsible; on the other, he is accused of being a structural determinist and, therefore, intellectually irresponsible. In either case, so say his critics, he undermines the possibility of action by transforming the world into discourse. Despite the argument in the previous section, we do not dismiss these charges: because they issue from all parts of the political spectrum, and because they are leveled against a theorist who linked his work with activism, they need to be explicitly addressed. As we demonstrate in this section, we think the charges ultimately boil down to a few uncontroversial observations about the working methods of historians. Nonetheless, a discussion of what appears to be Foucault's odd mixture of relativism and determinism will help demystify the notorious term "discourse."

In *The Archaeology of Knowledge,* Foucault analyzes "what history has become," by which he means what history has become *for him* (6). Now, he says, history "organizes the document, divides it up, distributes it, orders it, arranges it in levels, establishes series, distinguishes between what is relevant and what is not" (6). History, he continues, "does not try to reconstitute what men have done or said"; it is "the work expended on material documentation" (7). This kind of work, since it attempts to reconstruct—or simply construct—patterns of significance out of remains from the past, makes history "archaeological." History, as it was traditionally understood, waited to be discovered. By contrast, Foucauldian history—a reflection, to be precise, on the *making* of history—is created. It is not, however, created out of the historian's mind but rather out of documents. In this respect, history is not relative, but neither does it announce itself as the truth. This much working historians know and, by now, acknowledge as uncontroversial (conversations with Manfra and Dykstra made this last point clear; also see Veyne 3–30).

Yet, the way in which history is used in ideological debates, especially in this country, is something else again. Take, for example, the ongoing debate over multiculturalism and the canon. Cultural conservatives like Lynne Cheney and William Bennett still want to defend and preserve "*our* legacy," so that it may enrich future generations. For Cheney and Bennett, the content of the "legacy" and the identity of "we" who inherit it are self-evident truths, yet Foucault argues it is just these kinds of "truths" that certain groups construct through a selective use of historical documents. Or take the term "America," which Robert Hughes uses to defend a reactionary caricature of multiculturalism. "America," he says, "is a construction of mind, not of race or inherited class or ancestral territory" (44). But who lives in this "construction of mind"? To African-Americans and women, who as groups still earn less than white men and occupy fewer positions of corporate and political power, the U.S. is very much a construction of race and class—it is a walled city, in fact, to which few of their number are granted entrance. Hughes' "America," for its part, is very much an imaginary construction tacked together by Hughes himself and other traditionalists. Nonetheless, it serves to bolster a very real political movement: namely, the American radical right.

The literary critic Homi K. Bhabha draws attention to how terms like Cheney and Bennett's "legacy" and Hughes' "America" are used to further domination (127). Culture, says Bhabha, is always "crossed by the *différance* of writing or *écriture*" (129). Any given culture, in other words, receives its definition from what it is not.[4] To use Bhabha's formulation: Cheney, Bennett, and Hughes "attempt to dominate in the *name* of a cultural supremacy which is itself produced only in the moment of differentiation" (127). Hughes' "America," for example, gains its content from the "cult of the Abused Inner Child," the people Hughes considers not grown up enough to take their licks and keep quiet about it (45); the "legacy" so admired by Cheney and Bennett is visible only against the backdrop of the works they deem unfit to be part of it.

Yet, Hughes treats "America" as though he and others who share his beliefs did not create it, and the same goes for Cheney and Bennett's "legacy." When Foucault speaks of "organizing the document," in contrast, he is underscoring the act of creation which produces such an object as "America"—the kind of act in which all those who deal with history and culture engage. Never did he say that the U.S.—the real-life, flesh-and-blood country of 250 million people and the institutions that shape their lives—was a linguistic phantasm. Not much more needs to be said, really, about Foucault's supposed relativism.

But what about Foucault's determinism? In order to solve the agency/structure problem and, by extension, the problem of "discursive determinism," one has only to understand the nature of an object like "America" and how it is produced. To begin with, because "America" is the product of a selective use of documents—newspapers, laws, books, speeches, etc.—it is a *linguistic* object. Yet, it is not a deterministic discursive "structure" that somehow constrains epiphenomenal actors. Foucault would, instead, say that the term "America" receives its content from the definitions given of it, the statements made about it. Obviously, people have acted and will continue to act within "America"—or the U.S.—but the significance of their actions is a topic for debate among historians, cultural critics, philosophers, and so on. The actors and their actions Foucault calls, not without sarcasm, "living, fragile, pulsating 'history'"; the significance of those actions is a problem for what he calls the "methodological field of history," in which "structures" have a place (*Archaeology of Knowledge* 11). He disposes with the "conflict" between action—so-called agency—and structure in the following way:

> [I]t is a long time now since historians uncovered, described, and analyzed structures, without ever having occasion to wonder whether they were not allowing the living, fragile, pulsating 'history' to slip through their fingers. The structure/development opposition is relevant neither to the definition of the historical field, nor, in all probability, to the definition of a structural method. (*Archaeology of Knowledge* 11)

Foucault, for his part, defines the "historical field" as the archive —or, in simpler terms, the documents that survive from the past.

Whether or not the "actors" that appear in this field are free is a meaningless question, since they now exist in a time that has already occurred. Freedom, therefore, is beside the point when the historian is reading documents from the past.

If Foucault had intended his "archaeology" as an explanatory framework, then he might have opened himself to criticisms of the familiar sort made by Lazarus and Appiah. Foucault transforms social life into an "infinite text," Foucault argues for a "structural determinism," etc. But, in fact, he proposes "archaeology" as a methodological experiment: *methodological,* in that he wanted to see how the past would appear if historians analyzed it largely as groups of related "statements"; an *experiment,* in that he did not know what the result of such an analysis would be (on experimentation, see Moussa). Foucault never claims that history or social life is nothing more than a text, nor that it was a text at all. Moreover, he never claims *it* is anything: in using a phrase such as the "methodological field of history," he emphasizes that history has no essence but rather exists through the use of those documents that an historian has managed to uncover. The choice of the word "methodological" by itself suggests that Foucault hoped to forestall the quasimetaphysical debates that critics like Lazarus have tried to initiate. (The question "Are social actors free if they live within social structures?" is only the contemporary version of the problem of free will, debated by medieval and modern philosophers.) And even at the end of *The Archaeology of Knowledge,* his most sustained archaeological "experiment," Foucault has not convinced himself that archaeology holds great promise.

Take, for example, the dialogue Foucault conducts with an imaginary interlocutor in the conclusion of *Archaeology.*[5] Tentative throughout the book, Foucault is still uncertain of the value of his methodological proposals.

> [I]t may be that archaeology is doing nothing more than playing the role of an instrument that makes it possible to articulate, in a less imprecise way than in the past, the analysis of social formations and epistemological descriptions; or which makes it possible to relate an analysis of the positions of the subject to a theory of the history of sciences; or which makes it possible to situate the place of intersection between a general

theory of production and a generative analysis of statements. (208)

"It may be," "doing nothing more than," "makes it possible"—this is not the language of a systematizer, a metaphysician. In another passage, Foucault says that archaeology "simply indicates a *possible line of attack* for the analysis of verbal performances" (*Archaeology of Knowledge* 206, emphasis added). Elsewhere again, reflecting on the preceding chapters, he says "one *could* draw up a specific description of statements, of their formation, and of the regularities proper to discourse" (*Archaeology of Knowledge* 200). The point seems clear: history could be discussed otherwise. According to Foucault's own admission, then, archaeology is not the only, or even the best, method of understanding the past.

Moreover, as the quote set off above strongly suggests, Foucault the archaeologist is concerned with a particular kind of history: the history of thought. Note, in particular, his remark about "epistemological descriptions." The archaeologist, he says, subjects them to a "precise" analysis. This is science at the highest meta-level, an analysis of the analysis of phenomena. A Foucauldian archaeologist, for example, would not ask, "What is the nature of language?" but rather, "What was being said, and in what ways, about language during the Classical period?" When Foucault the archaeologist became Foucault the genealogist, he broadened the scope of his theoretical inquiry. A characteristic genealogical question would be, "What was being said, and in what ways, about normality during the nineteenth century, and how did that discursive formation support disciplinary practices in schools, prisons, and hospitals?" In any case, neither in the archaeological nor the genealogical period did Foucault claim that people were, or were not, fundamentally free. Consider, in this regard, Foucault's comments about explanation in the following quote:

> [I]t's been more than fifty years since we perceived that the task of description was essential in domains like those of history, ethnology and language. After all, mathematical language since Galileo and Newton doesn't function as an *explanation* of nature but as a *description* of a process. I don't see why one should contest the attempt of non-formalized disciplines

like history to undertake for themselves the first task of description. (*Foucault Live* 17)

Quite clearly, in his archaeological phase, Foucault is not concerned with actual occurrences in history—and not with *explaining* them—but rather with *describing* what historians said about history and, moreover, how and why they said it. The discourse of history, not history itself, is Foucault's subject.

Not only does Foucault always discourage readers from taking him to be discussing history and people as nondiscursive constructs, but he also explicitly anticipates those who would interpret him as a postmodern determinist. In a passage that his critics have apparently forgotten, Foucault debates with an interlocutor the problem of "agency," in exactly the terms used by those who describe Foucault as a determinist. The interlocutor begins by saying:

> You make curious use of the freedom that you question in others. For you give yourself the whole field of a free space that you even refuse to qualify. But are you forgetting the care with which you enclosed the discourse of others within systems of rules? Are you forgetting all those constraints that you described so meticulously? *Have you not deprived individuals of the right to intervene personally in the positivities in which their discourses are situated?* (*Archaeology of Knowledge* 208, emphasis added)

Such misguided objections lead to problems concerning the "place" from which Foucault analyzes the archive. "Is *he* not constrained by a discursive structure?" Foucault replies by pointing out the "double mistake" contained in this and related questions.

First, he says the positivities—or structures—"must not be understood as a set of determinations imposed from the outside on the thought of individuals, or inhabiting it from the inside, in advance as it were" (*Archaeology of Knowledge* 208). The positivities are rather the "set of conditions in accordance with which a practice is exercised." This formidable-sounding phrase can be explained simply: no one speaks or acts outside of a discursive or practical context. Hegel, for example, responds to Kant; the early 20th-century U.S. labor movement responds to unrestrained capitalism. In general, an action takes place only within *some* kind of context—discursive, practical, or otherwise. During his "archaeological" period, Foucault was trying to specify one way of understanding a context, and his analysis was admittedly slanted toward language. As he says, his archaeology is an attempt "to show that to *speak* is to do something—something other than to express what one thinks" (*Archaeology of Knowledge* 209, emphasis added).

Second, Foucault questions the notion of freedom that seems to inspire the criticism of his supposed "determinism." Those who offer such a criticism seem to assume that actors and thinkers, in order to be free, must somehow be absolutely spontaneous, unencumbered by past and current intellectual debates and political institutions. Foucault asks: "Has not the practice of revolutionary discourse and scientific discourse in Europe over the past two hundred years freed you from the idea that words are wind, an external whisper, a beating of wings that one has difficulty in hearing in the serious matter of history?" (*Archeology of Knowledge* 209). Or, as Marx put it: "Men make history, but they do not make it just as they please; they do not make it under circumstances chosen by themselves, but under circumstances directly found, given and transmitted from the past." How are those circumstances transmitted? *This* is the question Foucault asks. He describes it, during one phase of his career, as "archaeological."

Even archaeology, the most abstract—and apparently determinist—of Foucault's theoretical endeavors, can be considered political in our sense: the very demonstration that no discourse has an anchor in "Reality" might encourage the silenced to speak. As Foucault said, "[T]he return to history makes sense in the respect that history shows that that which is was not always so" (*Foucault Live* 252). In other words, there is liberation in recognizing things can be different. But again, no philosophical theory can map out the actions that follow from this recognition. What should be done is up to the makers of the counterdiscourse.

3. Engaging Archaeologies: Speaking With Others

In an attempt to move beyond the "activist vs. theorist" debate, Bhabha suggests:

> [I]t is a sign of *political maturity* to accept that there are many
> forms of political writing. . . . It is not as if the leaflet involved
> in the organization of a strike is short on theory, while a specu-
> lative article on the theory of ideology ought to have more
> practical examples or applications. (113–14, emphasis added)

We think it is precisely a lack of such political maturity that disposes many leftist academics to criticize Foucault for being too far
from the action. They want to see undeniable applications and liberatory effects coming from Foucault's archaeologies and genealogies. For our part, giving Bhabha's remarks a Foucauldian twist,
we might describe ourselves as attempting to note a kind of "maturity," one which recognizes the limits of what we have called "practical theorizing." The "mature" political theorist recognizes that
speaking up—not theorizing in the traditional sense and not even
practical theorizing by itself—is the truly progressive and liberatory act.

No doubt, many stigmatized groups speak up and produce
counterdiscourses in a discursive space cleared by means other
than Foucauldian practical theorizing. Yet, without abandoning
our argument, we can admit there are many ways to disrupt oppressive received wisdom. Likewise, Foucault himself never asserted any absolute political value for his work, never asserted he
had found *the* way to combat disciplinary power. Our aim up to
now has been to highlight Foucault's own distinctive, and modest,
political usefulness, which has been denied by many activist-
minded writers. A brief discussion of another writer who might be
considered a practical theorizer will provide an illustration of what
we mean, in this context, by "political usefulness."

We propose that bell hooks, through her articles, books, and
public appearances, challenges many of the established discourses
about race, class, and gender in a Foucauldian mode. hooks champions the position that academics and critics need to recognize the
political importance of oppressed people, whoever they might be,
speaking up for themselves. She argues that any genuine moment
of gaining a voice ought not to be simply confused with or reduced
to a merely bourgeois desire to be noticed. For hooks:

> True speaking is not solely an expression of creative power; it
> is an act of resistance, a political gesture that challenges politics

of domination that would render us nameless and voiceless. As such, it is a courageous act—as such it represents a threat. To those who wield oppressive power, that which is threatening must necessarily be wiped out, annihilated, silenced. (8)

hooks attempts to lend support to this threat in her own brand of practical theorizing, what we are tempted to call her "Foucauldian activism." Her work has been a sustained effort to create possibilities for people, including herself, to move from the silent objectification that sexism, racism, and class elitism maintain to being a genuinely speaking subject, a person who dares to counter the various discourses of power.

According to hooks:

> Moving from silence into speech is for the oppressed, the colonized, the exploited, and those who stand and struggle side by side a gesture of defiance that heals, that makes new life and new growth possible. It is that act of speech, of "talking back," that is no mere gesture of empty words, that is the expression of our movement from object to subject—the liberated voice. (9)

"Talking back," then, is tantamount to counterdiscourse. For hooks, her autobiographical explorations, her archaeological searches through the "documents" of her childhood, and her life since first "talking back" are examples of practical theorizing, a theorizing that we have suggested ought to be the focus of any discussion concerning the implications of Foucault's thought and political efficacy.

One could rightly argue that hooks offers a more immediate and concrete possibility for a counterdiscourse than Foucault by virtue of her willingness to be simultaneously the archaeologist as well as the archive under consideration. Hooks is able to produce both theory *and* counterdiscourse; she speaks, writes, and acts as a theorist, and speaks, writes, and acts as a black woman. Perhaps more so than any other social critic today, hooks courageously offers herself both as "document" and "counter-discourse"—for complicated reasons that may never be completely understood or endorsed, Foucault did not choose to be both. hooks' use of her own diaries, memories, and earlier writings, in addition to her narrative-presentations and interviews (her talks *with* people), are all moments of crisscrossing, if not erasing, the line separating theory and practice in the traditional sense. Because, like Foucault, she does not sit comfortably on either side of the line, hooks has had to endure the criticism that comes from those who insist on the purity of theory. She is often attacked for being merely autobiographical and not theoretically rigorous.

Nonetheless, we take the work done by hooks as an important example of what Foucault would call the "theoretico-active" commitment possible within an academic setting and which may have important consequences outside the academy.[6] Her work is among the best responses to those who contend that many social critics today merely present narratives of the totalizing effects of power which yield nothing more than stories of passive conformity to the ebb and flow of power itself. What the detractors fail to see is that hooks assembles her histories informed by the oppressive institutions of racism, classism, and sexism in order to break down the discourses supporting them. Like Foucault, moreover, she has often exposed oppression where it was previously undetected, as she did when she helped initiate a counterdiscourse within the largely white feminist movement of the 1970s in the U.S., particularly in *From Margin to Center.* Perhaps, if Foucault had chosen to offer a more "personal" narrative—to offer, for example, an analysis of his own status within the university, or of his own sexual practices—more people might be persuaded by his distinctive conception of theorizing.

Following hooks, we would emphasize that refusing to speak for others should not be reduced to an act of "liberal difference," of merely "permitting" others to express themselves. Instead, it is linked to a commitment to unite, in a practical way, the typically separate realms of theory and practice. As Deleuze remarks to Foucault: "You became aware of the necessity for confined individuals to speak for themselves, to create a relay [to activist groups]. . . . A theorizing intellectual, for us, is no longer a subject, a representing or representative consciousness. Those who act and struggle are no longer represented" (Deleuze and Foucault 206–07). Radical intellectuals who fail to realize that they are part of an oppressive network of authority when they seek to bring "consciousness" to the "masses" or legitimacy to their complaints only further oppress them precisely by virtue of speaking *for* them, by creating totalizing theories that explain and justify them.

Much like Deleuze and Foucault, Paulo Freire in his *Pedagogy of the Oppressed* issues a warning about "intellectual leaders" that still rings true:

> Those who work for liberation must not take advantage of the emotional dependence of the oppressed—dependence that is the fruit of the concrete situation of domination which surrounds them and which engendered their unauthentic view of the world. Using their dependence to create still greater dependence is an oppressor tactic. . . . [N]ot even the best-intentioned leadership can bestow independence as a gift. (53)

This is not to say that there is no place for theorizing at all, but rather that intellectuals should be suspicious of the impulse to do grand theorizing on behalf of the Masses, Women, History, or whatever fine-sounding abstraction might be appealing for the moment. In a similar spirit, what Foucault challenges, along with hooks and others, is the habit of theorists speaking for others without considering the real-world significance of that act. In her essay "The Problem of Speaking for Others," Linda Alcoff puts it bluntly: "The point is that the impetus to always be the speaker and to speak in all situations must be seen for what it is: a desire for mastery and domination" (24). We think Foucault can help theorists acknowledge the seriousness of such domination and, in addition, the importance of speaking *with* others. Whatever political goals academics and theorists may aspire to, Foucault has demonstrated the need to respect the dignity of others speaking for themselves and the potential benefits for the theorist of speaking with others.

Moreover, this kind of respect might help keep a counterdiscourse "counter." Given the tendency of oppositional political movements and theories to ossify into hidebound institutions of one sort or another, counterdiscourses almost inevitably become discourses. Foucault was especially concerned about such disturbing, even if inevitable, discursive transformations: because they cannot be avoided, he urged intellectuals and others to exercise a "hyper-activism" in seeking out sites of oppression. Every

The Practical Theorizing of Michel Foucault   107

new idea, every new political proposal, every new social movement—even if explicitly "progressive," they are all "dangerous"
because they could all generate oppressive discourses (see Foucault, "Genealogy of Ethics" 231–32). Yet, at least if those who "talk
back" remember that their opponents, too, should be offered the
same opportunity to speak for themselves, then perhaps dialogue
among progressives and conservatives might remain as fluid and
productive as it often is during times of acute social crisis. The aim
of "talking back," that is, ought to go beyond the attempt simply
to silence others—an increasingly troubling aspect, we think, of
current radical theorizing. We admit, however, that many politically active theorists today want to do more than keep their discourses "counter," want more than the modest possibilities inherent in practical theorizing.

4. "Enough Is Enough. Enough Isn't Everything": Politics and Truth

   Why have progressive academics dismissed the practical political value of Foucault's work? We think the answer lies in a metaphysical impulse that still animates much of the writing done in the
Marxist and post-Marxist traditions. In spite of numerous much-
discussed assaults during the twentieth century on truth, universal
claims, and philosophical "foundations," progressive academics
still hanker for an intellectual support built on something other
than human social practice (see Moussa, "Misunderstanding").
They fear that anything less would be open to charges of relativism
and, therefore, capable of nothing more than affirming the status
quo. As Christopher Norris recently wrote: "It is a sad reflection
on the currency of 'advanced' intellectual debate in the human
sciences that so much of what nowadays passes for radical theory
is, in fact, quite incapable of mustering resistance to a downright
conformist or consensus-based account of knowledge, truth and
reality" (1). Making an argument parallel to Lazarus', Norris attacks Richard Rorty and Stanley Fish as the most visible "intellectual conformists," a term he imposes on those who favorably dis-
cuss language-games, interpretive communities, and other ideas
that lead to a "retreat from issues of real-world political concern"

(25). In a similar vein, Barbara Ehrenreich asserts starkly: "Any possibility of a moral perspective gets erased by a position fashionable among some of our post-modernist academics, that there can be no absolutes, no truths, and hence no grounds for judgements. There can't be a left if there's no basis for moral judgement" (4).

In response to this defense of realism or various retooled versions of it mounted by Lazarus, Norris, and Ehrenreich, we want to pose the question, "What would be enough to justify or support an attack on the status quo?" It seems that for many neorealist progressives like them, social theory without some kind of foundation is not enough. What would be "enough," however, is not clear. For our part, borrowing a quote from John Austin, we would answer the question by saying: "Enough is enough. Enough isn't everything" (qtd. in Putnam 121).[7] Austin meant that "enough" is determined by what circumstances require or allow, while "everything" harks back to Enlightenment notions of objectivity or truth—notions that, as Hilary Putnam says, assume a description of the world can be given from "no particular point of view" or from "outside our own skins" (11, 17).

We understand Foucault as saying that, like it or not, historians and philosophers have to accept that the past and even the present exist largely in the form of extant documents, which can be interpreted only from particular points of view. Any account of social life, therefore, can be little more than an interpretation of the documents—little more, yes, but that is *enough.* Indeed, it has to be enough, unless one is willing to try recuperating traditional realism one more time. Settling for the interpretation of documents as "enough," however, does not transform social life into an "infinite text," at least not in the sense that Lazarus intends. Foucault, unlike, say, Jean Baudrillard, never made hard-to-swallow claims about social life or the world not being "real," nor about social actors being somehow the puppets of discourse. What Foucault said was that no brute social "datum" exists before which all intellectuals must stand in silence. It is in this sense that nothing speaks for itself. Oppression, in particular, does not speak for itself. Alternatively, according to Foucault, the oppressed should be *allowed* to speak for themselves, having traditionally been spoken for by those—intellectuals, often, and others in a position of "discursive power"—who exercise the power to label and categorize them.

As a way of testing our claims about social life and documents, we consider the 1991 Gulf War. According to Norris, academic progressives without a philosophical foundation lacked the means of answering the dominant political beliefs revealed by public discussion in this country about the war; he describes those beliefs as "narrow, parochial, self-serving, exploitative, class-based, chauvinistic [and] downright racist" (33). Only philosophical realists, implies Norris, can operate at the "level of rock-bottom factual appeal and ethical responsibility which may then be invoked by investigative journalists, critical intellectuals and others with a principled interest in exposing the extent of mass-media complicity" (28). Only realists, that is, possess the needed philosophical equipment to make contact with the "real world." Making a similar claim, Lazarus says "a great deal is lost" when "the social" is collapsed into "the discursive": what is lost, he suggests, is "political commitments and solidarities" (127–28).

Norris, Lazarus, and Ehrenreich all seem to assume that, if given the chance by committed journalists and philosophers, the "real world" of oppression, genocide, and racism will appear, in all its horrid undeniability, before the open eyes of the public. That, at any rate, is the philosophical "picture" behind such an assumption.[8] Yet, when Norris, for example, tries to fill in the details of that picture, he appeals to the sort of methods that Foucault or even Rorty would recommend for making political judgments critical of the status quo. Norris writes: "[W]e can only be in a position to make such judgements if we continue to seek out the best available sources of information, and moreover, *to interpret that evidence according to the standards of veridical utterance,* enlightened participant debate, and ethico-political accountability" (27, emphasis added). In Foucault's terms, this amounts to reading the documents in accordance with the accepted limits of interpretation. Public intellectuals committed to a progressive agenda, intellectuals like Stanley Aronowitz and Michael Berube, have been offering such "interpretations" for some time.

Yet the neorealists, in philosophizing about politics, are unwilling to settle for interpretation of any sort. What they seem to want is an event that speaks for itself, that forces its truth on those who witness it, that can be taken in only one way, namely as progressive. Such an event might someday appear, but it has not appeared yet. That it has not is what Foucault aims to underscore by speaking of his work as, by turns, "archaeological" and "genealogical." By listening to history itself, says Foucault, historians learn that behind it lurks "not a timeless and essential secret, but the secret that [things] have no essence or that their essence was fabricated in a piecemeal fashion from alien forms" ("Nietzsche" 142). At least up to now, in other words, the essence that Norris and Lazarus assume must be present for progressives to be justified in being progressive has never been found by those working in the archive. This essence would provide the "safe place," as Stanley Fish puts it, from where partisan struggle would be banished and Truth would shine forth (245). It is unfortunate, perhaps, that such a place has not been discovered. Still, there are reasons for being progressive, but those reasons do not add up to the undeniable Truth that ends all discussion.

Notes

1. On the question of agency, see Smith. Consider his claim that "Foucault's 'subject' is more incapable than not of becoming an agent of large social change" (168). Also see Alcoff, "Feminist Politics and Foucault." Nancy Fraser takes Foucault to task for lacking an alternative to liberalism. See her "Foucault on Modern Power." Charles Taylor and Jürgen Habermas have pounded away at Foucault's supposed tendency to dwell on the negative side of history; see Taylor and Habermas.

2. For a lengthy discussion of the supposed political consequences of rejecting truth, see Norris.

3. Derrida's repeated calls for rigor, which have become nearly obsessive, indirectly reveal his disdain for nonacademics, especially the hated journalists. See, in particular, his comments about journalists at the beginning of "Paul de Man's War."

4. For a discussion of the relationship existing among identity, lack, and violence, with regard to the issue of homelessness and the image of America, see Scapp.

5. The *Archaeology*, in this respect, is a book like Wittgenstein's *Philosophical Investigations*, where another imaginary interlocutor acts as the persistent metaphysical worrywart. One of us (M.M.) would like to thank Burton Dreben for his help in understanding such "self-deconstructing" books.

6. It is worth noting that both Foucault and hooks have had a significant impact on prisoners. The influence of Foucault's *Discipline and Punish* is well known; less well known, but certainly no less important, is the influence hooks' writing is currently having on African-American males in American prisons.

7. Our discussion in this section owes much to Putnam's essay as well as others in the collection edited by Conant.

8. We are using "picture" in Ludwig Wittgenstein's sense. See, for example, Wittgenstein, Remark #59.

Works Cited

Alcoff, Linda. "Feminist Politics and Foucault: The Limits to a Collaboration." *Crises in Continental Philosophy.* Ed. A. B. Dallery, C. E. Scott, and P. H. Roberts. Albany: SUNY P, 1990. 69–86.

———. "The Problem of Speaking for Others." *Cultural Critique* 29 (1991–92): 5–32.

Appiah, Anthony. "Tolerable Falsehoods: Agency and the Interests of Theory." *Consequences of Theory.* Ed. Jonathan Arac and Barbara Johnson. Baltimore: Johns Hopkins UP, 1991. 63–90.

Bhabha, Homi K. "The Commitment to Theory." *Questions of the Third Cinema.* Ed. J. Pines and P. Willemen. London: British Film Institute, 1989. 111–32.

Deleuze, Gilles, and Michel Foucault. "Intellectuals and Politics." *Language, Counter-Memory, and Practice.* Ed. Donald F. Bouchard. Ithaca: Cornell UP, 1977. 205–17.

Derrida, Jacques. "Like the Sound of the Sea Deep within a Shell: Paul de Man's War." *Critical Inquiry* 14 (1988): 590–652.

Ehrenreich, Barbara. "The Challenge for the Left." *Democratic Left* 19.4 (1992): 4.

Fish, Stanley. "There's No Such Thing as Free Speech and It's a Good Thing, Too." *Debating P. C.* Ed. Paul Berman. New York: Dell, 1992. 231–45.

Foucault, Michel. *The Archaeology of Knowledge.* Trans. A. M. Sheridan Smith. New York: Pantheon, 1972.

———. *Discipline and Punish: The Birth of the Prison.* New York: Vintage, 1979.

———. *Foucault Live: Interviews, 1966–84.* Ed. Sylvère Lotringer. New York: Semiotext(e), 1989.

———. *The History of Sexuality.* Trans. Robert Hurley. New York: Vintage, 1980.

———. "Nietzsche, Genealogy, History." *Language, Counter-Memory, and Practice.* Ed. Donald F. Bouchard. Ithaca: Cornell UP, 1977. 139–64.

———. "On the Genealogy of Ethics." *Michel Foucault: Beyond Structuralism and Hermeneutics.* Ed. Hubert L. Dreyfus and Paul Rabinow. Chicago: U of Chicago P, 1982. 229–52.

———. "Questions of Method: An Interview with Michel Foucault." *Philosophy: End or Transformation?* Ed. Kenneth Baynes, James Bohman, and Thomas McCarthy. Cambridge: MIT P, 1987. 100–24.

———. *The Uses of Pleasure.* Trans. Robert Hurley. New York: Pantheon, 1985.

Fraser, Nancy. "Foucault on Modern Power: Empirical Insights and Normative Confusions." *Unruly Practices: Power, Discourse and Gender in Contemporary Social Theory.* Minneapolis: U of Minnesota P, 1989.

Freire, Paulo. *Pedagogy of the Oppressed.* New York: Continuum, 1988.

Habermas, Jürgen. "Taking Aim at the Heart of the Present." *Foucault: A Critical Reader.* Ed. David Hoy. New York: Basil Blackwell, 1986. 103–08.

hooks, bell. *Talking Back.* Boston: South End P, 1989.

Hughes, Robert. "The Fraying of America." *Time* 3 Feb. 1992: 44–49.

Lazarus, Neil. "Doubting the New World Order: Marxism, Realism, and the Claims of Postmodern Social Theory." *differences* 3.3 (1991): 94–138.

Moussa, Mario. "Foucault and the Problem of Agency; or, Toward a Practical Philosophy." *Ethics and Danger: Currents in Continental Philosophy.* Ed. Arlene Dallery and Charles Scott. Albany: SUNY P, 1992. 255–72.

————. "Misunderstanding the Democratic 'We': Richard Rorty's Liberalism and the Radical Urge for a Philosophical Foundation." *Philosophy and Social Criticism* 17.4 (1991): 297–312.

Norris, Christopher. "The 'End of Ideology' Revisited: The Gulf War, Postmodernism and *Realpolitik.*" *Philosophy and Social Criticism* 17.1 (1991): 1–40.

Putnam, Hilary. "The Craving for Objectivity." *Realism with a Human Face.* Ed. James Conant. Cambridge: Harvard UP, 1990. 120–31.

Readings, Bill. "The Deconstruction of Politics." *Reading De Man Reading.* Ed. Lindsay Waters and Wlad Godzich. Minneapolis: U of Minnesota P, 1989. 223–43.

Scapp, Ron. "Lack and Violence: Towards a Speculative Sociology of the Homeless." *Practice: The Journal of Politics, Economics, Psychology, Sociology, and Culture* 6.2 (1988): 34–47.

Smith, Paul. *Discerning the Subject.* Minneapolis: U of Minnesota P, 1988.

Spivak, Gayatri Chakravorty. "Can the Subaltern Speak?" *Marxism and Interpretation of Culture.* Ed. Cary Nelson and Lawrence Grossberg. Urbana: U of Illinois P, 1988. 271–313.

————. "Criticism, Feminism, and the Institution." Inter. Elizabeth Grosz. *The Post-Colonial Critic: Interviews, Strategies, Dialogues.* Ed. Sarah Harasym. New York: Routledge, 1990. 1–16.

Taylor, Charles. "Foucault on Freedom and Truth." *Foucault: A Critical Reader.* Ed. David Hoy. New York: Basil Blackwell, 1986. 69–102.

Veyne, Paul. *Writing History: Essays on Epistemology.* Trans. Mina Moore-Rinvolucri. Middletown: Wesleyan UP, 1984.

Wittgenstein, Ludwig. *Philosophical Investigations.* Trans. G. E. M. Anscombe. New York: Macmillan, 1958.

Postcolonialism's Possibilities: Subcontinental Diasporic Intervention

Samir Dayal

The question of postcolonialism's possibilities is a grammatical as well as a practical—political—one. How is postcolonialism discursively articulated, and what can it promise as its directions or indirections? Is postcoloniality condemned to the "condition of pessimism" expressed by Anthony Appiah ("Is the Post- in Post-modern the Post- in Postcolonial?" 353)? Is it capable of productive transgressions, (sub)versions of the reigning cultural discourses of postmodernism, or "abstract liberal humanism," within which it is often in danger of being coopted?[1]

1. Postmodernity and Its Others

If the post- in postmodernism is not the same as the post- in postcolonial (to adapt Appiah's terms), then the significance of the distinction is critical, for at least three reasons. First, it is important that postcolonialism not be subsumed under the rubric of post-modernism because that would mean the subsumption—domestication or erasure—of the former's specific social and political contingencies under the latter. In Edward Said's terms, what is to be resisted is the condition of being "outnumbered and outorganized by a prevailing consensus that has come to regard the Third World as an atrocious nuisance" ("Intellectuals in the Post-Colonial World" 52). Second, there is a tendency in several quarters, even among well-meaning contemporary theorists and cultural critics, to entrench a hegemony of postmodernism over postcolonialism. This hegemony needs to be constantly destabilized. For the assimilation of the postcolonial into the postmodern is tantamount to always construing the "post-" of the latter as somehow more transcendent that the "post-" of the former. Third, postmodernism and postcolonialism are articulated from different discursive positionalities, different sites in the academy and in the global cultural economy. They theorize in divergent ways not only the discourse of nation, but the articulation of subject positions, gender assignations, racial and ethnic alignments, and class identifications. Postcolonialism can point up this critical difference and disallow the dilution of its particular agendas and the dissipation of what are for postcolonialism strategic or tactical imperatives—the "possibility of knowledge and of discovery of what it means . . . to be outside the whale" ("Intellectuals" 51), no longer in the abstract liberal humanist envelope but in the real, and secular, sphere of conflictual global culture.

Postcolonialism is not, in this view, merely a passing fad, and its current visibility in the Western academy is not evidence merely of the opportunism of certain conveniently situated intellectuals (despite what critics such as Arif Dirlik allege). Its possibilities can best be realized by developing—or setting in motion—a discourse that could articulate, at differentially constructed moments of emergence, a politics, an ethics, and even an erotics of intervention. A substantial contribution to that complex project can be made by diasporic postcolonials. Interstitially situated as they are in the global cultural economy, they can articulate the anomalies and contradictions of that situation, and explore the possibilities of theoretical, ludic, and transgressive intervention, annulling what might in Derridean language be termed a certain violence of the letter that comes with the "post-" of postmodernism's appropriation of the pre-postmodern other.

Appiah's pessimism about postcolonialism perhaps shares something with the postmodern disillusionment with the project of modernism. Postmodernism's much vaunted antifoundationalist skepticism about metanarratives, as evidenced most recognizably in Jean-François Lyotard's recommendation of "*petits récits*" instead of grand narratives, seems to necessitate a postmodern aesthetics of "quotation" (rather than of apodictic assertions). It is an ancillary condition, according to Roger Scruton, that "for the first time we are more inclined to think that something is finished, than that something new has begun" (4). This sense of an ending, paradoxically enough, provides a ground for the universal abandon with which First World postmodernism has debunked metanarratives and adopted the ironic stance associated with an aesthetic of quotation.

This aesthetic springs from within the context of a late capitalist cultural formation. Thus, the gesture of disavowal cannot be identical in the First and the Third Worlds. What then are the implications for postcolonialism? Is the problematic differently constructed for postcolonialism, defined with reference to an emergent albeit pre-postmodern cultural space, an economy that is "developing" (and is thus still within the developmentalist logic of modernism)? Other political questions rise. Is anything being jettisoned, finessed, or repressed by postmodern abandon that needs to be reinscribed by the postcolonial, such as Third World interiority and materiality? Is there a forgetting of the history of imperialism and Orientalism, or an inadequate awareness of a structure of fantasy wherein the other is fetishized as the opposite number of the Western Other? Is a neocolonialist logic at work within the Third World discourse of the nation? Does the willed innocence of a rhetoric of "progress" not require a corresponding critique of innocence on the part of the postcolonial critic? What does grasping a sense of the new mean for postcolonialism as opposed to postmodernism? What should the Third World expect or hope for, and how can postcolonialism articulate it?

What is clear is that transcultural debate (to use a phrase of Akbar Ahmed's) cannot be negotiated in the same way by postmodernists and postcolonialists. Simon During rightly suggests that there may well be hidden or subtextual postmodernist agendas that ought to be deconstructed by postcolonial criticism:

"the play of passions that we call postcolonial . . . wish once and for all to name and disclaim postmodernism as neo-imperialist . . . by accepting and using those practices and concepts (representation, history, evaluation) which postmodernism most strenuously denies" (368–69). On the other hand, perhaps there are cultivable productive affinities between postmodernism and postcolonialism that would help define the latter's political exigencies. I argue here that postcolonialism ought to maintain a skepticism or political wariness about postmodernism, even in engagement with its conceptual universe, and offer possible alternatives to, or (sub)versions of, the home truths of even the antifoundationalist discourse now in the ascendant in the Western academy. Otherwise, postcolonialism may inherit and labor under a false consciousness, particularly a false dualism or dilemma between reified subjecthood or an order of essentialist, mimetic representationalism—as against postmodern antifoundationalism, with its attendant assumptions and its unapologetic, even triumphalist, self-construction.

Even Gayatri Spivak's notion of the subject effect produced by the "*strategic* use of positivist essentialism" is problematic for postcolonialism, as Madhava Prasad points out, insofar as it implies that "theory itself is not a strategic necessity" (67). Instead of regarding a strategic essentialism as a necessity for the Third World subject, postcolonial criticism cannot uncritically adopt the metropolitan discourse of intersubjective relations, but must continually mark and demystify the phantasmatic place that the Third World occupies in that discourse. Essentialism, furthermore, risks isolationism and particularism: if one argues that the quiddities of the various Third World cultures can only be truly understood "from within" those Third World experiences, then the West too would seem to be closed to analysis by the postcolonial critic, and we would have a kind of totalized segregation, obviating truly transcultural debate. It is a companion bromide that Third World voices should be encouraged to conceive of themselves as springing from a native matrix—the immediacy of a cryogenized Third World "nature" (in every sense of the word) and materiality. Postcolonial critique can and must also go beyond a merely reactive analysis of social relations, beyond a hack postmodernism *manqué,* and reimagine itself as a transgressively ludic and (self-)transformative discourse.

Postmodernism in the West congratulates itself for its transcendence over a primitive mimetic representationalism and appropriates fixed forms, with the intention, for instance, of transforming them into sophisticated new hybridizations. That sophistication is deemed inconceivable for the Third World, in what Prasad describes as the grand narrative that "posits an epic battle between conceptuality and its unnameable opposite" (57). But postcolonialism effectively poses a challenge to this exclusivist and self-congratulatory postmodernity. Said rejects the notion that the disillusionment with metanarratives of emancipation, enlightenment, The Subject, and so on is exclusively a Western phenomenon, an Occidental secular ideal. Similarly, R. Radhakrishnan points to Fredric Jameson's influential agonization of the West against the Third World on the basis of the "official conviction that the Third World histories are a predictable repetition of the histories of the 'advanced world'; hence, the masterly confidence with which [Jameson] 'allegorizes' the Third World on its own behalf" (329). Jameson has earned the notoriety of arguing, with reference to Third World cultural production, that all personal identity is national identity and that only "national allegories" merit our attention.[2] Aijaz Ahmad questions this exclusionary formulation for its traffic in exclusionary and essentialist rhetoric.[3] He insists that there are many significant Third World cultural productions that give the lie to Jameson's reduction, and that "nationalism itself is not some unitary thing with some pre-determined essence and value" (8). In the Jamesonian split, postmodern sophistication is pitted against a less refined or premodern cultural production, one that is regressive, static, "undeveloped." Late capitalism's "pastiche energetics," its celebratory leveling of the high and the low, its cynical "depthlessness," which fetishizes the image as simulacrum, its heady textualism that is often also an ahistoricism, are implicitly the opposite of national allegory. In such opposition, the Third World is locked into a mimetic epistemology that throws into flattering relief the sophisticated and nuanced deprecations of precisely such an epistemology. Recall Ihab Hassan's catalogue of characteristic postmodern style multivalence, hybridity, and indeterminacy, to which one might add the deconstructionist catechism of decentering and abyssal. A critical elitism seems to be at work in this discourse, ultimately entailing the abjection of Third World cultural production and self-production in the global cultural economy.

Jameson's prescription is echoed, with modifications, even by other First World critics who are professedly sympathetic to the concerns of postcolonialism. Timothy Brennan writes of Salman Rushdie's *Grimus* that "[i]t would be hard to find a novel that demonstrated better the truth of Fanon's claim that a culture that is not national is meaningless. . . . they must be anchored in a coherent "structure of feeling," which only actual communities can create (*Salman Rushdie* 70). Brennan's recommendation seems a reasonable neocommunitarian credo, but his blanket "must" fails to emphasize the internal differences among postcolonial contexts. National culture, even nationalism, may *in some cases* indeed offer what Brennan has elsewhere called a "defensive bulwark" against, especially, North American hegemony in the global cultural economy ("India, Nationalism, and Other Failures" 144). But too often it effects a secondarization and marginalization of the Third World within that economy, as reactionary (petulant?) chauvinism or neonativism. It is crucial not to let nationalism degenerate into a form of nativism—what Said has described as an "especially besetting hobble of most post-colonial work" ("Intellectuals," 64).

The notion of the unsophistication of the Third World other is at least as old as the anthropological construction of the other as constitutively inferior (as Derrida points out in discussing Claude Lévi-Strauss's construction of the Nambikwara, for instance). In the Orientalist stereotype of the Eastern mind as self-defeatingly labyrinthine, the Third World is constructed as at once inadequately subtle and needlessly oversubtle. Where the Eastern mind most needs to be rational, it fails because it lacks the capacity, the discipline, and the necessary fineness (a notion critiqued in, for example, S. H. Alatas's *The Myth of the Lazy Native*). And where simplicity, purity, and clarity are virtues, the Third World is, in E. M. Forster's terms, a "muddle." James Snead observes that Europeans defined themselves not only against the rest of Europe's nations and against other compatriots, but also defined European culture as separate from African culture, "the ultimate otherness, the final *mass*. Only having now reached this stage can we make any sense whatever of the notion of 'black culture' and what it might oppose" (Snead 215). The word "culture" then acquires

"two fateful senses": the first involving a group's aggressive assertion of its superiority vis-à-vis another, and a "finer" one, between
haute and *basse* culture. For Hegel, blackness was the mark of the
"lowest stage of that laudable self-reflection and development
shown by European culture," and moreover black culture "simply
did not exist in the same sense as European culture did" (215). Hegel
described all non-Western cultures as destitute of self-expression
and of a refined sense of self, and thus needing the explanatory
apparatus of Western rationality. Marx concurred:

> Bourgeois society is the most developed and the most complex
> historic organization of production. . . . The intimations of
> higher development among the subordinate animal species
> . . . can be understood only after the higher development is
> already known. The bourgeois economy thus supplies the key
> to the ancient. (Marx, *Capital*, vol. 1, qtd. in Chakrabarty 4)

The decentering of "Europe" is a *critical* project if postcolonialism
wishes to offer resistance to the posting of the Third World as logically and culturally posterior, as lagging "behind."

But this critical imperative should not be construed as just an
inversion of a hegemonic structure. The critique of Eurocentrism
needs to resist the opposition of the Third World as logically and
culturally posterior (or should that be anterior?) to the possibilities
and positivities of the First World because that opposition consigns
the Third World to an irretrievable anachronism. It is important
also that that opposition is not adduced in a neocolonialist grammar reinscribing the invidious hegemony entailed by a Hegelian
description of the non-European other's "'strange form of self-
consciousness' unfixed in orientation towards transcendent goals
and terrifyingly close to the cycles and rhythms of nature" (Snead
217).

Rationality and cultural progress are notions central to the
mythos of modernity in the West. Recent cultural criticism seeks
to demystify modernism's premises, and this is especially important to postcolonial critics such as Ashis Nandy, who writes that
India is not antimodern or modern but nonmodern (212); for
Nandy, the "armed version" of modernism is colonialism itself. The
seductiveness of the modernist myth of progress lay (lies?) in the

implication that to be nonmodern is to be unregenerate, regressive. But nostalgia, ignorance, and recidivism are not the only postures available as rejections of this seduction. Snead proposes "repetition" as an effective and culturally proven alternative to progress. That a Third World culture is destitute of a Hegelian "goal," in Snead's account, may indicate not so much that Third World culture is retarded or regressive as that it has always already "arrived." Can the Third World not conceive of its history and its futures independently of the European models of modernity, progress, and development, in a separate possibilist discourse? The West, in its own description, must perennially aspire to its own completion, and therefore must remain forever imperfect and internally riven, in Walter Benjamin's conception, looking forward by always looking back. Repetition, conceived as a figure of Black aesthetics, exploits a parodic, ludic energy. And as Linda Hutcheon reminds us, "[p]astiche and parody are not simply the new games Europeans play . . . but offer a key to destabilization . . . of a repressive European archive" (x).

Progress and modernity for the First World subject are always cause for hope *as well as* nostalgia, occasions for regretful disillusionment, and a sense of real failure. This "modernity" the Third World can do without. It is politically and psychologically crucial for any subject marginalized in the global cultural economy to emancipate himself or herself from that myth of progress by conceptualizing his or her culture in terms of happy rather than vicious repetition.

But there are other strategies by which the performativity of Third World subjectivity can transgress the space-time of the First World. If the Third World concedes to being "explained," ethnographically rearranged, by a tropology fabricated in the West, then the Third World can hardly resist being articulated as chronically inferior and belated. As Spivak puts it, "[w]e are always *after* the empire of reason, our claims to it always short of adequate" ("Poststructuralism" 228). Thus, Christopher Miller can say that African philosophy, even as it seeks to assert the power of African thought, "assumes that the West does indeed have a philosophical 'secret' that permitted it to conquer the world" (23). In submitting to the West's description of its "nature," the Third World only confirms an alleged failure of self-determination. Similarly, for Chakrabarty, academic history constructs "Europe" as the "sovereign, theoretical subject of all histories, including the ones we call 'Indian,' 'Chinese,' 'Kenyan,' and so on." Furthermore, "all these other histories tend to become variations on a master narrative that could be called 'the history of Europe.'" As a result, "Indian" history itself is in a position of subalternity; one can only articulate subaltern subject positions in the name of this history" (1).

This "in-the-name-of" is the mark of a paternal signifier blocking access to the Symbolic: the vertiginous abyss the Third World subject plunges into when his or her own history is locked in an Imaginary that forbids him to imagine himself as anything but an aspirant to the First World subject's example, and condemned forever to lag behind. When he looks in the mirror, what he or she thinks he sees is never himself. If the Third World subject is female, invisible is perhaps the best she can hope to be, in this Western "his-tory" or optics of representation. If he is male, at best he can be a mimic man, although most frequently he is cast into a strange family romance where he is the feminized Asiatic eroticizing the colonial adventure, as in *A Passage to India,* or fulfilling some other specular role such as that of the pre-postmodern imitator of Western "nostalgia."

The anomalies of this specularity are a central theme of Pico Iyer's *Video Night in Kathmandu.* Real cultural and experiential differences between (and among) individuals outside the circuit of Western culture are suppressed or ignored, as indeed are those of minorities within that circuit. The minority subject is homogenized and effectively othered in the metropolitan discourse of the nation. Marginal history and culture disappear into the so-called depthlessness of the postmodern landscape, the flattened new world order. And the persistence of real socioeconomic power in the multinational corporation is concealed under the West's apparently benign cultural exemplariness (an appeal related to the colonizer's question, "[d]id we not do much to improve your country?"). Travelling in China, Iyer notes that the emphasis of postcolonial cultural struggle is consequently on the eclectic adaptation of Western methods, technology, and cultural capital without succumbing to (allegedly "decadent") Western values (114).

Instances of deliberate postmodern "forgetting" and homogenization of the other are underscored by Chakrabarty's argument that within discursive parameters laid down by a First World version of history, "a third-world historian [or, more generally, intellectual] is condemned to knowing 'Europe' as the original home of the 'modern,' whereas the 'European' historian does not share a comparable predicament with regard to the pasts of the majority of humankind" (19). Chakrabarty's interest is to anticipate a premature celebration of postcoloniality, which is to say he problematizes the very use of the postcolonial as a category (5). This caveat is seconded by Anne McClintock, who argues that the "post-" in postcolonialism should also be suspected of "reducing the cultures of peoples beyond colonialism to *prepositional* time" and conferring upon colonialism the "prestige of history proper" (86). Spivak, too, severely vetoes "postcolonial" in favor of "neocolonial"; she finds the word postcolonial "just totally bogus" ("Neocolonialism" 224).

Here again, while both postmodernist *and* postcolonialist (I will continue to use the terms for convenience) theorists may share a skepticism about binaries such as modern/nonmodern, or the Occidental/Oriental, there is often a failure within postcolonialist theory itself to nuance adequately the divergences in postcolonialist agendas. For instance, according to McClintock, while postcolonial theory appropriately questions the "grand march of western historicism with its entourage of binaries (self-other, metropolis-colony, center-periphery, etc.), the *term* 'post-colonialism' nonetheless re-orients the globe once more around a single, binary opposition: colonial/post-colonial" and thereby theory itself is "shifted from the binary axis of *power* (colonizer/colonized—itself inadequately nuanced, as in the case of women) to the binary axis of *time*, even less productive of political nuance" because it does not distinguish between the beneficiaries and the victims of colonialism—or of neocolonialism (85–86). What is missing—or suppressed—is a full recognition of not only the multiplicity of different cultural contexts, which McClintock remarks, but of the multiplicity and polyvocality *within* any given cultural context. The near chaotic possibilities of such multiplicity are evoked by Achille Mbembe when he observes that "the postcolony is made up of not one coherent 'public space' but a plurality of spheres and arenas" (5). An emphasis on multiplicity and difference, furthermore, should be nuanced (as it often is not) by a recognition that such an emphasis is always at risk of degenerating into a form of particularism, so that "multiplicity" becomes a slogan taken up with alacrity even by those who would insist on cultural incommensurability; it may be conveniently at hand for those who would insist on the (customarily hierarchized) separateness of First and Third Worlds. This failure of nuance infects even the work of some of the most influential postcolonial theorists.

Postcolonial cultural critique must, first, recognize that the postcolonial is always already placed in an adversative relation to the postmodern. Second, it should problematize the position of postmodernism as cultural dominant, and trouble the positioning of postcolonialism as exiguous.[4] Third, it must resist assimilation into postmodernism. Fourth, postcolonialism must be reconceived under a new sign, one that does not *necessarily* appeal, even for contrast, to postmodernism qua territorialized metropolitan discourse but remains open to the contingencies and fissures in the global cultural flow. Finally, it must find possible a transgressive, self-transformative, and even ludic energy, for only this sort of energy can promise postcolonialism a future. None of this should imply a willed ignorance of postmodernist agendas, a hiding of the head in the sand; indeed, my argument is quite to the contrary.

2. The Sequestration of the Third World

The postmodern incredulity toward the metanarratives of Truth and reality entails the reign of simulacrum in Western metropolitan discourse as a displacement of the real. At face value, therefore, it might appear that there is good political reason to recommend that Third World literature should hew to a realism based on local givens, on lived experience—in order to preserve the heterogeneity as well as the materiality of marginal or subaltern figures, to resist assimilation to the devices of Western hegemony, and to enable the subaltern to speak from a situation and in a way that cooptation by the West is forestalled.

As I have suggested, however, the emphasis on immediate materiality for the Third World is often accompanied by the presumption that a reflective immediate mimeticism, discredited within postmodernism, is adequate foundation for Third World epistemology. This results in the sequestration of that world in a contained hothouse of exoticism and exemplary primitivism, and effects a secondarization of its discursive modes as premodern, not to mention pre-postmodern. Kumkum Sangari writes that "[m]odernism in fact derives its energy from a steady opposition to realism: realism is the implied or habitual mode of perception that has to be countered or subverted" (178). Here, Sangari is evidently drawing on Lyotard's definition of modernity: "in whatever age it appears, [it] cannot exist without a shattering of belief and without discovery of the 'lack of reality' of reality, together with the invention of other realities" (77).

The limitation of Sangari's approach can be seen in her embrace of "magical realism" as a *characteristic* Third World narrative. Gabriel García Márquez' "preoccupation with circular time and the rejection of linear time," Sangari writes, are "often read as evidence either of his fatalism or of his primitivism." She suggests that the "absence of a single linear time need not be read as the absence of a historical consciousness but rather as the operation of a different kind of historical consciousness" (172). García Márquez "avoids the familiar 'Third World' bind, the swing from disillusionment with an inadequate rationalism to an easily available mysticism—in some sense mutually constitutive categories brought into play by colonialism" (162).

But Third World alterity can also be articulated as a constitutive "symptom" of the modern and the postmodern, so that the dialectical pairing of the Third and the First Worlds, and that of the subaltern and the hegemonic, can also be understood as mutuality and interdependence. The purported decentering of the global cultural flow should not blind us to the West's investment in maintaining a hegemony. Instead, the persistence of these double disjunctions suggests an arena for postcolonial deconstruction. Thus, a fundamental task for the postcolonial must be to finger these double disjunctions, to disturb the reification of a Third World as a symptom of the First World and trouble the appropriative gesture that domesticates the non-West as other.[5] A starting point may be the observation, adroitly put by Sangari, that on the one hand, "the world contracts into the West . . . and the postmodern problematic becomes *the* frame of reference through which the cultural products of the rest of the world are seen." On the other hand, "the West expands into the world," to create a new colonialism, muffling the globe and threatening to homogenize cultural production (183).

Again, however, Sangari's analysis slides toward nationalist particularism even as she warns that "[t]he writing that emerges from this [neocolonialist] position . . . gloomily disempowers the 'nation' as an enabling idea and relocates the impulses for change as everywhere and nowhere." But the deconstruction of, or disillusionment with, monolithic narratives of "nation" need not be gloomy.[6] Sangari herself observes that "the postmodern crisis of meaning is not everyone's crisis (even in the West)" (184), so we are not locked into First World problematizations of "nation." An effective way of troubling such presumptions is to reject the alleged universality of Western crises of meaning, so as to focus on local problems in a global frame, and to claim for the postcolonial a ludic and hybrid ambivalence that has a political urgency. It may not always be necessary to invoke a "national" culture, to frame the calculus of all cultural production as approaching but never exceeding the limit or orbit of a narrative of the nation. It could be a tragic failure if one disqualified or preempted ex cathedra, as it were, other, exorbitant strategies and categories, such as what Appadurai calls *"transnation"* ("Patriotism and Its Futures" 424).

One would have thought that Sangari's own words would yield a recognition that there is not always a parallel anxiety about meaning and reality in Western and non-Western discourses.[7] The "nonmimetic narrative modes" of a García Márquez or a Salman Rushdie, writes Sangari, "inhabit a social and conceptual space in which the problems of ascertaining meaning assume a political dimension qualitatively different from the current postmodern skepticism about meaning in Europe and America." Marvelous realism responds to an emergent society's need for a redescription of itself beyond the West's construction of it as a convenient alterity, and mediates between "a real *and* a possible." And this is perhaps the chief importance of his contribution, since "the brutality of the *real* is equally the brutality and terror of that which is *immanent,* conceivable, potentially possible. . . . the difficulty of distinguishing between fact and fiction becomes a *political* possibility that bears upon the ethical difficulty of functioning as 'real' human beings" (163). It is important, within the orbits of cultural studies, not to cycle magical realism as an index of *all* Third World or postcolonial literary production, as its sole alternative. Spivak rightly rejects the elevation of magical realism to the status of "characteristic" mode (*Outside in the Teaching Machine* 57–58). She would recognize, of course, the problem of what I have called the sequestration of Third World cultural production. Nor are epistemological issues about meaning and reality identically formulated in the First and the Third Worlds. But that does not mean that these are entirely discrete language games, for as I have argued, there is a symptomatic interdependence between First and Third Worlds. It is sometimes a question of perceived *levels* or *paradigms* of factuality and reality. Realizing the "possible" admittedly involves reinventing givens such as the opposition of the real and the factitious, rationality and irrationality, essence and construct. The possible, for the Third World, *need* not depend for its conceptualization on an already realized schema in more "advanced" countries.

In this light, it is not difficult to see the catachrestic simplification that informs Stephen Slemon's recommendation of a dual agenda for the Third World, which is

> to continue the resistance to (neo)colonialism through a deconstructive reading of its rhetoric *and* to retrieve and reinscribe those post-colonial social traditions that in literature issue forth on a thematic level, and within a realist problematic, as principles of cultural identity and survival. (5)

Slemon's "dual" agenda is *unstable;* he acknowledges that it is "perhaps theoretically contradictory" (6). Undaunted, he wants to locate, in postcolonial writing, an *originary* awareness of referential slippage (as in postmodernism) and simultaneously a development of strategies for signifying an order of mimesis.[8] This process of reinstalling the referent in the service of colonized and postcolonial societies, even if postcolonialist criticism "draw[s] on poststructuralism's suspension of the referent in order to read the social 'text' of colonialist power," tends to reterritorialize the Third World cultural production within a schematic of mimesis. Inevitably, the postcolonial moment is adduced as somehow more innocent than the postmodernist.[9]

If the postcolonial cultural production does gravitate toward mimeticism, even fully aware of intertextuality as overdetermined, it finds itself doomed to a Utopianism marked within high (metropolitan) theory as always already deconstructed. From the postmodernist perspective, postcolonialist endeavors thus remain (reassuringly?) naive, circumscribed within the orbit of the primitive, the childlike, the quaint, not to mention the untheoretical. Postcolonialism is thus recuperated within what Jean Franco identifies as stereotypes about the Third World, and reassimilated and domesticated within postmodernism.

Certainly, some postcolonialist writing has in fact turned toward an autochthonous mimetic mode. But it is an impoverished aesthetics that sees cultural production as necessarily a copy of "reality." Solomon O. Iyasere invokes Susan Langer's argument that artistic form "is a projection, not a copy," and John V. Hagopian's argument that the literary artist makes a "metaphorical model of the subject-object dialectic" (447). For Iyasere, the art work aspires only to simulacrum, and a novel is great only if it demonstrates mastery of the "craft of fiction" and "the ability to renovate language to explore and pattern the chaos of experience and perception" (454). Nevertheless, even this line of argument, if I read it correctly, offers no support for the prescription of a special agenda for Third World cultural production. The various sociopolitical realities of the Third World cannot be homogenized under the rubric of an *essentially* different attitude to the "real," as though the "real" and the "natural" remained unproblematic for an untheoretical Third world, uninfected, and uninflected, with the poststructuralist difference that has beset the postmodern West.[10] One cannot endorse, then, Slemon's presumption that while postmodernity springs from a disillusionment with realism (it is no wonder that he does not recommend his dual agenda for the postmodern West), the mimeticism he is proposing for Third World cultural production is adequate to Third World epistemology. His recommendation can be understood under a Derridean "archeology" of the European self-image: "Non-European peoples were not only studied as the index to a hidden good Nature, as a native soil recovered, of a 'zero degree' with reference to which one could outline the structure, the growth, and above all the degradation of our society and our culture" (Derrida 115).

This faux anthropological construction is not so different from the contrast between the modern or postmodern capitalist

world and the premodern and precapitalist. Writing about Claude
Lévi-Strauss's *Tristes Tropiques,* Derrida identifies an *anthropological*
war, "the essential confrontation that opens communication between peoples and cultures, even when that communication is not
practiced under the banner of colonial or missionary oppression"
(107). Students of the "primitive," as Marianna Torgovnick remarks, "usually begin by defining it as different from (usually opposite to) the present. . . . the needs of the present determine the
value and nature of the primitive" (8–9). She notes

> the common, problematical view in certain discussions of
> global culture, a view that energizes critics like James Clifford
> who argue . . . for recognizing that the third world now in-
> cludes many signs of the West, signs we should conceive of not
> as "cultural impurities," but as cultural facts that can lead to a
> number of future possibilities. The problem is one of *sprezza-
> tura,* of carnivalesque rejoicing, of celebrating the crossing and
> recrossing of things, of believing that contact and polyphony
> are inherently liberating. (40)

What cannot be ignored are "social and economic facts," which
add up to the "cost of the global village" (Torgovnick 40–41). She
admits that isolation for "third world nations and primitive groups
is no longer possible or even, perhaps, desirable" (Torgovnick 41).
The violence of the "post-" in postmodernism is visible in the reduction to such "thirdness" necessary for the consignment of the
other to "ante-"rooms of postmodernity. Thus Slemon's position
is open to Helen Tiffin's charge, of replicating on the local level
the "often imperialist and racist essentialisms" and of failing to
"perceive that the old, if cryptic[,] comparison—with Britain and
Europe—thus remains authorised within both national cultural institutions and within the academy" (Tiffin xii). She cites Diana Bry-
don's rejection of the "idea of authentic indigenity" on which postcolonialism is based, arguing that postmodernism's "fetishization
of simulacra inevitably sponsors a counter 'cult of authenticity'"
(xii). Tiffin's discussion is chiefly an *aesthetic* objection. But this objection about sponsoring a counter-cult does not go far enough.

   The more insidious danger is the sequestration of the Third
World in a *conceptual* postmodern premodernity—a premodernity
that is continuously produced and re-produced *for the West* as exig-

uous or "othered" to postmodernism, assuring postmodernism a First World space even as it confines the premodern to a contemporary Third World space that is always past. The premodern, when thus produced by and for the West, is reinscribed in Orientalist or neocolonialist modes. But when produced by the postcolonial for the West, it traces the trajectory of what must be a deliciously ironic complicity. For the complicitous reproduction of the other by the other fully satisfies the phantasmatic dictates that quicken the dialectic of othering (not to mention sustains the global tourist market). And no one is more vertiginously poised to stage the contradictions of that complicity than the diasporic, distanced from the Third World in the First.

3. Subcontinental Diasporic Intervention: Situational Politics, Ethics, and Erotics

Many diasporic postcolonial critics insist that the socioeconomic conditions of Third World India make postmodernism an inappropriate discursive and political category for India, because postmodernism is predicated upon a condition of surplus capital. But the alternative to postmodernism is not necessarily a cultural and political reification, a mimetic reflection of some unreconstructed "real" givens that can allegedly never be transcended by the Third World (on the tautological grounds that they are what determine its "thirdness"). Third World reality is presumed in First World representations to determine postcolonial discourse exhaustively, whereas postmodernity is able to constitute its own groundless ground rules. Geeta Kapur prefers to speak instead of an "enlightened eclecticism" (Jayamanne 116). If postmodernism prides itself on its alert deconstruction of any and all master narratives, then postcolonialism too can benefit from alertness to deconstructive strategies. Postcolonialism need not acquiesce to the askesis recommended for it by some varieties of postmodern discourse, need not disavow a ludic, transgressive energy usually identified as postmodernist just because of some notion that the Third World ought to be uncontaminated, wedded to its specificities, "authentic."

And transgression is not just the inversion of hierarchies such as high/low, intellectual/bodily, West/East, pure/contaminated; it is also a transvaluation of values. Nor is it a utopian stasis. Transgression recognizes the possibility of deracination as well as liberation. Whatever political, ethical, or erotic gain attaches to transgression, its contingent character can be fully thematized. Thus, a mere "positive" rhetoric of nationalism is hardly an adequate model for *all* postcolonial cultural activity.

Slemon is sensitive to the erasure effected "in the intersection between post-colonial cultural work and the debate over post-modernism" and even agrees with Ketu Katrak that the First World debate over the "semiotics of difference" has "systematically ignored the 'theoretical' work of Third World and post-colonial subjects;" he concedes that this may be because that theory is articulated "*in* literary texts and *as* social practice, not in the affiliative theoretical language of Western intellectual institutions" (8). In the face of this erasure, if Third World or postcolonial writing were to be caught in a reflective mimeticism, even with a "dual agenda," might this mimetic mode not abet the erasure, make it easier for Western intellectual discourse to ignore or coopt Third World or postcolonial cultural and theoretical work? I would argue that postcolonialism should seek an interventionist mode, should become not more restricted to the local and particular "reality" but more engaged with the transnational circuits of theoretical debate. It should pursue more, not less, theoretical sophistication, a more self-reflexive politics.

We might well ask whether Slemon's diagnoses of postcolonialist writing are accurate. Are Rushdie's *The Satanic Verses* or Yambo Oulouguem's *Bound to Violence,* or Tayeb Salih's *Season of Migration to the North* interested in making "truth claims" or upholding a dual agenda? Should they be? In what significant sense are these texts mimetic in a way that a Western postmodernist text is not? On the other hand, what room is there in Slemon's sweeping notion of the postcolonialist text for the ambivalences and complicities of V. S. Naipaul's *An Area of Darkness*?

In a discussion of Rushdie's *Midnight's Children,* Slemon argues that Padma, "the lotus goddess, who embodies the creative power of maya and who even at the text's moment of seemingly total cultural dissolution may be 'writing' the text of a post-colonial future not through the indeterminacies of interpretive slippage

and 'freedom' but from a solid grounding in pre-colonized cultural and religious agency" (8). Padma's role is crucial in the text,
but everywhere it is secondary to Saleem's. Saleem acknowledges
frequently the importance, to him, of Padma as well as of other
women in the novel (Dayal 441). But to locate in Padma a sort of
central intelligence seems perverse. It is Saleem's imaginative, if
crazy, narrative energies that drive the book. Padma is no more
than an enabler and check, a minor realist who functions as coun-
terweight to Saleem's fantastical. To see her as "'writing' the text of
a post-colonial future . . . from a solid grounding in pre-colonized
cultural and religious agency" is at best an exaggeration. Slemon's
word "pre-colonized" begins to look like an unflattering euphe-
mism. There are other dynamics of gender, race, nation, and class,
as well as different narrative impulses that cannot be represented
by Padma's earthy mimetic mode. Even Tai the boatman, who de-
fends the autochthonous or indigenous in the book, cannot be said
to represent a viable alternative: his purist nationalist narrative is
represented as obsolescent within the context of Rushdie's tale. He
is deeply chagrined to discover that he cannot deflect the modern-
izing inertia of Aadam, Saleem's grandfather, who has returned
from Germany, bringing with him the contamination of Europe
and breaking with the local and national traditions that Tai (his
mentor) would have liked to see him continue.

Rushdie's "problem," as Catherine Cundy puts it, "in *Grimus*
and beyond it, [is] producing a new kind of literature; a new kind
of cultural representation that is an amalgam of both the Eastern
and Western influences that comprise his experience" (128). His
novels are about dislocation, or at least about always problematic
location. If postcolonial writing truly engages with deconstruction's antifoundationalist force, can it really *be* both deconstructive
and truly realistic as Slemon's dual agenda would have it? Can it
have it both ways: affirming a center in "lived experience" and
decentering the lived experience by textualizing it? I find it hard
to take comfort from Slemon's confidence that there is already a
satisfactory program ready to hand for the postcolonialist (while
no such program is satisfactory for the incomparably sophisticated
postmodernist).

We should also recognize a certain "protective" gesture in the
work of some First World critics—the desire to shield a theoreti-

cally feeble and callow Third World from the culturally ruinous and fragmenting power of postmodern deconstruction of "authenticity." Slemon professes commitment to "the project of reiterating the colonialist's 'pretext' [. . .] not only the figuration of textual resistance but also the recuperation—the remembering or relearning—of 'the role of the native as historical subject and combatant, possessor of another knowledge and producer of alternative traditions'" (Parry 34, qtd. in Slemon 6–7). But in fact Slemon underemphasizes the multiple *other* knowledges and *alternative traditions* that Parry would allow for. Lisa Lowe, developing a Foucauldian notion of *heterotopia,* properly insists that "on discursive terrains, such as the one on which orientalism is one formation, articulations and rearticulations emerge from a variety of positions and sites, as well as from other sets of representational relations, including those that figure class, race, nation, gender, and sexuality" (15). Moreover, plurality, I have argued above, is not simply the plurality of different realities in different social and cultural circumstances but multiple and unpredictable possibilities *within* a given cultural context, and is even constitutive of cultural "identity" itself.

Appiah stresses the plurality of cultural contexts and cultural productions in different regions of the globe and the multiplication of distinctions. He champions hybridity and recognizes that "we are all already contaminated by each other, that there is no longer a fully autochthonous *echt*-African culture awaiting salvage by our artists;" he notes that in some postcolonial writing there is a "clear sense" that the "postulation of a unitary Africa over against a monolithic West—the binarism of Self and Other—is the last of the shibboleths of the modernizers that we must learn to live without" (*In My Father's House* 155). It is all the more remarkable then that his description of postcoloniality is so harsh: "postcoloniality is the condition of what we might ungenerously call a comprador intelligentsia: of a relatively small, Western-style, Western-trained, group of writers and thinkers who mediate the trade in cultural commodities of world capitalism at the periphery" (149). Dirlik may be right in suggesting that this description misses the point because "the world situation that justified the term *comprador* no longer exists, but only obscures the issue by proposing that postcoloniality "is the condition of the intelligentsia of global capitalism"

(356). It conflates (or fails to distinguish among) too many different perspectives, including the postmodern with the postcolonial,
and the left-oriented intelligentsia with the neoconservative.

But, leaving aside this definitional quibble, what does the plurality and intercultural hybridity acknowledged by Appiah actually
mean for postcolonialism, in terms of political effectivity? The postcolonial is neither simply a geographical (spatial) category nor just
a temporal, but a discursive one (Dirlik 332, 352), and one that
has a political significance. And one ought to distinguish among
individuals and groups with divergent interests and loyalties: the
diasporic located in the First World academy who actively intervenes in the discourse of postcoloniality or makes a profession of
it, the postcolonial who is barely aware of his or her postcolonial
situation, and the postcolonial who is not an intellectual but either
individually or as a member of a group lays claim to the national
product and has awakened to his political and cultural significance
(this is evident in the obstreperousness of the Bharatiya Janata
Party—BJP—in the Hindu-Muslim agon over the mosque at Ay-
odhya in India as well in the ethnic tensions in Germany or Bosnia-
Hercegovina). For what is at issue is the possibility of an intervention that embraces hybridity but is alive to its contingencies.
Meaningful political intervention, for the postcolonial (and especially for the diasporic postcolonial), can mean among other things
strategically posing a challenge to Eurocentrism in such a way that
new forms of participation in a global culture can be conceived. It
can also mean resisting a totalizing conceptualization of the nation.
For instance, it can mean questioning the rhetoric to which Indira
Gandhi unwisely appealed when she invoked the "non-Hindu" as
an embodiment of the antinational, a rhetoric that tends to ossify
identity and unify the nation on false pretexts. As such, that rhetoric calls for analysis of presumed political identities in a nation-
state that is defined by nothing so much as its diversity of linguistic-
cultural and class allegiances. Postcolonial criticism can mean a
kind of "internal" criticism of the Third World informed by a diasporic forum of debate outside the Third World. It can direct its
own consciousness and cultural aspirations rather than following
someone else's, not to mention work out its own neuroses rather
than take a bit part in someone else's.

Extending Benedict Anderson, Appadurai proposes that we

theorize the multiple imagined worlds "which are constituted by the historically situated imaginations of persons and groups spread around the globe ("Disjuncture and Difference" 7). I would add to Appadurai's suggestion that equally important is the constitution of multiple imagined selves, without fetishizing identity. And identitarian theory should remain open to the problematics of subject-constitution, and indeed at some level seek to theorize those problematics. Not only are global communities aligned fluidly within large-scale cultural configurations, but individuals too make unpredictable alliances and agential identifications. The diasporic postcolonial is a special case, being constituted as transnational. Inhabiting an interstitial space-time that displaces the unipolarity of the global cultural economy, the diasporic postcolonial can call attention to the splitting of the cultural authority of the postmodern. Postmodernism, habitually conceptualized as a First World aesthetic, abets the unipolarization of the cultural economy by making paradigmatic Euro-American cultural values, even as the narrative of capitalism is displaced from the position it formerly enjoyed as the narrative of Europe. The diasporic can, by representing transnational identity, disturb the borders of any unipolarized structuration of the cultural economy.

The decentering of the global economy implied by the rise of the transnational corporations should not be allowed to blind us to either the concentration of power and capital in transnational corporations and in Euro-American cultural capital(s) or to the differential access to capital and resources. The postcolonial development of India is rather different from the abrupt transition to postcoloniality in the case of Britain's African colonies and from the workings of neocolonialism in Hong Kong. Subcontinental diasporic postcoloniality is different from other diasporic postcolonialities, in terms of language and cultural position.

Postcolonial space cannot be constituted in terms of the tired binaries pitting the First versus the Third World. A world systems approach or one that recognizes the complex heterogeneities as well as homogeneities of the global cultural flow is preferable because it acknowledges, for instance, that we have a new regionalism of the North versus the South, overlaid on the equally problematic division between East and West.

Instead of reterritorializing the Third World under the sign of a culturally correct anxiety, it is better, politically, for the postcolonial intellectual to acknowledge and even participate in the complex play of allegiances and ad hoc alignments of the globalized cultural economy. In this sense, postcolonial cultural production can usefully elaborate the complex inscapes of complicities.

The diaspora from the Indian subcontinent provides a striking demonstration of postcolonialism's possibilities. Alongside Bharati Mukerjee's work, one could mention the work of Raja Rao, Anita Desai, Salman Rushdie, Sara Suleri, Zulfikar Ghosh, and perhaps even include V. S. Naipaul, as well as the films of Hanif Kureishi and Mira Nair, and the nonfiction of writers such as Pico Iyer. There is also the theoretical work of Homi Bhabha, Spivak, the Subaltern Studies Collective, R. Radhakrishnan, Lata Mani, Appadurai, and Chandra Mohanty, to name only a few. This diasporic cultural production suggests possibilities for intervention in the debates about postcolonialism and postmodernism.

Perhaps not surprisingly, the theoretician and the creative elements of diasporic subcontinental cultural production are complementary and supplementary. The "ambivalence" that Homi Bhabha celebrates is just one of the strategies of discursive cross-dressing available to the diasporic as a way to insist on the split enunciation of diasporic intervention, and as a way to destabilize postcolonialism's relegation to the position of postmodernism's poor cousin. Iyer's diasporic voice in *Kathmandu* confounds a simple mimetic enunciation of identity by exploiting a labile diasporic homelessness. He presents as his credentials his postcolonial and transnational status:

> For more than a decade while I was growing up, I spent eight months a year at boarding school in England and four months at home in California—in an Indian household. As a British subject, an American resident and an Indian citizen, I quickly became accustomed to cross-cultural anomalies and the mixed feelings of exile. Nowhere was home, and everywhere. (24)

Iyer speaks of being at "home" in Santa Barbara, Cambridge, and New York (102) even as he designates the East as home. But in the East, when asked where he comes from, he replies both truthfully, and with a deep ambiguity presumably lost on the territorialized

Easterner who inquires: "Eyes flashing, my slim-hipped new friend asked me where I came from. New York" (44). In Nepal, like the Hessean hippies he mocks, he himself admits to travelling to rediscover the "wisdom" of the East, a phrase he uses both to disavow any credulous belief in so nakedly Orientalist a cliché, and to align himself with the West (81). The man from the East effortlessly slips between identities. He becomes, in the Western-contaminated East, an American in search of an innocent Americanness more uncontaminated than he might have found at Haight and Ashbury, and which he was "too young" to know. But this identificatory rhetoric is always already undercut by his critical distance from the topos called "America"—an *innocent* America—which he is in fact studying: "I was," he writes, "interested to find out how America's pop-cultural imperialism spread through the world's most ancient civilizations" (Iyer 5).

Similarly, in Hanif Kureishi's films *My Beautiful Laundrette* and *Sammy and Rosie Get Laid,* the contradictions of identity are modulated through anxieties and ambivalences about sexuality and gender, and about nationality. In *Sammy and Rosie,* a Black man prefers to be called "Victoria," exploiting the deliberate sexual confusion of the name. Similarly, Sammy says, "We're not British, we're Londoners." But this apparent hybridity needs further analysis, rather than being understood as savvy cosmopolitanism.[11] Sammy and Rosie's politically correct disapproval of Sammy's father's questionable political activities in the "home country" is witheringly turned on its back by the father: Sammy is not aligned in the same way as Rosie against his father. For one thing, he is "Black" in Britain and she is white, and therefore his problematization of his Britishness has a special enunciative modality. In claiming status as a Londoner and simultaneously denying Britishness, he is attempting to situate himself as a metropolitan citizen of a global economy, but at the same time suppressing his ethnic difference, which seems increasingly to be a sticking point in the definition of European national identity—though perhaps not, in Britain, as strongly as it is in Germany (where nobody who is not ethnically German can be granted citizenship) and Bosnia-Hercegovina.

It profits nothing and nobody to worry about the purity or authenticity of a culture or to deprecate, as Dirlik seems to do, postcolonial subcontinental critics for pressing their current advantages (if these really exist) in the contemporary academic environment. Not all the credit for their current success is due to the alleged enterprise of postcolonials themselves; some of it accrues to larger forces circulating in the academy and in the global culture-scape.

This understanding of the political possibilities of the situation of the diasporic postcolonial renders somewhat less formidable the attack mounted on the postcolonial by Rey Chow. Chow levels charges of opportunism and complicity against some Chinese diaspora intellectuals: "While enjoying the privilege of living in the West, they cling, in their discourse, to the status of the neglected 'other'" (109). Such charges slough away easily if the issues of complicity, privilege, perspective, situation, and so on are *theorized*, if they become not silent sins but elements of the discursive and political intervention of the diasporic postcolonial. There is no theoretical or conceptual advantage in glossing over the conditions of the postcolonial intellectual's interstitial location. The postcolonial can only benefit from being fully aware of the privileges of living in the West, the blandishments and seductions of exile, as well as the languors and problematics, whether strategic or tactical, of assimilation and complicity with metropolitan postmodern discourse, even if that assimilation and that complicity are engaged to enable internal criticism. It cannot but be productive to make the privileges, prejudices, and problems of the diasporic postcolonial objects of study, even to situate postcolonialism and raise questions about its "political agency" (Shohat 100). Only a misguided postcolonial intellectual would nurture pretensions of speaking for the territorial postcolonial back "at home." Perhaps there is some purchase to be gained on the moral high ground of "sincerity" in Chow's call to the postcolonial to come clean, but I see no crisis of bad faith.

The irreducibly split enunciation of the diasporic postcolonial most instructively problematizes key determinants of contemporary global cultural formations and thus makes possible an understanding of a postcolonial politics. In addition, the inauguration of an ethics and an erotics of postcolonial intervention might provide a forum for examining the phantasmatic play of desire that regulates a logic of othering. If hell is other people, then the *jouissance* of the Other, as Žižek conceptualizes it (following Lacan), is death, or at least the enjoyment of the other threatens our own by its very excess. This is at the basis of the constitutive belief in the national Thing, for *das Ding* exists only as long as members of the community believe in it: "it is literally an effect of this belief in itself" (*Tarrying with the Negative* 202, 203). Thus, to return to a theme from the beginning of this essay, in Eastern Europe as in the East, the West

> seeks for its own lost origins, its own lost original experience of "democratic invention." In other words, Eastern Europe functions for the West as its Ego-Ideal (*Ich-Ideal*): the point from which [the] West sees itself in a likable, idealized form, as worthy of love. The real object of fascination for the West is thus the *gaze,* namely the supposedly naive gaze by means of which Eastern Europe [or, the non-West] stares back at the West, fascinated by its democracy. It is as if the Eastern gaze is still able to perceive in Western societies its own *agalma,* the treasure that causes democratic enthusiasm and that the West has long ago lost the taste of. (Žižek 200)

The West's fascination is rooted in the hatred of its own enjoyment since "the Other is the Other in my interior" (Žižek 203): the West stares fascinatedly at the spectacle of the non-Western other's enjoyment of a constitutive aspect of its own democracy, an enjoyment that the West has come to recognize, jadedly, as unsophisticated. The Black's or Slovene's or Asian's excessive enjoyment is hated as excessive self-enjoyment is hated in the Western European's own circuit. At the same time the West fears a "theft" of its enjoyment (Žižek 203), so that there is an anxiety at some level to remain in a superior position in the cultural economy of desire. What Žižek calls the (Western) Nation-Thing is contradictory in that it is taken to be inaccessible to the Eastern "other" even as the other is phantasmatically constructed as the "constant menace." That menace is always threatening to accede to precisely that which is most precious about the Nation-Thing, namely its enjoyment of a way of life (for instance, the "American lifestyle"). This is the logic that drives the universal abandon of the postmodern West. Attempts to align Third World societies more or less with some species of local particularity or mimetic realism are necessary to exclude the non-Western other as being unready for postmodern abandon, not having benefited from the developmental and "progressive" fruits of modernity—the *agalma* for which the West has now lost the taste even as democracy purportedly is breaking out in Russia and Eastern Europe, even as the Japanese begin to "enjoy" themselves as Western people do, and even as Cuba falters and peasant agitation is quelled by the Mexican police.

The postmodern attitude can thus be seen as a way of organizing enjoyment, of structuring desire. As I have been arguing, it is to this desire that the Third World is imagined to aspire. Hence the unipolarity of the global culture flow. We can recognize here the springs of the rhetoric of "tolerance" purveyed in First World metropolitan discourse: the postcolonial is to be tolerated, if only as long as the hegemony of the postmodern is not seriously challenged and only as long as the Third World is kept in a recognized, albeit inferior, position. Is this a new version of the *mission civilisatrice*?[12]

It is also a structural effect of the unipolarity of the global cultural flow that the Third World is left to occupy a place of secondarized, imitative desire and belated or even regressive "development" (if that is not just an oxymoron). Thus, the East remains in the position that the past of the postmodern present would occupy if access could be had to it. The stereotype of the "mystic" East survives the deflation of the imperialist and Orientalist moment in Euro-American history. And this stereotype is precisely the target of a novelist such as Gita Mehta, who in *Karma-Cola* throws the gaze of the West's fascination with (and desire for) the exotic back in its teeth. She well understands that the East must be demystified if it is to be regenerated from its inferior status in the global cultural economy. Her more recent novel, *The River Sutra*, is almost as good an example of the ludic energy. In both books the mystic East jettisons its aura in the age of global capitalism, but it does so with an irony that explicitly avoids the "sincerity" and naiveté with which the East is often expected to represent its reassuringly ancient culture. The rejection of "sincerity" has quite properly become a locus of a great deal of postcolonial diasporic literature (literary merit is an issue beyond the scope of this essay).

Like *Jasmine* and several other works, Bharati Mukherjee's recent novel *The Holder of the World* reconstructs the Western woman's desire for the non-Western man as an implicit and teasing reversal of Western *male* desire for and fascination with the mysterious and exotic Eastern feminine. In Mukherjee's novel, the image of the Western male gaze at the Eastern woman is a central issue, and it is an exemplary illustration of the nexus of political, ethical, and erotic issues. The India hands are all expected to have native "bibis," and their wives tolerate this on the basis of a carefully maintained illusion that no Indian woman could be more attractive to their men than a European. The illusion is crucial to the European women's confidence in their own desirability and adequacy as women. But this illusion is maintained in the face of an even more inescapable and unspeakable realization that no European wife could hope to satisfy the torrid desire aroused in tropical climes in ordinary European men—and not just the perpetually libidinous Gabriel Legges—who are at home so much less animal. What are the ethical ramifications of turning a blind eye to the desire of the European for Indian women? On the other hand, how regulate or even comprehend Hannah Easton's often coextensive faithfulnesses and promiscuities particularly in the instances where Indian masculinity eclipses English manhood? The regulation and containment of desire becomes an extraordinarily delicate and threatening matter for the Europeans.

It is no accident that these delicious ironies are recognized and retailed so pungently by a diasporic postcolonial. A fellow postcolonial diasporic, Pico Iyer similarly develops the irony with which the non-West returns the gaze of the West even in everyday cultural contexts, sometimes inadvertently, often playfully. Several observers have noted that Western economic strategies and attitudes are viewed with suspicion while Western fashions and ways of life are embraced: this irony is visible in the form of the popularity of T-shirts worn even by leftist guerrillas in some Third World countries. The apparently universal celebration of, even "yearning after," aspects of Western cultural capital reflects the "Coca-Colonization" of Third World societies and the irresistible rise of global media capitalism. Yet, the West's triumphalism about the globalization of the cultural economy is threatened by the fact that the non-Western other's desire is not ultimately in the control of the West, as Žižek helps us see. The phantasmatic does not yield itself to manipulation. Again, few structural positions in the global cultural economy better facilitate a critique of these ironies and contradictions than the diasporic postcolonial's.

The diaspora in the United States is, as Appadurai notes, a particularly good illustration of the "unruliness, the rank unpredictability, the quirky inventiveness, the sheer cultural vitality of this [cultural] free trade zone" ("Patriotism and Its Futures" 427). On a more global scale too, it is "possible to detect in many . . . transnations (some ethnic, some religious, some philanthropic, some militaristic) the elements of a postnational imaginary" (427, 428). The retrieval of a supposedly a priori hypostatized subjectivity within a sphere of mimetic realism and monolithic national identity are challenged most effectively in the work of diaspora postcolonialist intellectuals. Above all, diasporic cultural production usefully problematizes cultural boundaries, and reinscribes the "other" geopolitically not only as marginal but as constitutive, as necessary to the constitution of the "sameness" of the West.

For the diasporic postcolonial, it is above all a question of forging a new discourse, a new conception of cultural politics and of the structuring of ethics and desire. It is a matter of representing satisfactorily the imbricated but different interests of individuals and groups in a variety of complex cultural contexts and political situations, thus always contingently articulated. But it is by no means easy to reconfigure the social and cultural Imaginary in which that diasporic postcolonial now conceives political participation. I am not talking about just a relational matrix here. Rather, what is needed is an endless critical reconstruction of desire itself, or at least a constant vigilance to and redescription of how the global cultural flow enables the construction of desire. As Žižek conceives it, it is not the subject who manipulates or controls the economy of desire, but rather the global cultural flow of capital and its quite mobile army of images that clear a space for the subject's self-articulation. The problem of identity is then not so much consolidation of self, but rather of being critically self-aware of the images that regulate desire and of the performativity of the self.

A naive individualism is exactly the wrong frame in which to understand this economy of desire. Indeed, as Michel de Certeau observes, the social atomism that such individualism implies has been discredited by "more than a century of sociological, economic, anthropological, and psychoanalytic research"; he notes that "each individual is a locus in which an incoherent (and often contradictory) plurality of . . . relational determinations interact" (xi). The postcolonial's location troubles in an exemplary way the nexus of several such relational determinations. The split enunciation of the diasporic checks an aesthetics of bourgeois individualism, for that way lies a domestication of the postcolonial in well-worn categorization; but it also resists a simply imitative antiessentialism of the subject. Bharati Mukherjee's and Anita Desai's fictions often risk such a bourgeois individualism, evacuating subjectivity by facilitating the assimilation of the dynamics of selfformation to Western models, for instance by conceiving the struggle of the individual as the crisis of anomie in the modern city. An inadequately theorized articulation of subjectivity is perilous, and even some of the more sophisticated theory must be vigilant about its conceptualization of subjectivity. Gyan Prakash points out that "the early phase of the *Subaltern Studies* was marked by a desire to retrieve the autonomous will and consciousness of the subaltern," but "[t]his is no longer the case in [the group's] more recent writings" and "even in their earlier writings the desire to recover the subaltern's autonomy is repeatedly frustrated because subalternity, by definition, signifies the impossibility of autonomy" (9).

Postcolonial diasporic discourse can be critically interposed among various discourses and interests, First and Third Worlds, interrupting the metropolitan gaze of the West upon its "other." Thus, the diasporic can challenge a kind of abjection of the Third World subject within postmodern fables of society. But it is also turned inward (self-reflexively), which might mean for instance that the diasporic can scrutinize claims to liberal democracy made within the Third World from a perspective informed by the insights of metropolitan theory. The diasporic can usefully interrogate the development of a discourse of nation. Despite his recommendation of Third World nationalism, Brennan himself recognizes that "at present, anticolonial struggle seems to belong more to the West than the East Indies, for it is there that the peasant peoples seem most fully conscious, and most fully capable of challenging imperial policy" ("India" 132). This is because often there is a "depressing"—and I would even say blinding—"cycle of communalist violence, religious corruption, and voiceless village life on the Indian subcontinent" that disables the territorial postcolonial. This is not meant to endorse a hierarchy of the diasporic over the territorial postcolonial: on the contrary, it is absolutely clear that there is a great need for collaboration between and among these groups. The possible directions in which diasporic postcolonials can work are abundant. They include Said's politics of secular interpretation, the Subaltern Studies Collective's work, which draws heavily on deconstruction and other modes canonized within the Western academy, Lata Mani's discussion, greatly indebted to Western feminism, of sati in India and Fatima Mernissi's application of metropolitan discourse to study the place of women in Algeria, and the study of the neocolonialist exploitation of female peasants in Africa by Africans. Another instance is Appiah's critique of the "conservation of 'race'" or an exploration of the interiorities of individuated cultural experience that are tied to no delusions or anxieties about mimetic authenticity, and are not necessarily circumscribed within cultural forms already digested within Western practices ("Conservation of 'Race'"). Finally, critique of discourses of nationalism *from the interstitial position of the diasporic* is crucial, as demonstrated in a collection such as Bhabha's *Nation and Narration* or the collection entitled *Nationalisms and Sexualities,* edited by Parker, Russo, Sommer, and Yaeger.

Of course, there is a danger of cooptation where diasporic postcolonialism becomes wittingly or unwittingly complicitous with the usually metropolitan discourse. But this is precisely why intervention must strive to be both self-reflexive and critical, neither sequestering the minority discourse nor domesticating within the Western cultural dominant of postmodern discourses. Hybridity, ambivalence, and bricolage can provide reconstruction as well as "analysis" of the reigning dicourse of postmodernism. Diasporic postcolonial intervention is eminently positioned to show that transculturality can point beyond the limited choice between a monotonic global culture and cultural anarchy. The diasporic intellectual or cultural worker can explore indirection, even open up a space for the aleatory or for the ineffable and possibly subversive *jouissance* of the other (a possibility suggested by, among others, Julia Kristeva, in her discussion of Chinese women, for instance).[13] As a flâneur in the circuit of this discourse, the diasporic can negotiate conflicting, changing desires and emerging possibilites for intervention, drawing on the insights of postmodern discourse without relinquishing the fluid agendas of emerging cultural formations. But these interventions can also be creative bricolage. Enunciated as interstitial or ambivalent (polyvalent), the diasporic postcolonial can negotiate the commutation between momentary condensations of identity and more stable strategic cultural alignments, and thus remain open to the necessity for cultural border crossings and the deconstruction of boundaries, such as those constitutive of nation or subjectivity. Diaspora postcoloniality can also be a perspective from which to examine afresh the structuring force of desire, which appears at first glance to distance the agency (the one who desires) from the structure of desire itself. It is in this sense that postcolonial politics can be linked to an ethics and erotics of intervention.

Notes

1. See Gregory S. Jay, "The End of 'American' Literature: Toward a Multicultural Practice," 265.
2. See Fredric Jameson, "Third World Literature in an Era of Multinational Capitalism," in *Social Text* 15 (1986): 65–88, esp. 65. Jameson writes,

> Judging from recent conversations among third-world intellectuals, there is now an obsessive return of the national situation itself, the name of the country that returns again and again like a gong, the collective attention to "us," and what we have to do and how we do it, to what we can't do and what we do better than this or that nationality, or unique characteristics, in short, to the level of the "people." This is not the way we American intellectuals have been discussing "America," and indeed one might feel that the whole matter is nothing but that old thing called "nationalism," long since liquidated here and rightly so. (65)

Jameson's arrogant dismissal leads him to maintain that "[w]hat all third world cultural productions seem to have in common and what distinguishes them radically from analogous cultural forms in the first world" is "that all third world texts are necessarily allegorical." They are to be read, specifically, "as what I will call *national allegories* even when, or perhaps I should say, particularly when their forms develop out of predominantly western machineries of representation, such as the novel" (69).
3. See Aijaz Ahmad, "Jameson's Rhetoric of Otherness and the 'National Allegory,'" in *Social Text* 17 (1987): 3–27, esp. 3. Prefacing his comments with a profession of his admiration for Jameson's work, Ahmad aligns himself politically with the former, saying that he had formerly thought of "us, Jameson and myself" as

"birds of the same feather," although "we never quite flocked together." Now, however, Ahmad recognizes with "no little chagrin," that "the man whom I had for so long, so affectionately, even though from a physical distance, taken as a comrade was, in his own opinion, my civilizational Other. It was not a good feeling" (4).

4. Appiah points out that instead of emphasizing formal criteria such as an aesthetic of *textuality*, depthlessness (even the depthlessness of historicity), the death of the subject, the notion of simulacrum, the society of the spectacle, and so on, Jameson conceptualizes the postmodern in terms of periodization and cultural context (*In My Father's House* 143). Even if all the formal features of high modernism as oppositional and marginal are present in postmodernism, the significance of those formal features changes "when they become a cultural *dominant* with a precise socio-economic functionality" (Jameson, *The Ideologies of Theory* 195, qtd. in Appiah 142). Similarly, Appiah reminds us that Jürgen Habermas's project is "surely intended (though in the name of a most un-Lyotardian metanarrative) to provide a modus operandi in a world in which pluralism is, so to speak, waiting for some institutions" (144). Appiah's understanding of postmodernism, then, is *functional*. Appiah defines it thus:

> in philosophy, it is the rejection of the mainstream consensus from Descartes through Kant to logical positivism on foundationalism (there is one route to knowledge, which is exclusivism in epistemology) and of metaphysical realism (there is one truth, which is exclusivism in ontology). Similarly, in architecture, postmodernism reacts against exclusivism of function (as it embraces a taste for pastiche). In literature, postmodernism refuses the high seriousness of modernism, and in political theory it rejects the "monism of Big-M Marxist (though not . . . the newer little-m marxist and liberal conceptions of justice). (143)

5. Even Slemon recognizes the doubly disjunctive symptomatic logic that I have pointed to, for he notes that postmodernism

> *needs* its (post-) colonial Others in order to constitute or to frame its narrative of referential fracture. But it also needs to exclude the cultural and political specificity of post-colonial representations in order to assimilate them to a rigorously Euro-American problematic. This . . . is a typically self-sustaining post-modern contradiction; and yet in this contradiction there could perhaps reside a fissuring energy which could lay the foundation for a radical change of tenor within the post-modern debate. (9)

It is ironic then that his own recommended "dual agenda" conceals a more insidious assimilation of postcolonialism by postmodernism.

6. Of course, First World discourse is neither monolithic nor destitute of self-critique. In Western feminist ontology too, for instance, resistance to essentialism has been critical (one recent example is the work of Judith Butler). Tania Modleski, for instance, worries "that the position of female anti-essentialism as it is being theorized by some feminists today is a luxury open only to the most privileged women," leaving other women to one or other variety of essentialism (22). Indeed, in its complexity, it can be a model: it is precisely from the model of self-reflexive criticism that postcolonialism might most profit, because there is sometimes a tacit agreement that "subaltern" critical voices should not be subject to critique "from within the fold."

7. Sangari herself seems to caution against forms of essentialism:

> nonmimetic, non-western modes also seem to lay themselves open to
> the academized procedures of a peculiarly western, historically singu-
> lar, postmodern epistemology that universalizes the self-conscious
> dissolution of the bourgeois subject, with its now characteristic stance
> of self-irony, across both space and time. (157)

8. Slemon acknowledges Hutcheon's insistence that postmodernist discourse's
truth claims are made only *sous rature* (2). Nevertheless, for him, an "*interested*
post-colonial critical practice would want to allow for the positive production of
oppositional truth claims in these texts [and] to retain for post-colonial writing
. . . a mimetic or referential purchase to textuality," and at the same time to "recognize in this referential drive the operations of a crucial strategy for survival in
marginalized social groups" (5).

9. Slemon is careful to agree with During that

> a post-colonial "affect" needs always to be specified in relation to, and
> within, each post-colonial society . . . But in general terms, a post-
> or anti-colonial critical or disidentificatory discourse can be seen to
> energize an enormously heterogeneous set of social and representa-
> tional practices from within a large number of post-colonial (and
> sometimes, latently, within colonialist) social configurations. (3)

Slemon cautiously locates *part* of this "differential post-colonial discourse" within
the contemporary poststructuralist project of anticolonialist critique and defines
another part within postcolonial literary activity.

Slemon enlists During and Hutcheon in defense of his own analysis although
Hutcheon disagrees with During's definition of postcolonialism as "the need, in
nations or groups which have been victims of imperialism, to achieve an identity
uncontaminated by universalist or Eurocentric concepts and images" (During,
qtd. Hutcheon 183). She understands that there is no uncontaminated space-
time for the postcolonial. Perhaps there never was. Postcolonialism may have at
its disposal a variety of strategies for internal subversion of the dominant culture
(irony, allegory, parody, self-reflexivity) that it "shares with the complicitous critique of post-modernism, even if its politics differ in important ways" (183). But
these ironic forms cannot sufficiently describe the trajectory or the telos of postcolonial theory.

10. Slemon quotes Craig Tapping to the effect that

> despite theory's refutation of such absolute and logocentric categories
> as these—"truth" or "meaning," "purpose" or "justification,"—the
> new literatures . . . are generated from cultures for whom such terms
> as "authority" and "truth" are empirically urgent in their demands.
> Land claims, racial survival, cultural revival: all these demand an un-
> derstanding of and response to the very concepts and structures
> which post-structuralist academicians refute in language games, few
> of which recognize the political struggles of real peoples outside such
> discursive frontiers. (qtd. in Slemon 5–6)

This quotation from Tapping is intended to support Slemon's argument for the
"dual agenda."

11. I have benefited from reading Spivak's discussion of this scene in *Outside in
the Teaching Machine*. But my take on it diverges considerably from hers, as I hope
will be evident.

12. David Spurr's recent analysis of colonial discourse suggests that there is a well-defined rhetoric of the territorialized native as untutored, debased, or undisciplined in his desire. This rhetoric constructs "uncivilized society" as the very body of the colonized subject "writ large" (77). Thus, the civilizing mission was a kind of sentimental education of the other, which is linked to the desire to regulate the *jouissance* of the other.

13. Julia Kristeva, *About Chinese Women*, in *The Kristeva Reader*, 146–47.

Works Cited

Adam, Ian, and Helen Tiffin, eds. *Past the Last Post*. New York: Harvester Wheatsheaf, 1991.

Ahmad, Aijaz. "Jameson's Rhetoric of Otherness and the 'National Allegory.'" *Social Text* 17 (1987): 3–27.

Ahmed, Akbar S. *Postmodernism and Islam: Promise and Predicament*. London: Routledge, 1992.

Anderson, Benedict. *Imagined Communities: Reflections on the Origin and Spread of Nationalism*. London: Verso, 1983.

Appadurai, Arjun. "Disjuncture and Difference in the Global Cultural Economy." *Public Culture* 2.2 (1990): 1–24.

———. "Patriotism and Its Futures." *Public Culture: Bulletin of the Society for Transnational Cultural Studies* 11 (1993): 411–29.

Appiah, Kwame Anthony. "The Conservation of 'Race'." *Black American Literature Forum* 23.1 (1989): 37–60.

———. "Is the Post- in Postmodernism the Post- in Postcolonial?" *Critical Inquiry* 17 (1991): 336–57.

———. *In My Father's House: Africa in the Philosophy of Culture*. New York: Oxford UP, 1992.

Brooker, Peter, ed. *Modernism/Postmodernism*. London: Longman, 1992.

Bhabha, Homi K. *Nation and Narration*. New York: Routledge, 1990.

Brennan, Timothy. "India, Nationalism, and Other Failures." *South Atlantic Quarterly* 87.1 (1988): 131–46.

———. *Salman Rushdie and the Third World*. London: Macmillan, 1989.

Butler, Judith. "Imitation and Gender Insubordination." *Inside/Out: Lesbian Theories, Gay Theories*. New York: Routledge, 1991.

Chakrabarty, Dipesh. "Postcoloniality and the Artifice of History: Who Speaks for 'Indian' Pasts?" *Representations* 37 (1992): 1–26.

Chow, Rey. *Writing Diaspora: Tactics of Intervention in Contemporary Cultural Studies*. Bloomington: Indiana UP, 1993.

Cundy, Catherine. "'Rehearsing Voices:' Salman Rushdie's *Grimus*." *Journal of Commonwealth Literature* 27.1 (1992): 128–38.

Dayal, Samir. "Talking Dirty: Salman Rushdie's Midnight's Children." *College English* 54.4 (1992): 431–45.

De Certeau, Michel. *The Practice of Everyday Life*. Trans. Steven F. Rendall. Berkeley: U of California P, 1984.

Derrida, Jacques. *Of Grammatology*. Trans. Gayatri C. Spivak. Baltimore: Johns Hopkins UP, 1976.

Dirlik, Arif. "The Postcolonial Aura: Third World Criticism in the Age of Global Capitalism." *Critical Inquiry* 20 (1994): 328–56.

During, Simon. "Postmodernism or Postcolonialism?" *Landfall* 39.3 (1985): 366–80.

Ferguson, Russell, Martha Gever, Trinh T. Minh-ha, and Cornel West, eds. *Out There: Marginalization and Contemporary Cultures.* New York: New Museum of Contemporary Art and MIT P, 1991.

Hassan, Ihab. *The Dismemberment of Orpheus: Postmodern Literature.* New York: Oxford UP, 1982.

Hutcheon, Linda. "Circling the Downspout of Empire." *Past the Last Post.* Ed. Ian Adam and Helen Tiffin. New York: Harvester Wheatsheaf, 1991. 167–89.

Iyasere, Solomon O. "Art, A Simulacrum of Reality—Problems in the Criticism of African Literature." *Journal of Modern African Studies* 11.3 (1973): 447–55.

Iyer, Pico. *Video Night in Kathmandu and Other Stories: And Other Reports from the Not-So-Far-East.* New York: Vintage, 1989.

Jameson, Fredric. *The Ideologies of Theory: Essays 1971–1986, vol. 2, Syntax of History,* 178–208.

———. "Third World Literature in an Era of Multinational Capitalism." *Social Text* 15 (1986): 65–88.

Jay, Gregory S. "The End of 'American' Literature: Toward a Multicultural Practice." *College English* 53.3 (1991): 264–81.

Jayamanne, Laleen, Geeta Kapur, and Yvonne Rainer. "Discussing Modernity, 'Third World,' and *The Man Who Envied Women.*" *Art and Text* 23 Part 4 (1987): 41–51. Rpt. Peter Brooker, ed. *Modernism/Postmodernism.* London: Longman, 1992. 113–21.

Kristeva, Julia. *The Kristeva Reader.* Ed. Toril Moi. New York: Columbia UP, 1986.

Kureishi, Hanif. *My Beautiful Laundrette.* Dir. Stephen Frears. Cinecom, 1986.

———. *Sammy and Rosie Get Laid.* Dir. Stephen Frears. Cinecom, 1987.

Lowe, Lisa. *Critical Terrains: French and British Orientalisms.* Ithaca: Cornell UP, 1991.

Lyotard, Jean-François. *The Postmodern Condition: A Report on Knowledge.* Trans. Geoff Bennington and Brian Massumi. Minneapolis: U of Minnesota P, 1984.

Mbembe, Achille. "The Banality of Power and the Aesthetics of Vulgarity in the Postcolony." Trans. Janet Roitman. *Public Culture: Bulletin of the Project for Transnational Cultural Studies* 4.2 (1992): 1–30.

McClintock, Anne. "The Angel of Progress: Pitfalls of the Term 'Post-Colonialism.'" *Social Text* 31/32 (1992): 84–98.

Mehta, Gita. *Karma Cola: Marketing the Mystic East.* New York: Fawcett Columbine, 1979.

Miller, Christopher. *Theories of Africans: Francophone Literature and Anthropology in Africa.* Chicago: U of Chicago P, 1990.

Modleski, Tania. *Feminism Without Women: Culture and Criticism in a "Postfeminist" Age.* New York: Routledge, 1991.

Mukherjee, Bharati. *The Holder of the World.* New York: Knopf, 1993.

Nandy, Ashis. *The Intimate Enemy: Loss and Recovery of Self under Colonialism.* Delhi: Oxford UP, 1983.

Parker, Andrew, Mary Russo, Doris Sommer, and Patricia Yaeger, eds. *Nationalisms and Sexualities.* New York: Routledge, 1992.

Parry, Benita. "Problems in Current Theories of Colonial Discourse." *Oxford Literary Review* 9.7 (1987): 27–58.

Prakash, Gyan. "Postcolonial Criticism and Indian Historiography." *Social Text* 31/32 (1992): 8–19.

Prasad, Madhava. "On the Question of a Theory of (Third World) Literature." *Social Text.* 31/32 (1992): 57–83.

Radhakrishnan, R. "Poststructuralist Politics: Toward a Theory of Coalition." Douglass Kellner, ed. *Postmodernism/Jameson/Critique.* Washington, D.C.: Maisonneuve P, 1989. 268–300.

Said, Edward, ed. "Intellectuals in the Post-Colonial World." *Salmagundi* 70–71 (1986): 44–64.

———. Introduction. Rudyard Kipling. *Kim.* New York: Penguin, 1987. 7–46.

———. "Representing the Colonized: Anthropology's Interlocutors." *Critical Inquiry* 15 (1989): 205–25.

Sangari, Kumkum. "The Politics of the Possible" *Cultural Critique* 6 (1987): 157–86.

Scruton, Roger. "In Inverted Commas: The Faint Sarcastic Smile on the Face of the Postmodernist." *Times Literary Supplement* 4681 (Dec. 18, 1992): 3–4.

Shohat, Ella. "Notes on the 'Post-Colonial.'" *Social Text* 31/32 (1992): 99–113.

Slemon, Stephen. "Modernism's Last Post." *Past the Last Post.* Ed. Ian Adam and Helen Tiffin. New York: Harvester Wheatsheaf, 1991. 1–11.

Snead, James. "Repetition as a Figure of Black Culture." *Out There: Marginalization and Contemporary Cultures.* Ed. Russell Ferguson, Martha Gever, Trinh T. Minh-ha, and Cornel West. 213–30.

Spivak, Gayatri Chakravorty. "Neocolonialism and the Secret Agent of Knowledge." Interview with Robert Young. *Oxford Literary Review* 13.1–2 (1991): 220–51.

———. *Outside in the Teaching Machine.* New York: Routledge, 1993.

———. "Poststructuralism, Marginality, Postcoloniality and Value." *Literary Theory Today.* Peter Collier and Helga Geyer-Ryan, eds. London: Polity P, 1990.

Spurr, David. *The Rhetoric of Empire: Colonial Discourse in Journalism, Travel Writing, and Imperial Administration.* Durham: Duke UP, 1993.

Tiffin, Helen. Introduction. *Past the Last Post.* Ed. Ian Adam and Helen Tiffin. vii–xvi.

Torgovnick, Marianna. *Gone Primitive: Savage Intellects, Modern Lives.* Chicago: U of Chicago P, 1990.

Žižek, Slavoj. *Tarrying with the Negative: Kant, Hegel, and the Critique of Ideology.* Durham: Duke UP, 1993.

Paulo Freire and the Academy: A Challenge from the U.S. Left

Peter McLaren

We are living the hallucinatory wakefulness of nightmare reason. It is a time in which U.S. culture and history threaten the autonomy of the human spirit rather than exercise it. As early as 1975, Henri Lefebvre warned that those who inhabit this present historical conjuncture suffer from an alienation from alienation—that is, from a disappearance of our consciousness that we exist in a vertiginous and toxic state of alienation. Today, we can only gasp in horror at the current conditions surrounding the neoliberal public sphere with its hate-filled languages of white supremacy, its militant siege mentality, its antigovernment and anti–civil rights rhetoric, its love affair with firearms, explosives, and covert, steely-eyed militias.

Educators and cultural workers in the U.S. living in this twilight of reason are facing a crisis of democracy. The democratic aspiration of U.S. schooling and social, cultural, and institutional practices in general have been carried forth to an unheralded present moment in what retrospectively appears to have been an

© 1996 by *Cultural Critique*. Spring 1996. 0882-4371/96/$5.00.

act of bad faith. The consequences of such an act for future generations are only faintly visible and are bathed in an ethos eerily reminiscent of earlier swindles of hope. The "democratizing" imperatives of private enterprise, wage labor, free trade, and other
fundamental axes for the new capitalist world system ushered in
by the third industrial revolution of computer technology have
shrouded individuals in a web of promotional logic patterned by
the conquering dynamism of Eurocentrism. Colonization has gone
transnational and corporatist (Miyoshi). As Jacques Attali warns,
"From Santiago to Beijing, from Johannesburg to Moscow, all economic systems will worship at the altar of the market. People will
sacrifice for the gods of profit" (120). We live in an age in which
desires, formerly tilted inward, are now constructed on the surface of bodies like pathologically narcissistic tattoos that reflect lost
hopes and empty dreams—forfeited identifications turned into
serpentine grotesqueries, unable to escape the circuit of deceit and
despair constructed out of capitalist relations and rationalizations
and new modes of social regulation that produce not persons nor
individuals, but "subjects."

Capitalism carries the seeds of its own vulnerability and frailty
even though its cunning appears inexhaustible and its mechanisms
of production and exchange irreproachable and unchallenged. Its
vulnerability is, ironically, the most steadfast and dangerous precondition for its further development. So long as it has bourgeois
universal reason and the epistemic privilege of science as its
spokesperson and Eurocentrism as its cultural anchor, and white-
ness as its foundation of cultural calculability, its very constitution
as a discourse of power within an increasingly homogeneous
"world culture" needs to be challenged by popular movements of
renewal within a polycentric cultural milieu.

Educators in the U.S. have no special immunity to these conditions but bear a signal responsibility to understand them and, in
turn, help their students to do the same. Students are particularly
vulnerable in these dangerous times, as they are captured in webs
of social and cultural meaning not of their own making, motivated
to remember in specific ways, and silently counseled through advertisements, the media, and religious and political "others" to respond to the logic of commodity fetishism as if it were a natural
state of affairs. Teachers and students together face New Right

constituencies of all types and stripes—in particular, fundamental-ist Christians and political interest groups who are exercising an acrimonious appeal to a common culture monolithically unified by a desire for harmony in sameness.

The forms of ethical address which have been constructed by the sentinels of our dominant political, cultural, and educational systems—even under cover of abstract endorsements of diver-sity—are bent on draining the lifeblood out of difference by install-ing an invisible ideological grid through which appeals to nor-malcy, decency, and citizenship may be filtered and differences extorted into reconciliation. They are effectively limiting the range of meanings which are being stockpiled in the name of democracy. E. D. Hirsch wants to reduce culture to a politically denuded the-saurus, a paraphrasable core of necessary ideas; the English Only movement desires to ontologically and epistemologically fix the re-lationship between citizenship and language so that "real Ameri-cans" won't be bothered anymore by a babel of foreign tongues; educational reformers under the sway of marketplace logic are im-plored to get youth off the streets and into the declining job mar-kets, where they can then be conscripted into the corporate wars with Germany and Japan.

Insinuated into grand narratives of progress, these contest-able sets of assumptions and social practices effectively reproduce the systems of intelligibility that further the interests of the privi-leged and powerful. Against the backdrop of the global underclass, the growing influence of neoconservatism and neoliberalism in po-litical life in general and education in particular, and the struggle for democracy exists the work of Paulo Freire, one of the great educational revolutionaries of our century. It is important to make clear that Freire's work cannot be articulated outside the diverse and conflicting registers of indigenist cultural, intellectual, and ideological production in the Third World. The "Third World" is a term that I use most advisedly after Benita Parry and Frantz Fanon to mean a "self-chosen phrase to designate a force indepen-dent of both capitalism and actually existing socialism, while re-maining committed to socialist goals" (Parry 130). As such, it offers a starting point for a critique of imperialism and "retains its radical edge for interrogating the Western chronicle." In other words, the discursivities of Freire's pronouncements cannot be decapitated from their sociohistorical and geopolitical location or the contextual specificities of their production, circulation, and reception. While the historically specific content of Freire's thought should not be accorded a stable, transcendent status that suggests his work has travelled unproblematically to the intellectual shores of North American leftist traditions, I will argue that his work can certainly be adopted not as a once-and-for-all knowledge, but as part of a larger critique of the U.S. academy.

One of the most important implications surrounding the distinction between First and Third Worlds involves the politics of underdevelopment. Andrew Ross describes the classic model of underdevelopment as one that benefits the small, indigenous elites of Western developed nations. Foreign markets such as those in Latin America provide a consumption outlet for the developed nations of the First World for absorbing the effects of a crisis of overproduction in the core economy. According to Ross, the peripheral economy (Latin America) underproduces for its domestic population. He reports that "The Economic surplus which results from peripheral consumption of core products is appropriated either by core companies or by the domestic elites; it is not invested in the domestic economy of the peripheral nation" (129). Of course, what happens as a result is that the domestic economies of Latin America and foreign capital certainly do encourage peripheral economies to develop but such development—if you can call it that—is almost always uneven and consequently such contact forces the peripheral economy to undevelop its own domestic spheres.

When there is economic dependency, cultural dependency often follows in its wake. However, the capitalist culture industry is not simply superstructural but constitutive in that the masses—both in First and Third Worlds—do not simply consume culture passively as mindless dupes. There is often resistance at the level of symbolic meaning and in terms of exercising a "hidden transcript" that prevents the culture industry from serving only as a vehicle of repressive homogenization of meaning (Martin-Barbero; McLaren, "Collisions"; James C. Scott). According to Andrew Ross, the elites of the peripheral nations are the first to acquire access to Westernized popular culture but because of the limited access of the indigenous population to the media, the media generally serve to encourage affluent groups to adopt the consumer values of the most developed countries. The elites basically serve in a supervisory capacity when it comes to the cultural consumption of the indigenous peasantry. However, the continuing ties of the peasantry to their own ethnic cultures does help them become less dependent on Western information. Foreign mass-produced culture is often interpreted and resisted at the level of popular culture and we must remember that First World cultural values can also be affected by its contact with the cultures of less developed countries. And, further, not everything about contact with Western culture is to be shunned, although the emergence of a new, transnational class appears to have all the ideological trappings of the older, Western bourgeoisie. My own contact with Brazilian feminists has revealed to me that, for instance, oppositional feminist critique in the U.S. can be successfully appropriated by Brazilian women in their struggle against the structures of patriarchal oppression, structures which can permit men to kill their wives if they suspect them of infidelity on the grounds that their "male honor" has been violated.

The image of Freire that is evoked against this recurring narrative of the decline and deceit of Western democracy and the cultural hegemony of developed nations is that of a distant voice in a crowd, a disturbing interloper among the privileged and powerful—one who bravely announces that the emperor has no clothes. Ethically and politically Freire remains haunted by the ghosts of history's victims and possessed by the spirits that populate the broken dreams of utopian thinkers and millenarian dreamers—a man whose capacities for nurturing affinities between disparate social, cultural, and political groups and for forging a trajectory toward moral, social, and political liberation exceeds the disasters that currently befall this world.

Freire's internationally celebrated praxis began in the late 1940s and continued unabated until 1964, when he was arrested in Brazil as a result of a literacy program he designed and implemented in 1962. He was condemned, imprisoned, and exiled by the leaders of Brazil's military coup, who accused him of being an "international subversive" and "a traitor of Christ and the Brazilian people," and his writing was denounced as comparable "to that of Stalin, Hitler, Peron, and Mussolini" (McLaren and Giroux xiv).

Freire was imprisoned by the military government for 70 days, and exiled mainly for his work in the national literacy campaign, of which he had served as director. Freire's 16 years of exile were tumultuous and productive times: a five-year stay in Chile as a UNESCO consultant with the Chilean Agrarian Reform Corporation, specifically the Reform Training and Research Institute; an appointment in 1969 to Harvard University's Center for Studies in Development and Social Change; a move to Geneva, Switzerland, in 1970 as consultant to the Office of Education of the World Council of Churches, where he developed literacy programs for Tanzania and Guinea-Bissau that focused on the re-Africanization of their countries; the development of literacy programs in some postrevolutionary former Portuguese colonies such as Angola and Mozambique; assisting the governments of Peru and Nicaragua with their literacy campaigns; the establishment of the Institute of Cultural Action in Geneva in 1971; a brief return to Chile after Salvador Allende was assassinated in 1973, provoking General Pinochet to declare Freire a subversive; designing literacy methods for "base communities" organized worldwide by priests and lay workers responsive to the initiatives of Liberation Theology; and his eventual return to Brazil in 1980 to teach at the Pontifícia Universidade Católica de São Paulo, the Universidade de São Paulo, and the Universidade de Campinas. These events were accompanied by numerous works, most notably, *Pedagogy of the Oppressed, Cultural Action for Freedom,* and *Pedagogy in Process: Letters to Guinea-Bissau.* Little did Freire realize that on November 15, 1988, the *Partido dos Trabalhadores* (Workers Party or PT) would win the municipal elections in São Paulo, Brazil, and he would be appointed Secretary of Education of the city of São Paulo by Mayor Luiza Erundina de Sousa.

Relentlessly destabilizing as *sui generis* and autochthonous mercenary pedagogy—i.e., spontaneous pedagogy wantonly designed to stimulate the curiosity of students yet imposed in such a bourgeois manner so as to "save" those who live in situations of domestication only when they are reinitiated into the conditions of their own oppression—Freire's praxis of solidarity, that is, his critical pedagogy speaks to a new way of being and becoming human. This "way of being and becoming" constitutes a quest for the historical self-realization of the oppressed by the oppressed themselves through the formation of collective agents of insurgency. Against the treason of modern reason, Freire aligns the role of the educator with that of the organic intellectual. It should come as no surprise, then, that against perspectives generated in the metropolitan epicenters of education designed to serve and protect the status quo Freire's work has, even today, been selected for a special disapprobation by the lettered bourgeoisie and epigones of apolitical pedagogy as a literature to be roundly condemned, travestied, traduced, and relegated to the margins of the education debate. That Freire's work has been placed under prohibition, having been judged to be politically inflammatory and subversive and an inadmissible feature of academic criticism, is understandable given the current historical conjunction. But it is not inevitable.

It is not the purpose of this essay to address the often egregious misrepresentations of Freire's work by mainstream educators, nor to simply situate Freire unproblematically within the context of First World efforts to ground liberation struggles in pedagogical practices. I intend merely to elaborate on one of the central themes of Freire's work, which is the role of the educator as an active agent of social change.

Critical Pedagogy Versus the Academy

While their political strategies vary considerably, critical educators of various stripes (many of whom have been directly influenced by Freire's work) generally hold certain presuppositions in common, which can be summarized as follows: pedagogies constitute a form of social and cultural criticism; all knowledge is fundamentally mediated by linguistic relations that inescapably are socially and historically constituted; individuals are synecdochically related to the wider society through traditions of mediation (family, friends, religion, formal schooling, popular culture, etc.); social facts can never be isolated from the domain of values or removed from forms of ideological production as inscription; the relationship between concept and object and signifier and signified is neither inherently stable nor transcendentally fixed and is often mediated by circuits of capitalist production, consumption, and social relations; language is central to the formation of subjectivity (conscious and unconscious awareness); certain groups in any society are unnecessarily and often unjustly privileged over others and, while the reason for this privileging may vary widely, the oppression which characterizes contemporary societies is most forcefully secured when subordinates accept their social status as natural, necessary, inevitable, or bequeathed to them as an exercise of historical chance; oppression has many faces and focusing on only one at the expense of others (e.g., class oppression vs. racism) often elides or occults the interconnection among them; power and oppression cannot be understood simply in terms of an irrefutable calculus of meaning linked to cause and effect conditions, and this means that an unforeseen world of social relations awaits as domination and oppression are implicated in the radical contingency of social development and our responses to it; and mainstream research practices are generally and unwittingly implicated in the reproduction of systems of class, race, and gender oppression (Kincheloe and McLaren 1994). Some criticalists, myself included, follow Niklas Luhmann in arguing that "[r]eality is what one does not perceive when one perceives it" (68). In other words, knowing anything presupposes a paradoxical understanding; cognition depends upon a necessary blind spot, a collusion with self-reference. Hence, the importance of multiple observers in dialogue as part of any critical inquiry.

Freire's work certainly reflects this list of assumptions to different degrees, and while his corpus of writing does not easily fall under the rubric of poststructuralism, his emphasis on the relationship among language, experience, power, and identity give significant weight to certain poststructuralist assumptions. For instance, Freire's work stresses that language practices among individuals and groups do more than reflect reality, they effectively organize our social universe and reinforce what is considered to be the limits of the possible while constructing at the same time the faultlines of the practical. To a large extent, the sign systems and semiotic codes that we use are always already populated by prior interpretations since they have been necessarily conditioned by the material, historical, and social formations that help to give rise to them. They endorse and enforce particular social arrangements since they are situated in historically conditioned social practices in which the desires and motivations of certain groups have been culturally and ideologically inscribed, not to mention overdetermined. All sign systems are fundamentally arbitrary, but certain systems have been accorded a privileged distinction over others, in ways that bear the imprint of race, class, and gender struggles (Gee). Sign systems not only are culture-bound and conventional but also are distributed socially, historically, and geopolitically (Berlin). For U.S. educators, this implicates our language use in Euro-American social practices that have been forged in the crucible of patriarchy and white supremacy (Giroux, *Border Crossings*).

Knowledge does not, according to the view sketched above, possess any inherent meaningfulness in and of itself but depends on the context in which such knowledge is produced and the purpose to which such knowledge is put. If there is no preontological basis for meaning that is extralinguistically verifiable, no philosophical calculus that can assist us in making choices—then we can come to see language as a form of power that apprentices us to particular ways of seeing and engaging the self and others and this, in turn, has particular social consequences and political effects (McLaren and Leonard). Few educators have helped us to judge the political effects of language practices as much as Paulo Freire. And few educators have been as misused and misunderstood. Clearly, Freire does not see individuals and groups to be agentless beings invariably trapped in and immobilized by language effects. Rather, human beings are *politically accountable* for their language practices and as such, agency is considered immanent (McLaren and Lankshear; McLaren and Giroux). Freire's position reflects Gramsci's notion that the structural intentionality of human beings needs to be critically interrogated through a form of *conscientization*, or *conscientizaçao* (this Portuguese word is defined by Freire as a deep or critical reading of commonsense reality).

The Educational Institution as (a) Moral Agent

When the surgical pick of Egas Moniz was poised to perform the first medical lobotomy (a procedure that, it may be recalled, won him the Nobel Prize and which led reactionary advocates to consider lobotomies for individuals subversive of good citizenship practices), it was inconceivable at that time to think that such an act of cerebral terrorism could be achieved at a cultural level more effectively and much less painfully through the powerful articulations of new and ever more insidious forms of capitalist hegemony. The emancipatory role of university and public intellectuals has been greatly diminished by this process, as has the function of the organic intellectual. In fact, emancipatory praxis has been largely orphaned in our institutions of education as educators are either unable or refuse to name the political location of their own pedagogical praxis. Part of the problem is that postmodern traditions of mediation have become simulacra whose ideological dimensions cannot easily be identified with or organically linked to the most oppressive effects of capitalist social relations and material practices. The redoubled seduction of new information technologies not only rearticulates a submission to multinational financial strategies, but creates possibilities for a resignification of, resistance to, and popular participation in the politics of everyday life. The fact that relationships between the specific and the general have become blurred by these new electronic forces of mediation has both increased a reorganization and liberation of difference but has also posed a danger of further cultural fragmentation and dissolution limiting the struggle for strategic convergences among sites of intellectual production, the formation of new moral economies, and the expansion of new social movements. This disaggregation of public spheres and the massification of *mestizaje* identities makes it difficult to establish the solidarities necessary for developing liberating idioms of social transformation (Martin-Barbero; McLaren, "Collisions"). Rey Chow poses an urgent question to U.S. intellectuals: "How do intellectuals struggle against a hegemony which already includes them and which can no longer be divided into the state and civil society in Gramsci's terms, nor be clearly demarcated into national and transnational spaces?" (16). Chow remarks that most oppositional university intellectual work derives from *strategies* which deal (after de Certeau's conceptualization of urban spatial practices) with those who wish to solidify a place or barricade a field of interest. What we need instead of strategies, argues Chow, are *tactics* to deal with calculated actions outside of *specific sites*. Strategic solidarities only repeat "what they seek to overthrow" (17). In discussing de Certeau's distinction between strategies and tactics, Michael Shapiro notes that strategies belong to those who have legitimate positions within the social order and consequently are part of "a centralized surveillance network for controlling the population" (103). Tactics, on the other hand, "belong to those who do not occupy a legitimate space and depend instead on time, on whatever opportunities present themselves" (103). Tactics are associated with the performative repertoire—i.e., "the slipperiness of the sophistic stance"—of displaced, disenfranchised, and dominated people (Conquergood 83). Tactics, in other words, are the "techniques of the sophist" in which the ethos of the formal meaning of sophistry is replaced by a resistant praxis of the contingent, the available, the possible (Conquergood 82). In a world of scarce options, tactics can serve to camouflage resistance as a form of what Conquergood calls "improvisational savvy" (82). There are the actions of the class clown, the student who "goofs off," the teacher who seizes the space of a classroom lesson to engage in a dialogue with students about issues not on the formal curriculum. De Certeau describes tactical operations and maneuvers as follows:

> [A] tactic is a calculated action determined by the absence of a proper locus. . . . The space of a tactic is the space of the other. Thus it must play on and with a terrain imposed on it and organized by the law of a foreign power. It does not have the means to keep to itself, at a distance, in a position of withdrawal, foresight, and self-collection: it is a maneuver "within the enemy's field of vision," . . . and within enemy territory. It does not, therefore, have the option of planning, general strategy. . . . It operates in isolated actions, blow by blow. It takes advantage of opportunities and depends on them, being without any base where it could stockpile its winnings, build up its own position, and plan raids. . . . This nowhere gives a tactic mobility, to be sure, but a mobility that must accept the chance offerings of the moment, and seize on the wing the possibilities that offer themselves at any given moment. It must vigilantly make use of the cracks that particular conjunctions open in the surveillance of proprietary powers. It poaches in them. It creates surprises in them. . . . It is a guileful ruse. (qtd. in Conquergood 82)

According to Conquergood, rationality itself is linked to the domain of strategy in that it derives its legitimacy (after de Certeau) in an established locus or place. Against the strategic imperatives of formal rationality founded on established rights and property, Conquergood posits what he calls "sophistic tactics" that "resist systematizing and totalizing discourses because they are dispersed and nomadic; they are difficult to administer because they cannot be pinned down." He further adds: "Artful dodgers and tacticians of resistance are branded disreputable by proprietary powers because they are always on the move and refuse to settle down" (83). It should be emphasized that the realm of resistance that can be tactical is not only classroom behaviors deemed counter-hegemonic but also the practice of theory, as Giroux has pointed out ("Paulo Freire").

Chow elaborates on the distinction between strategies and tactics as it relates to the politics of insurgent university educators:

> We need to remember as intellectuals that the battles we fight are battles of words. Those who argue the oppositional standpoint are not doing anything different from their enemies and are most certainly not directly changing the downtrodden lives of those who seek their survival in metropolitan and non-metropolitan spaces alike. What academic intellectuals must confront is thus not their "victimization" by society at large (or their victimization-in-solidarity-with-the-oppressed), but the power, wealth, and privilege that ironically accumulate from their "oppositional" viewpoint, and the widening gap between the professed contents of their works and the upward mobility they gain from such words. (When Foucault said intellectuals need to struggle against becoming the object and instrument of power, he spoke precisely to this kind of situation.) The predicament we face in the West, where intellectual freedom shares a history with economic enterprise, is that "if a professor wishes to denounce aspects of big business . . . he will be wise to locate in a school whose trustees are big businessmen." Why should we believe in those who continue to speak a language of alterity-as-lack while their salaries and honoraria keep rising? How do we resist the turning-into-propriety of oppositional discourses, when the intention of such discourse has been that of displacing and disowning the proper? How do we prevent what begin as tactics—that which is "without any base where it could stockpile its winnings" (de Certeau: 37)—from turning into a solidly fenced-off field, in the military no less than in the academic senses? (17)

Chow reminds us that oppositional tactics within the university—often undertaken as the practice of Freirean "critical pedagogy"—can become dangerously domesticated precisely because they can be conscripted by leftist educators into the service of career advancements. Even employed with the best of intentions, Freirean pedagogy can unwittingly locate itself as a voguish set of systematized strategies that carries with it the imprimatur of leftist high theory (McLaren and Lankshear). Its adoption can be used for accruing one's academic property rights for those who wish to keep resistance a form of ludic play, a form of mimesis as distinct from praxis. To enact resistance as a tactical performative undertaking, a subversive maneuver designed to rupture and displace the unitary cohesiveness of the academy's master discourses and develop a pedagogy that operates outside of mainstream pedagogy's founding binarisms, would be considered too risky for educators who wish to enjoy the appearance of being radical without facing the hard decisions that could risk one's job security or possibilities for tenure. It is to a deeper understanding of the strategic and tactical relationships between the role of hegemony in the formation of public intellectuals and the function of the university itself in the context of wider social and political formations that Freire's work needs to be engaged. Freire's work also needs engagement with oppositional discourses dealing with higher education and the role of the intellectual that appropriate postmodernist criticisms.

What can be loosely described as postmodern social theory has been influential in, among other things, offering criticisms of material and economic causality and the Cartesian notion of subjectivity by placing an emphasis on reading social reality as a text, on language as a model of representation that helps "construct" social reality, on power as both a condition and effect of discourse, on world-construction as an interplay of signifying relations and on unmasking Enlightenment conceptions of truth as the aesthetic effectiveness of the rhetoric of reading and writing practices. Freire's work has not addressed in any extended commentary current political debates surrounding the pedagogy and politics of postmodernism (McLaren and Leonard), but recent remarks situate these debates as ongoing "discoveries" that center around two possibilities: the denial of history and human agency or the recognition of history as a necessary human experience, one that is historically constituted (Freire, Foreword, and *A Note*). Freire writes:

> I would like to actively follow the discussions about whether the issue of postmodernity is an historical province in itself, a kind of sui generis meant in History as the starting point of a new History, almost without continuity with what went before or what is to come; without ideologies, utopias, dreams, social classes or struggles. It would be a 'round time', 'filled out', 'smooth', without 'edges', in which men and women would eventually discover that its main feature is neutrality. Without social classes, struggles or dreams to fight for, without the need for choice or, therefore, for changes, without the game of conflicting ideologies, it would be an empire of neutrality. It would be a denial of history itself.
>
> I would like to discover whether, on the contrary, postmodernity, like modernity, and traditionalism, on which presses a substantial number of connotations, implies a necessary continuity which characterizes History itself as a human experience whose form of being can filter from one moment in time to another. In this sense, each moment in time is characterized by the predominance and not by the exclusivity of its connotations.
>
> For me, postmodernity today, like modernity yesterday, by conditioning men and women caught up in it, does not destroy nor did it destroy what we call their nature, which[,] not being a priori of History, has been socially constructed exclusively through it. (*A Note* 2)

Freire describes pedagogical practice within postmodernity as "one that humbly learns from differences and rejects arrogance" (3). It is a practice that does not forcefully reject prior historical struggles but rejects the arrogance and certainty that often accompanied them.

Writing from a postmodernist perspective, Sande Cohen has recently offered a forceful challenge to the timid and frequently duplicitous role which university intellectuals have assumed in relation to the sociality of capital and the "catastrophe of socialized expectations." Cohen's analysis has much to offer Freirean educators who wish to enter into conversation with postmodern social theory and who also wish to situate the challenge of critical pedagogy within university settings. Following the persistent contentions of Baudrillard, Nietzsche, and others, Cohen maintains that objectivity can no longer hide or deny its subjectively based interests—a situation that has serious implications for the role of the intellectual in contemporary North American society. He writes:

> For the intellectual it is suggested that our texts and objects now fail to connect with everything but *our own simulacra, image, power, formation of exchange.* In doubting and negating everything, in affirming and consecrating everything, intellectuals remain prisoners of the futile role of the subject-in-consciousness and enforce the pretense that our efforts translate and represent for the truth of others, the reality of the world. (154, emphasis in original)

For Cohen, as for Freire, the dilemma of the intellectual lies in the failure to forcefully challenge the perils of capitalism. In response to this dilemma, Cohen mounts an articulate and vigorous attack on the U.S. professoriate. University discourse and practices are condemned as mobilizing the academicization and domestication of meaning through a modernist process of historicization—a process which, in effect, amounts to creating various self-serving theologies of the social that enable professors to speculate on the future in order to justify their social function as intellectuals. Resulting from this process are acute forms of antiskepticism leading in many instances to a debilitating cynicism. According to Cohen, universities and their academic gentry operate as a discursive assemblage directed at creating a regime of truth, a process that fails to undertake the important task of "inventing systems independent of the system of capital" (3). In this instance, academic criticism is crippled by its inability to break from conventional categories such as "resemblance." Critical languages forged in the theoretical ovens of the academy simply and regrettably pursue their own hegemony through the production of pretense and the desire for power. Further, in face of the cultural logic of late capitalism, "the category of the intellectual is disengaged from any possible antimodernist argument" (68). This situation recenters "high status" knowledge within the liberal tradition of thera-

peutic discourse. According to Cohen, "Universities cannot speak
to their own participation in the destruction of events without undoing their 'need' and control structures" (114).

Even Habermas' now popular appeal for a rational means of
resolving differences and restoring democratic social life in the
ideal speech situation is described as "psychologically based moral
economy" (67) in which "intellectuals are empowered so long as
they stay in the precut grooves of providing resocialization with
concepts, theory, sophistication, the seductions, one might say, of
bureaucratic integration" (70). With this dilemma in mind, Cohen
asks the following:

> Why isn't capitalism—which makes mincemeat of real argu-
> mentation by its homogenization of signifiers, accomplished,
> for example, by the media's ordinary excessive displacement
> of analysis or the marginalization of unfamiliar cultural and
> social voices—rendered more critically? . . . Why is the eco-
> nomic mode so accepted in the first place as an unalterable
> form of social relation? Why is criticism so often an opposition
> that acts under the identity of a "loyal opposition?" (70)

In order to escape the inevitability under capitalism of a modernist historicist recoding of knowledge, Cohen astutely adopts Lyotard's notion of "dispossession." Dispossession is recruited in this
context in terms of "the dispossession of historicizing, narrating,
reducing, demanding" (72). More specifically, it refers to a form of
"uncontrolled presentation (which is not reducible to presence)"
(73). It also points to the suspension of identification—including
negative identification. Cohen also conscripts into the service of a
critique of capitalism Hannah Arendt's concept of "active critique"
of ends and goals "that never identif[ies] with time valuations
which are, unavoidably, always already atrophied" (113). We are
advised here to "strangify"—a term he employs in tandem with an
unyielding commitment to resubjectification—to making subjectivity different outside the acts of negation and opposition through
the creation of insubordinate signifiers which loosen and "neutralize . . . the Platonic control on the power to select" (118). To strangify is to engage in a nonreduction of meaning that terrorizes all
forms of equational logic, positive and negative (119).

Cohen's project of strangification—a type of postmodern extension of Freire's term of conscientization—is directed at destabilizing and decentering the monumentalization of the already known and the militarization of existing sign systems established by the academic gentry and mandarins of high status knowledge whose participation is aimed at the legitimization of their own power. Along with smashing through the Western arcs of destiny—those supposedly unassailable narratives of individual freedom arching toward Disneyland, Aztecland, Inca-Blinka, San Banadov, or Gangsterland—strangification unsettles foundational myths which anchor meaning in a sedentary web of contradictory appearances and precode the world in such a way that entrance to the world of "success" depends on the imprimatur of one's cultural capital and the potential for earning power.

A number of questions are raised by Cohen's analysis for those who are developing Freirean-based pedagogical work. These questions include, among others, the following:

• Of what importance does "postmodern theory" and "resistance postmodernism" have for the Brazilian sociopolitical context?
• The recent thesis on "the death of the subject" advanced by many poststructuralists (the individual is constituted by discourse or is simply a position in language, systems of signification, chains of signs) has called into question the feasibility of historical agency of political praxis. How can we think of agency outside of a transhistorical and prediscursive "I" and yet not fall into the cynical trap that suggests that individuals are simply the pawns of the interpretive communities in which they find themselves? If the subject has been aestheticized and reduced to simply a "desiring machine," how are we to address the concepts of morality and ethics and multidimensional forms of agency?
• How are we to react to those who proclaim the "death of History" thesis which decries the metanarratives of the Enlightenment as misguided beliefs in the power of rational reflection? If we are to reject "grand theories" that essentialize others and speak for their needs from a perspective that refuses to critically interrogate its own ideological constitutiveness, then are we simply left with a micropolitics of local struggles? In other words, is it possible to build

global alliances in the postmodern era that do not produce the same forms of technocratic capitalism that are part of the problem?
• If master narratives are colonizing practices that repress both differences and the recognition of multiple subjectivities; if all our observations are produced by contingent observers; if the social is always virtual, partial, and perspectival; and if it is virtually impossible to represent the real outside the constraints of regimes of representation, how should we begin to rethink and practice liberation?
• While postmodern theorists have developed new understandings of desire as a means of criticizing the disabling effects of instrumental reason, how can we address *pragmatically* the project of human freedom?

Postmodern critiques of educational institutions such as those advanced by Cohen can be helpful to Freirean educators in placing social and educational critique within a wider contemporary problematic. While I do support certain inflections of criticalist postmodernist critique, I am wary of some aspects of postmodernist pedagogies. The radical posturing, flamboyant marginality, and fashionable apostasy of such pedagogies can put forward a smoke screen for a sellout liberal humanism. No divine intervention by a floating signifier can draw our attention away from the materiality of suffering under current conditions of capitalism. Freire remains with Marx when he stresses that it is not enough to problematize representations at the conceptual, imagistic level of signification alone; we need to examine their epistemological embeddedness in the historical social relations of their production.

The Nocturnal Academy and the Politics of Difference

Western intellectuals need to further understand that while affirming the experiences of subaltern groups is exceedingly important within a praxis of liberation, it is a highly questionable practice to render the "other" transparent by inviting the other to speak for herself. Freire and other critics make this point very clear (Freire and Macedo; Freire, *Pedagogy of the Oppressed* and *The Politics of Liberation*). As Gaurav Desai (following Gayatri Spivak,

Lata Mani, and Partha Chattergee) notes, the position of permitting the other to speak for herself is uncomfortably "complicitious with a Western epistemological tradition that takes the conditions of the possibility of subaltern counterinvention for granted without engaging in a critique of the effects of global capitalism on such counterinvention" (137). Since the oppressed speak for themselves within a particular sign structure, the language of critique adopted by the insurgent intellectual needs to be able to analyze the embeddedness of such a sign system in the larger episteme of colonialism and white supremacist, capitalist patriarchy. Insurgent intellectuals must apply the same critique to their own assumptions about the other as they do to the other's self-understanding. In fact, critical educators need to counterinvent a discourse that transcends existing epistemes (Desai). "We can," Linda Alcoff argues, "engage in a 'speaking to' the other that does not essentialize the oppressed and nonideologically constructed subjects." Summarizing Spivak, Alcoff points out that Western intellectuals must allow "for the possibility that the oppressed will produce a 'counter-sentence' that can then suggest a new historical narrative" (23). We need to question how events "position" Western intellectuals as authoritative and empowered speakers in ways that reinscribe the oppressed in discourses of colonization, patriarchy, racism, and conquest (Alcoff). Jim Merod poses the challenge of the intellectual as follows:

> The critic's task is not only to question truth in its present guises. It is to find ways of putting fragments of knowledge, partial views, and separate disciplines in contact with questions about the use of expert labor so that the world we live in can be seen for what it is. (188)

The problem, as Merod sees it, is that there exists within the North American academy no political base for alliances among radical social theorists and the oppressed. He writes:

> The belief among liberal humanists that they have no "liberation strategy" to direct their steps is a vivid reminder of the humanities' class origin. Yet intellectuals always have something to fight for more important than their own professional position. North American intellectuals need to move beyond

theory, tactics, and great dignified moral sentiments to support, in the most concrete ways possible, people harmed or
endangered by the guiltless counter-revolutionary violence of
state power. . . . The major intellectual task today is to build a
political community where ideas can be argued and sent into
the world of news and information as a force with a collective
voice, a voice that names cultural distortions and the unused
possibilities of human intelligence. (191)

One important task of the critical educator is to translate cultural difference. This is certainly the challenge for Freirean educators. The act of translation is, in Bhabha's terms, "a borderline
moment" (314). As Walter Benjamin pointed out, all cultural languages are to a certain extent foreign to themselves, and from the
perspective of otherness it is possible to interrogate the contextual
specificity of cultural systems (Bhabha). It is in this sense, then,
that "it becomes possible to inscribe the specific locality of cultural
systems—their incommensurable differences—and through that
apprehension of difference, to perform the act of cultural translation" (Bhabha 314).
    All forms of cultural meaning are open to translation because
all cultural meanings resist totalization and complete closure. In
other words, cultural meanings are hybrid and cannot be contained within any discourse of authenticity or race, class, gender,
essences. Bhabha describes the subject of cultural difference as
follows:

> [T]he subject of cultural difference is neither pluralistic nor
> relativistic. The frontiers of cultural differences are always be-
> lated or secondary in the sense that their hybridity is never
> simply a question of the admixture of pre-given identities or
> essences. Hybridity is the perplexity of the living as it inter-
> rupts the representation of the fullness of life; it is an instance
> of iteration, in the minority discourse, of the time of the arbi-
> trary sign—"the minus in the origin"—through which all
> forms of cultural meaning are open to translation because
> their enunciation resists totalization. (314)

The subaltern voices of minority cultures constitute "those
people who speak the encrypted discourse of the melancholic and

the migrant" (Bhabha 315). The transfer of *their* meaning can never be total. The "desolate silences of the wandering people" (Bhabha 316) illustrate the incommensurability of translation which confronts the discourse of white supremacist and capitalist patriarchy with its own alterity.

As translators, critical educators must assume a transformative role by "dialogizing the other" rather than trying to "represent the other" (Hitchcock). The site of translation is always an arena of struggle. The translation of other cultures must resist the authoritative representation of the other through a decentering process that challenges dialogues which have become institutionalized through the semantic authority of state power. Neither the practice of signification nor translation occurs in an ideological void, and for this reason educators need to interrogate the sign systems that are used to produce readings of experience. As Joan Scott notes, "experience is a subject's history. Language is the site of history's enactment" (34). All language circulates within a conceptual economy that does not function as a static repository of knowledge, but rather, shifts discourses continuously from context to context of interpretation. It is Freire's particular strength that he has developed a critical language and vernacular which can help to translate both the other's experience and his own experience of the other in such a way that ideological representations may be challenged. The challenge here is to rethink authoritative representations of the other in a critical language that does not simply reauthorize the imperatives of "First World" translation practices (McLaren, *Critical Pedagogy*). To do otherwise would open translation to a form of cultural imperialism. Experiences never speak for themselves, even those of the oppressed. Freire is careful to make sure his language of translation provides the oppressed with tools to analyze their own experiences while at the same time recognizing that the translation process itself is never immune from inscription in ideological relations of power and privilege (Freire and Gadotti).

While Freire's dialogue does not centrally address the politics of race, his pedagogy can be employed in uncovering and disclosing stereotypes or hypostatized negative and otherizing differences within the conceptual economy of university work. His message can be elaborated and critically extended through an engagement with the work of Black insurgent intellectuals. Cornel West blames what he perceives as a decline in Black literate intellectual activity on the "relatively greater Black integration into postindustrial capitalist America with its bureaucratized, elite universities, dull middlebrow colleges, and decaying high schools, which have little concern for and confidence in Black students as potential intellectuals" (137). He is highly critical of "aspects of the exclusionary and repressive effects of White academic institutions and humanistic scholarship" (137) and, in particular, "the rampant xenophobia of bourgeois humanism predominant in the whole academy" (142). West sketches out four models for Black intellectual activity as a means of enabling critical forms of Black literate activity in the U.S. The bourgeois humanist model is premised on Black intellectuals possessing sufficient legitimacy and placement within the "hierarchical ranking and the deep-seated racism shot through bourgeois humanistic scholarship" (138). Such legitimation and placement must, however, "result in Black control over a portion of, or significant participation within, the larger White infrastructures for intellectual activity" (140).

The Marxist revolutionary model, according to West, is "the least xenophobic White intellectual subculture available to Black intellectuals" (140). However, West is also highly critical of the constraints Marxist discourse places on the creative life of Black intellectuals in terms of constructing a project of possibility and hope, including an analytical apparatus to engage short-term public policies. According to West,

> [t]he Marxist model yields Black intellectual self-satisfaction which often inhibits growth; also highlights social structural constraints with little practical direction regarding conjunctural opportunities. This self-satisfaction results in either dogmatic submission to and upward mobility with sectarian party or pre-party formations, or marginal placement in the bourgeois academy equipped with cantankerous Marxist rhetoric and sometimes insightful analysis utterly divorced from the integral dynamics, concrete realities, and progressive possibilities of the Black community. The preoccupation with social structural constraints tends to produce either preposterous chiliastic projections or paralyzing, pessimistic pronouncements. (141)

It is important to point out amidst all of this criticism that West does recognize the enabling aspects of the Marxist revolutionary model in its promotion of critical consciousness and its criticisms of dominant research programs within the bourgeois academy.

The Foucauldian postmodern skeptic model invoked by West investigates the relationship among knowledge, power, discourse, politics, cognition, and social control. It offers a fundamental rethinking of the role of the intellectual within the contemporary postmodern condition. Foucault's "political economy of truth" is viewed by West as a critique of both bourgeois humanist and Marxist approaches through the role of Foucault's specific intellectual. The specific intellectual, according to West,

> shuns the labels of scientificity, civility, and prophecy, and instead delves into the specificity of the political, economic, and cultural matrices within which regimes of truth are produced, distributed, circulated, and consumed. No longer should intellectuals deceive themselves by believing—as do humanist and Marxist intellectuals—that they are struggling "on behalf" of the truth; rather the problem is the struggle over the very status of truth and the vast institutional mechanism which account for this status. (142)

West summarizes the Foucauldian model as an encouragement of "an intense and incessant interrogation of power-laden discourses" (143). But the Foucauldian model is not a call to revolution. Rather, it's an invitation to revolt against the repressive effects of contemporary regimes of truth.

Selectively appropriating from these three models, West goes on to propose his own "insurgency model," which posits the Black intellectual as a critical, organic catalyst for social justice. His insurgency model for Black intellectual life recovers the emphasis on human will and heroic effort from the bourgeois model, highlights the emphasis on structural constraints, class formations, and radical democratic values from the Marxist model, and recuperates the worldly skepticism evidenced in the Foucauldian mode's destabilization of regimes of truth. However, unlike the bourgeois model, the insurgency model privileges collective intellectual work and communal resistance and struggle. Contrary to the Marxist model, the insurgency model does not privilege the industrial working class as the chosen agent of history but rather attacks a variety of forms of social hierarchy and subordination, both vertical and horizontal. Further, the insurgency model places much more emphasis on social conflict and struggle than does the Foucauldian model. While Freire's critique of domesticating forms of pedagogy gives a specifically Latin American context for the development of the insurgent intellectual, West's own typology extends some central Freirean themes in order to deepen its engagement with issues of race.

Bell hooks describes an intellectual as "somebody who trades in ideas by transgressing discursive frontiers . . . who trades in ideas in their vital bearing on a wider political culture" (152). However, hooks argues that White supremacist capitalist patriarchy has denied Black women, especially, "the opportunity to pursue a life of the mind." This is a problem that is also firmly entrenched in the racist White university system that involves "persecution by professors, peers, and professional colleagues" (157). Hooks rightly notes that "any discussion of intellectual work that does not underscore the conditions that make such work possible misrepresents the concrete circumstances that allow for intellectual production" (158). She further elaborates:

> Within a White supremacist capitalist, patriarchal social context like this culture, no Black woman can become an intellectual without decolonizing her mind. Individual Black women may become successful academics without undergoing this process and, indeed, maintaining a colonized mind may enable them to excel in the academy but it does not enhance the intellectual process. The insurgency model that Cornel West advocates, appropriately identifies both the process Black females must engage to become intellectuals and the critical standpoints we must assume to sustain and nurture that choice. (160)

I have employed criticisms of the academy by West, hooks, and Cohen because concerns dealing with postmodern social conditions and theory and those of race and gender help to widen

Freire's criticisms by situating his insights more fully within the context and concerns of North American liberation struggles, specifically as they address struggles of the poor, of women, and people of color (McLaren and Leonard; Freire, *A Note*). Of course, there is room to broaden the context even further in relation to the struggles of indigenous peoples, of gays and lesbians, and other cultural workers within and outside of university settings. Freirean-based educators need to raise more questions related to race and gender so that these issues are given a more central focus in the struggle for social transformation. These include the following:

• In what ways have pedagogical practices been colonized by racialized discourses?
• What is the relationship between racial differentiation and subordination and dominant discourses about race and ethnicity? How are these relationships reproduced by white supremacist discursive regimes and communicative practices?
• While the struggle for racial and gender equality is deemed worthwhile, those who struggle on behalf of this worthy goal are often deemed deviant when they step outside of the legitimating norms of what is considered to be the "common culture." How is race and gender inequality reproduced within liberal humanist discourses?
• If there is no necessary racial teleology within the educational practices of most U.S. schools, how does the reproduction of racist discourses occur in most school sites?
• How does the hypervisibility of white cultures actually hide their obviousness in relations of domination and oppression?
• How does race constitute a boundary constraint on what is considered normal and appropriate behavior?
• In what ways are the conditions within the dominant culture for being treated justly and humanely predicated on utilitarian forms of rationality and the values inscribed and legitimated by bourgeois, working class, and elite forms of white culture? How do these forms of rationality work within the episteme of a larger discourse of colonialism?
• How can criticalists develop a cultural politics that is able to phenomenologize ideology critique and critical analyses at the level of

lived experience in a way that avoids a leftist elitism? How can a public vernacular develop around critical studies that is inclusive and life-world sensitive?

Despite these absent discourses, Freire's work remains vitally important in the current debates over the role of universities, public schools, and educational sites of all kinds throughout North America (Freire, *Politics of Liberation*). Freire warns educators that the activity of reading the word in relation to the social world has been regrettably pragmatic rather than principled (Freire and Macedo). In other words, schooling (in relation to both universities and public schools) revolves around the necessity of differentially reproducing a citizenry distinguished by class, race, and gender injustices. The challenges of educators in both First and Third World contexts is to transform these reproductive processes. But I need to nuance this idea. Freirean pedagogy is set firmly against what Kristin Ross calls "the integral 'pedagogicizing' of society," by which she refers to the "general infantilization" of individuals or groups through the discourses and social practices of "the nineteenth-century European myth of progress" (669).

Kristin Ross conceives of critical pedagogy through what she refers to as the "antidisciplinary practice" of cultural studies. Drawing upon revisionist theories of allegory of Walter Benjamin, Paul de Man, and others, Ross moves away from the essentialist conceptions of cultural identity informed by a symbolic (mimetic and synecdochical) model of experience and representation in which one part timelessly and ahistorically reflects the whole. According to this model, the plight of, say, white women in New York reflects the plight of Black women in the Southern U.S. Rather than viewing this relationship as an unmediated one in which the plight of Black women constitutes an authentic reflection of the plight of white women, Ross prefers to see this and similar relationships as allegorical rather than mimetic. According to Ross,

> Allegory preserves the differences of each historically situated and embedded experience, all the while drawing a relationship between those experiences. In other words, one experience is read in terms of another but not necessarily in terms of establishing identity, not obliterating the qualities particular to each. (672)

E. San Juan Jr. maintains that allegory as a formal device has specific advantages for shattering illusion:

> What happens in allegory is this: instead of inducing an easy reconciliation of antimonies, an existential leap into faith where all class antagonisms vanish and rebellious desire is pacified, allegory heightens the tension between signifier and signified, between object and subject, thereby foiling empathy and establishing the temporary distance required for generating critical judgment and, ultimately, cathartic action. (46)

Further, San Juan notes that allegory constitutes "a process of misaligning opposites." As such, it

> focuses on the crux of the contradictions and discharges a call, a polemical challenge. It images the transitional movement of difference from passive contemplation to active involvement, converting objects into process: the process of social production rupturing social relations. (46)

Laura E. Donaldson remarks on the importance of allegorical vision in a feminist approach to the issues of homogeneity and universality. She does this by articulating allegory as a form of metanarrative that can negotiate "the contradiction between a radical politics of identity and a postmodern skepticism, an unqualified opposition and purely affirmative action, which threatens feminism from within" (20).

According to Donaldson, "[a]llegory not only exposes the ideological underpinnings of discourse, but also problematizes a symbolic metaphysics of presence, or in the case of a feminist standpoint, a radical politics of identity" (21). Whereas symbol is antiparadoxical, excluding the logic of its two opposing units, allegory "implies a much more discontinuous relation between signifier and signified, since an extraneous principle rather than some natural identification determines how and when the connection becomes articulated."

Donaldson's characterization of allegory in relation to feminism proves instructive:

> Allegory creates meaning metonymically by temporally displacing reference from one sign to the next; in other words,

it's always mobile. Construction of meaning resists a representational truth or the attempt to find an invariant signified for the narrative which can then be placed before the
reader for acceptance or rejection. Likewise, an allegorical
feminism resists not only a representational view of women's
truth but also the unified Cartesian subject which such a view
presupposes. Allegory highlights the irrevocably relational nature of feminist identity and the negations upon which the assumption of a singular, fixed, and essential self is based. (22)

Citing anthropologist James Clifford, Donaldson goes as far
as asserting that all meaningful levels of a text, including theories
and interpretation, are allegorical or are comprised of multiple
allegorical registers or "voices" (22). No one register necessarily
privileges the rest.

Kristin Ross conscripts similar insights about allegory into the
service of a critical teaching about cultural identity. Since it is impossible to represent every cultural group in the curriculum, the
task of critical pedagogy, in Ross' terms, is to construct cultural
identity allegorically—for each group to see his or her cultural
narrative in a broader and comparative relation to others and
within a larger narrative of social transformation.

For students to recognize the historical and cultural specificity
of their own lived experiences allegorically—i.e., in allegorical relations to other narratives—is especially urgent. As Kristin Ross
puts it,

at a time of growing global homogenization the non-West is
conceived in two, equally reductive ways: one whereby differences are reified and one whereby differences are lost. In the
first, the non-West is assigned the role for the repository for
some more genuine or organic lived experience; minority cultures and non-Western cultures in the West are increasingly
made to provide something like an authenticity rush for blasé
or jaded Westerners, and this is too heavy a burden for anyone
to bear. In the second, non-Western experiences are recoded
and judged according to how closely they converge on the
same: a single public culture or global average, that is, how far
each has progressed toward a putative goal of moderniza-
tion. (673)

An emancipatory curriculum cannot present First and Third World cultures in the context of binary oppositions as relations of domination and resistance, since this move usually permits the First World perspective to prevail as the privileged point of normative civilizations (Kristin Ross). While Freire's work calls attention to the danger of a reductive dichotomization of First and Third World cultures, his interpreters often attempt simply to transplant Freire's perspective into First World contexts as a fortuitous equivalence or natural counterpart to subaltern resistance without recoding Freire's arguments sufficiently in terms of First World contexts (Giroux, *Paulo Freire*). This leads to an unwitting embrace of pedagogy as a Western "civilizing" practice. Freirean criticalists working in the West need to be wary of the processes through which liberal democracy represses the contingency of its own selectivity. Democracy is negatively prejudiced by the choice of its definitional terms, its articulation of freedom. U.S. democracy, in particular, is undergirded by an opportunistic celebration of pluralism that disavows its own purging of oppositional views and refuses to seriously confront its hierarchies of privilege.

As a teacher, Freire has provided the pedagogical conditions necessary to better understand how Enlightenment humanism and its specifically Eurocentric (and Euro-American) "voice of reason" has not always been insightful or even reasonable in exercising its transcontinental thinking in the service of truth and justice (Giroux, *Paulo Freire*). Freire's work helps us to further confront this issue as well as many others of concern to educators and cultural workers.

The perspectives of Freire can help deepen the debate over the role of the university in contemporary North American culture and, by extension, can also help to situate the struggle of Latin American educators within the concerns of postmodern and insurgent criticisms of the academy as exemplified by the perspectives of West, hooks, and Cohen.

In a world of global capitalism, we need global alliances through cultural and political contact in the form of critical dialogue. Samir Amin notes that we collectively face a problem that "resides in the objective necessity for a reform of the world system; failing this, the only way out is through the worst barbarity, the genocide of entire peoples or a worldwide conflagration" (114).

In attempting to develop a project premised on the construction of an emancipatory cultural imaginary that is directed at transforming the conditions that create the victims of capitalist expansion, educators need to go beyond simply severing their arterial connections to the forces of production and consumption that defraud them through the massification and commodification of their subjectivities. Rather, they need to create new alliances through a politics of difference. Otherwise, they face the prospect of becoming extensions of multinational corporations within the larger apparatus of capitalist expansion in the service of unequal accumulation and further underdevelopment in the peripheral and semiperipheral countries of Latin America. In short, what is needed is a politics of radical hope. Hope needs to be conjugated with some aspect of the carnal, tangible world of historical and material relations in order to be made a referent point for a critically transformative praxis.

We are reminded by Freire and his colleagues not to engage in controversies about difference but rather to be encouraged to dialogue about difference. It is in this sense that the university is invited to become truly plural and dialogical, a place where students are not only required to read texts but to understand contexts. A place where educators are required to learn to talk about student experiences and then form this talk into a philosophy of learning and a praxis of transformation. Clearly, we need to work within an ontological and intersubjective articulation of strategic pluralism within what has come to be known as a "politics of location." That is, we need to work from—and feminist theory has been at the forefront here—our diverse subjective positions, from the context of our partial, contingent, and situated knowledges.

I have recently witnessed in Brazil an experiment using Freire's work in conjunction with contributions by critical educators in Europe and the U.S. at Escola de 1° e 2° Graus Jose Cesar de Mesquita (a public school and high school consisting of 1,000 students who live in an industrial zone in Porto Alegre). The project is currently supported by the Sindicato dos Trabalhadores nas Indústrias Metalúrgicos, Mecânicas e Material Elétrico de Porto Alegre, and Nize Maria Campos Pellanda, who serves as Consultora Pedagógica. Here, the curriculum has been forged out of dialogues among teachers, researchers, and scholars from many different countries in both First and Third Worlds. Both elementary and high school students are encouraged to make active alliances with social movements and link their classroom pedagogies directly to social issues facing the larger community. While there exists a great deal of political opposition to this school for workers from both reactionary and neoliberal educators, administrators, and politicians, the experiment itself is a testament to the Freirean vision of transcultural alliances and geopolitical realignment.

Freirean pedagogy argues that pedagogical sites, whether they are universities, public schools, museums, art galleries, or other spaces, must have a vision that is not content with adapting individuals to a world of oppressive social relations but is dedicated to transforming the very conditions that promote such conditions. This means more than simply reconfiguring or collectively refashioning subjectivities outside of the compulsive ethics and consumerist ethos of flexible specialization or the homogenizing calculus of capitalist expansion. Enjoined on all of us working from a criticalist perspective is the creation of new forms of sociality, new idioms of transgression, and new instances of popular mobilization that can connect the institutional memory of the academy to the tendential forces of historical struggle and the dreams of liberation that one day might be possible to guide them. This is a mission that is not simply Freirean but immanently human.

Rather than ground his pedagogy in a doctrinal absolutism, Freire's attention is always fixed on both the specific and generalized other. Categories of identity, when confronted by Freire's practice of conscientization, are vacated of their pretended access to certainty and truth (Giroux, *Border Crossings*). What has endeared several generations of critical educators to Freire, both in terms of a respect for his political vision and for the way he conducts his own life, is the manner in which he has situated his work within an ethics of compassion, love, and solidarity.

To disentangle hope from the vagaries of everyday life, to disconnect human capacity from the structures of domination and then to reconnect them to a project where power works as a form of affirmation and a practice of freedom is, these days, to invite more cynical critics to view Freire's work as a nostalgic interlude in a world whose modernist dream of revolutionary alterity has been superseded by the massifying logic of capitalist accumulation

and alienation. Yet Freire's work cannot be so easily dismissed as
an anachronistic project that has failed to notice history's wake-up
call from recent postmodernist critiques. Many, but not all, of these
critiques have relegated human agency to the dustbin of history,
along with modernist projects of emancipation, including those,
like Freire's, that continue to be informed by socialist and humanistic ideals. To argue in this climate of the simulacrum, as does
Freire, that freedom can be both true and real is to instantly arouse
skepticism and in some quarters, to provoke derision.

For both the oppressed and non-oppressed alike, Freire's life
and work have served as a life-affirming bridge from private despair to collective hopefulness to self and social transformation. Insofar as Freire addresses individuals as more than the capricious
outcomes of historical accident, or exceeding the abstract boundaries of metaphysical design, his work presupposes a subject of history and a culture of redemption.

At a time in U.S. culture in which history has been effectively
expelled from the formation of meaning and hope has been quar-
antined in the frenetic expansion of capital into regions of public
and private life hitherto unimaginable and unthinkable, Freire's
pedagogy of liberation is one we dismiss at our peril.

Note

This article is a substantially revised version of my introduction to *Paulo Freire
on Higher Education: A Dialogue at the National University of Mexico,* edited by Miguel
Escobar, Alfredo Fernandez, and Gilberto Guevara-Niebla, with Paulo Freire (Albany: SUNY P, 1994, ix–xxxiii). The original, unrevised introduction will also
appear in *Mentoring the Mentor: A Critical Dialogue with Paulo Freire,* edited by Paulo
Freire, with James W. Fraser, Donaldo Macedo, Tanya McKinnon, and William T.
Stokes (Albany: SUNY P, forthcoming).

Works Cited

Alcoff, Linda. "The Problem of Speaking for Others." *Cultural Critique* 20 (1991–
    92): 5–32.
Amin, Samir. *Eurocentrism.* New York: Monthly Review P, 1989.
Attali, Jacques. *Millennium.* New York: Random House, 1991.
Berlin, Jim. "Literacy, Pedagogy, and English Studies: Postmodern Connections."
    Critical Literacy: Politics, Praxis, and the Postmodern. Ed. Colin Lankshear and Pe-
    ter McLaren. Albany: SUNY P, 1993. 247–70.

Bhabha, Homi K, ed. *Nation and Narration*. London: Routledge, 1990.
Chow, Rey. *Writing Diaspora: Tactics of Intervention in Contemporary Cultural Studies*. Bloomington: Indiana UP, 1993.
Cohen, Sande. *Academia and the Luster of Capital*. Minneapolis: U of Minnesota P, 1993.
Conquergood, Dwight. "Ethnography, Rhetoric, and Performance." *Quarterly Journal of Speech* 78 (1992): 80–123.
De Certeau, Michel. *The Practice of Everyday Life*. Trans. Steven Rendall. Berkeley: U of California P, 1984.
Desai, Gaurav. "The Invention of Invention." *Cultural Critique* 24 (1993): 119–42.
Donaldson, Laura E. "(Ex)changing (Wo)man: Towards a Materialist-Feminist Semiotics." *Cultural Critique* 11 (1988–89): 5–23.
Freire, Paulo, and Donaldo Macedo. *Literacy: Reading the Word and the World*. South Hadley: Bergin and Garvey, 1987.
Freire, Paulo, and Moacir Gadotti. "We Can Re-invent the World." *Critical Theory and Educational Research*. Ed. Peter McLaren and Jim Giarelli. Albany: SUNY P, 1995. 257–70.
Freire, Paulo. Foreword. *Paulo Freire: A Critical Encounter*. Ed. Peter McLaren and Peter Leonard. London: Routledge, 1993.
———. *A Note From Paulo Freire. Communication and Development in a Postmodern Era: Re-Evaluating the Freirean Legacy*. International Conference Programme. University Sains Malaysia, Penang, Malaysia. December 6–9, 1993.
———. *Paulo Freire and Higher Education*. Ed. Miguel Escobar, Alfredo Fernandez, and Gilberto Guevara-Niebla, with Paulo Freire. Albany: SUNY P, 1994.
———. *Pedagogy of the Oppressed*. New York: Seabury P, 1971.
———. *The Politics of Liberation: Culture, Power, and Liberation*. South Hadley: Bergin and Garvey, 1985.
Gee, Jim. "Postmodernism and Literacies." *Critical Literacy: Politics, Praxis, and the Postmodern*. Ed. Colin Lankshear and Peter McLaren. Albany: SUNY P, 1993. 271–96.
Giroux, Henry. "Paulo Freire and the Politics of Postcolonialism." *Journal of Advanced Composition* 12.1 (1992): 15–26.
———. *Border Crossings*. New York: Routledge, 1993.
Hitchcock, Peter. *Dialogics of the Oppressed*. Minneapolis: U of Minnesota P, 1993.
hooks, bell, and Cornel West. *Breaking Bread: Insurgent Black Intellectual Life*. Boston: South End P, 1991.
Kincheloe, Joe, and Peter McLaren. "Rethinking Critical Theory and Qualitative Research." *Handbook of Qualitative Research*. Ed. Norm K. Denzin and Yvonna S. Lincoln. Newbury Park: Sage, 1994. 138–57.
Lefebvre, H. *Metaphilosophie*. Frankfurt: Suhrkamp, 1975.
Luhmann, Niklas. "The Cognitive Program of Constructivism and a Reality that Remains Unknown." *Self Organization: Portrait of a Scientific Revolution*. Ed. Wolfgang Krohn, Gunter Kuppers, and Helga Nowotry. Dordrecht: Kluwer, 1990.
Martín-Barbero, Jésus. *Communication, Culture, and Hegemony: From Media to Mediation*. London: Sage, 1992.
McLaren, Peter, and Henry Giroux. Foreword. *Reading Paulo Freire: His Life and Work*. Ed. Moacir Gadotti. Albany: SUNY P, 1994. xiii–xvii.
McLaren, Peter, and Colin Lankshear, eds. *Politics of Liberation: Paths from Freire*. London: Routledge, 1994.
McLaren, Peter, and Peter Leonard, eds. *Paulo Freire: A Critical Encounter*. London: Routledge, 1993.
McLaren, Peter. "Collisions with Otherness: Multiculturalism, the Politics of Dif-

ference, and the Ethnographer as Nomad." *American Journal of Semiotics* 9.2–3 (1992): 121–48.

——. *Critical Pedagogy and Predatory Culture: Oppositional Politics in an Age of Despair.* London: Routledge, 1995.

Merod, Jim. *The Political Responsibility of the Critic.* Ithaca: Cornell UP, 1987.

Miyoshi, Masao. "A Borderless World? From Colonialism to Transnationalism and the Decline of the Nation-State." *Critical Inquiry* 19 (1993): 726–51.

Parry, Benita. "A Critique Mishandled." *Social Text* 35 (1993): 121–33.

Ross, Andrew. *No Respect: Intellectuals and Popular Culture.* New York: Routledge, 1989.

Ross, Kristin. "The World Literature and Cultural Studies Program." *Critical Inquiry* 19 (1993): 666–76.

San Juan, E., Jr. *Ruptures, Schisms, Interventions: Cultural Revolution in the Third World.* Manila: De La Salle UP, 1988.

Scott, James C. *Domination and the Arts of Resistance: Hidden Transcripts.* New Haven: Yale UP, 1990.

Scott, Joan W. "Experience." *Feminists Theorize the Political.* Ed. Judith Butler and Joan W. Scott. New York: Routledge, 1992. 22–40.

Shapiro, Michael J. *Reading the Postmodern Polity: Political Theory as Textual Practice.* Minneapolis: U of Minnesota P, 1992.

Torres, Carlos Alberto. *Democratic Socialism, Social Movements and Educational Policy in Brazil: The Work of Paulo Freire as Secretary of Education in the Municipality of São Paulo* (in preparation).

Black Bodies of Knowledge: Notes on an Effective History

John Fiske

Recently, I've been listening to M'banna Kantako on *Black Liberation Radio*. I've also been reading Foucault. They come together productively. Foucault has helped me understand the importance of what *Black Liberation Radio*'s "information guerrillas" are doing, and *Black Liberation Radio* has helped me clarify why I find Foucault's notion of "an effective history" both one of his more productive and one of his more frustrating. M'banna Kantako is a blind, unemployed African American living in the John Hay Homes, an almost exclusively African American housing project in Springfield, Illinois. With the help of his wife Dia and their children, he runs from his tiny front room an unlicensed and therefore illegal micro radio station that is dedicated to improving his people's understanding of white oppression. He has been broadcasting now for five years, the FCC has tried to stop him, and the police regularly harass him, but he continues to disseminate his oppositional knowledge. His one-watt station was assembled for about $600 from catalogues and mall electronic stores, and although its signal can travel less than a couple of miles, Springfield

© 1996 by *Cultural Critique*. Spring 1996. 0882-4371/96/$5.00.

is so ghettoized that it reaches, by Kantako's estimate, 75% of the city's Black population.[1]

Following Foucault's emphasis on the discontinuities of counterhistory, I offer some fragments that M'banna Kantako and his Black activist intellectuals, whom he calls "knowledge gangsters," have broadcast in their efforts to produce an oppositional way of knowing, a Black counterknowledge:

> **Fragment 1:** As the slave ship's cargoes were auctioned off, their damaged goods, too battered or sick for productive work in the plantations, were sold for about a dollar apiece to businessmen, who kept them alive until hospitals needed their bodies for research. They were then killed carefully, often by being strapped to a chair and bled to death through a cut in the foot. Their bodies were sold and turned into white profit, bodies of knowledge that were the equivalent of the bodies of labor on the plantation.
>
> **Fragment 2:** Nat Turner, the leader of a slave rebellion, has been captured. He is sick, injured, and dying. His white captors offer him food on condition that he signs away his body to them, to do with it what they will after his death.
>
> **Fragment 3:** In 1932, the U.S. Public Health Service recruited 400 Black men suffering from syphilis in Tuskegee, Alabama, and charted the course of the disease through their bodies for 40 years, denying them treatment for the whole period, during which at least 254 died as a result of their infection. None of the men knew they were taking part in an experiment; rather, they believed they were undergoing treatment.
>
> **Fragment 4:** Between 1880 and 1910, a Black man, Sam McKeever, lived in Washington, D.C. He earned his living in the daytime picking up old rags in a push cart for resale. At night, he caught and killed other Blacks and sold their bodies to local hospitals.
>
> **Fragment 5:** Two advertisements in *The Charleston Mercury* in the 1830s: The South Carolina Medical College advertises:
>
>> Some advantages of a peculiar character are connected with this institution, which it may be proper to point out. No place in the United States offers as great opportunities for the acquisition of anatomical knowledge. Subjects being obtained from among the colored

population in sufficient numbers for every purpose, and proper dissections carried on without offending any individuals in the community!

Dr. T. Stillman (who had nothing to do with the S.C. Medical College) also advertised:

> To Planters and Others—Wanted fifty negroes. Any person having sick negroes, considered incurable by their respective physicians, and wishing to dispose of them, Dr. S. will pay cash for negroes affected with scrofula or king's evil, confirmed hypocondriasm, apoplexy, diseases of the liver, kidneys, spleen, stomach and intestines, bladder and its appendages, diarrhea, dysentery, etc. The highest cash price will be paid on application as above (Fry 174).

Fragment 6: In 1953, in Chicago, a Black woman called Henrietta Lack died of cervical cancer. Her tumor was kept alive, and it has now become the standard medium for cell culture, for viral and bacteriological development in laboratories.

In his discussion of Nietzsche's theory of genealogy as a counter to traditional history Foucault suggests some characteristics of an "effective history" that I find inadequately useful in helping me tackle these fragments. But part of interpretation must be the story of how I came across them. I am no historian but a cultural theorist and analyst. Most of these fragments came to my attention through my listening to *Black Liberation Radio,* and the others, Fragments 4 and 5, from reading suggested by it. *Black Liberation Radio* exists only to empower its Black listeners in their daily struggles against white power: to achieve this it mixes affirmations of the creativity, imagination, and resilience of Black culture through its music and writings with trenchant and tireless analyses of white power in action.

Let me turn first to what I find useful in Foucault's theorizing before passing on to his inadequacies. An effective history must counter traditional history through its emphasis on the particularities of events and upon bodies: it is genealogical in that it is "situated within the articulation of the body and history . . . Its task is to expose a body totally imprinted by history and the process of history's destruction of the body" (Foucault, "Nietzsche" 148). In this task, effective history inverts traditional history's prioritization of distance, or the grand view, over proximity, whereas effective history "shortens its vision to those things nearest to it," particularly the body.

Effective history emphasizes events, discontinuities, and multiplicities over the homogenizing trend of the grand narrative of traditional history. An event, for Foucault, is not, as in traditional history, a treaty, a reign, or a battle, but "a reversal in the relationship of forces" (Foucault, "Nietzsche" 148), a moment when power is most nakedly experienced, resisted, turned, evaded, or even merely exposed. An event is an instance in what he calls "the hazardous play of dominations," which is to be found not in structural social relations, such as those between classes, races, or genders, but in the "meticulous procedures that impose rights and obligations" (Foucault, "Nietzsche" 154).

His emphasis on the microphysics of power introduces discontinuities and multiplicities into the story of history. The body and the self are destabilized and multiplied. The useless slave (about to made useful) bleeding to death in the chair has many bodies and identities, some torn from Africa, others commodified by whites, dehumanized, made into a specimen, and, once dissected, discarded as inert lumps of flesh and bone. The discontinuities between Nat Turner and Henrietta Lack, both with their multiplied bodies, are what make their similarities so effective, and an official history would miss both or would dismiss the similarity within discontinuity as coincidence or as nonsignifying.

And the final characteristic of an effective history is that it must contain its own perspective; it cannot aspire to a transcendent objectivism, but must be effective for somebody, and that social body must be explicit in the history.

I selected these fragments from my listening to *Black Liberation Radio* as a hypothetical example of what a counterhistory might look like. There can be no singular counterhistory, for its effectiveness is dependent upon the conditions of the body—of the individual through to the social—that constructs it as it is only in those conditions that its effectiveness can be traced. I selected them, too, as examples of "events" where social power is meticulously inscribed upon the body and which, as a result, embody an "affect," an intensity of feeling whereby the social forces of history are experienced in the body and its senses; in their retelling, such events evoke in the bodies of their listeners traces of those original experiences. When I first heard them, I experienced a shudder, a bodily *frisson,* that is a necessary part of their effectiveness. But for whites, these retold events must produce a different bodily affect and, thus, a different historical effectiveness than for African Americans. In effect, it is not the white body that experienced this power, and it is not in that white body that that power can be countered or resisted. For African Americans, however, these events can carry their histories into the present, not just as understandings of the continuity between past and present, but as experiences of it. They are historical events, but the effectiveness of their history depends upon their historians embodying them and imbricating them into the experience, and therefore understanding, of the present.

The embodying of these fragments may be relatively straightforward, but their fragmentary disjunction is more problematic. Foucault promotes the discontinuities of events as a counter to the abstracting thrust of the "grand narrative" history that he opposes. These radio fragments—in effect, fragments of life—are locations that witness the application of the microphysics of power to bodies, and it is in this context that one must understand that power. The fragments are where the action is, and the action is the interplay between history and the body. In these microtechnological moments, power stops being an abstract system and becomes a material force applied both technologically and discursively.

A common misreading of Foucault's concept of discontinuity as a proposal for fragmentation rather than a strategy against a master narrative underemphasizes the systematicity of the power that buys a fit slave for $40 and an injured one for $1; that power becomes material at the moment of economic exchange when one body is taken to the plantation and the other to the holding pen. When the power passes beyond the discursive, a matter of exchange, to the technological as it is applied instrumentally to the body, its materiality becomes inescapable. The applied technology of the whip transforms the fit body into a body of labor. Similarly, the technology of the knife that opens a vein in the body bound to a chair and of the knife that dissects it on the operating table transforms the sick body into a body of knowledge. These are the events in that "hazardous play of dominations" that transform the Black body into a white body of knowledge or of labor.

Positively, the discontinuity of events inherently denies any absolute hierarchy of evidential reliability. In the forementioned fragments, for instance, the advertisements in the *Charleston Mercury* exist in archives which anyone can read. How they are interpreted and how they are integrated into a history, of course, are not archived and not equally available to everyone. In essence, they are the product of the specific researcher's work. Similarly, in Fragment 4, there is documentary evidence of the existence of a man called McKeever, his address, and his daytime occupation. *Boyd's Directory of the District of Columbia,* an annually published list of the name, address, and occupation of each resident, regularly includes the names of both Samuel and Eliza McKeever from 1883 until 1907, the last date Eliza's name appears. It also lists his daytime occupation variously as laborer; rags, junk, buyer; and, in his later years, elevator operator. His nighttime occupation, of course, remains undocumented and exists only in oral history.

Gladys-Marie Fry has collected a fascinating number of Black oral histories about him, whose proliferating details, through their imaginative power, act as authenticators by which belief is made into truth. Such details include the thick rubber soles on his shoes, the burlap on the wheels of his cart, and his long dark cloak. Perhaps most vivid of all, though, is the fact that one of the bodies he sold was that of his wife, whom he killed unwittingly in a dark street. Provided orally and not in the traditional form of archives, these facts are not equally available to all. Gathering them involves becoming familiar with their circulation, gaining the trust of those who own and use them, and offering assurances that neither the trust nor the knowledge will be abused. One cannot walk into this knowledge as one walks into a library, and the fact that Fry is African American has much to do with her ability to gather it. These "weak" facts, weak only because the social formation with access to them is disempowered, are effective because their truths are functional. They warn African Americans of their vulnerability and lack of protection in white cities; the rubber shoes and muffled wheels command a vividness that, in turn, evokes a shudder from the body of the listener, recalling the fear within the Black body in the street. One is also operating here within the realm of a situated logic: body snatchers disguise their approach—not being able to hear or see them does not mean that they are not there. Equally, the knowledge of McKeever mistakenly killing and selling his own wife carries the prophetic truth that Black people who collaborate with whites for selfish and short-term rewards will inevitably end up not only harming their race but themselves.

The effective history of McKeever's nighttime occupation counters not only the documented truth about McKeever, that he was an ordinary Black citizen, but it challenges the production of that truth and the hierarchization of evidence involved. Some facts, which are documented by white information collectors, editors, and publishers, are made "strong" by being technologized into books or journals, and institutionalized into the archive. They, then, contrast and overpower the "weak" facts that are circulated orally among Black people. The strong white facts emerge independent of the social formation experiencing them as events. In a white knowledge system, this exteriority guarantees their objectivity, but in a Black one, it guarantees only their inadequacy: for in this knowledge, whites can know only what Blacks allow them to know. The knowledge of those occupying the same social formation as the object of that knowledge will know truths that are necessarily invisible to the outside observer.

Equally, effective history actively demonstrates that official history represses knowledge whose truth would challenge the social interests of the power bloc that produces and validates it. To document McKeever's nighttime work would be to give it credibility that would, in turn, hinder white power; the repressive and self-interested effects of power are best secured when its benign and productive side is the only visible one. Thus, the exclusion of McKeever's nighttime work from white documentation contains the truth of how whites can write history. This history cannot, therefore, be used to invalidate a Black effective history, in which his night job is thoroughly and accurately articulated, as opposed to simply documented.

Collecting, recording, and documenting information is an urgent concern of the power bloc, as information remains essential to its social control. Selectively documenting others while excluding them from the process of documentation is a strategy of disempowerment against which effective history struggles. The knowledge of the power bloc, with all its technologies and institutionalization of literacy and numeracy, of information collection, storage, and retrieval, necessarily produces more socially powerful truths than those of disenfranchised social formations who are historically and systematically denied equal access to those technologies and institutions of knowledge. Power is always two-faced, always both productive and repressive, benign and selfish; it is most effective, however, when it puts forward its productive, benign face and hides its repressive, selfish one. The benignity with which *Boyd's Directory* makes its facts open and freely available to all hides the repression by which it denies other events, such as McKeever's nighttime job, the status of fact. Contrarily, then, it is these embodied experiences, which strong knowledge systems overlook, that carry the effective truths of the disempowered.

The politics of a counterhistory do not inhere essentially within it; instead, they result from and must be understood according to how it is put into effect. The counterhistory of these body snatchers, for instance, could be put to a very different political use. In the early years of this century, white employers in the South, predominantly former slave owners, were losing their labor force in the great northward migration of African Americans. To counter this, they disseminated among their work force the knowledge that the cities of the North were full of "night doctors," prowling their streets looking for Black bodies to sell to hospitals. In essence, Southern employers exploited for their own purposes a knowledge that ironically resembled a traditional Black tactic. The belief in "night doctors" was already widespread among the Black communities in most Northern cities at the turn of the century. Its origins stemmed from both the Black experience of mysterious disappearances of family and neighbors and from these rumors started by white Southerners. The contradiction between these disparate "origins" exists and persists without one source cancelling out the other because neither touches upon the truth— the knowledge that whites use Black bodies for their own purposes, both for labor and for science. This tradition and the truth it represents long precede either "origin" and continue long after the historical pertinence of both. Each is a tactical appropriation of a more generalized knowledge that uses it effectively in local conditions. This generalized truth and its local application are mutually authenticating, and the two-way exchange between the macro and micro levels of social experience is definitive in the effectiveness of a particular economy of power.

These competing ways of knowing, identified for the moment as white and Black, do not compete on equal terms. The power of knowledge to produce and circulate truth always has technological and institutional dimensions. The white truth of McKeever was technologized into a book and institutionalized into an archive. The Black truth of McKeever remained in oral circulation, with neither technological nor institutional support, until a Black historian, half a century after its active life, inscribed it in a book in a library and, thence, via a white academic, into this article.

The differential power of competing knowledge systems is determined partly by the social evaluation of their epistemological structure, logo-rationalism versus oral "logic"; partly by their material instrumentality, logo-rationalism having more immediate, visible, and measurable effects; partly by the social, economic, and political power of the social formation that uses them; and partly by their access to technology and institutions. Depriving a social formation of knowledge involves limiting access to technology and institutions. The fact that the socially weak are denied equal access to society's technologies and "institutions of truth" does not mean, however, that they are totally excluded from them. The Rodney King case demonstrates that video technology *can* be used to circulate a truth involving the weak; *Black Liberation Radio* does much the same with radio technology. As knowledge has to be stored and circulated for its power to be realized, it is inherently vulnerable to guerrilla raids, much as a raid upon an armory would equip those whom the weapons were intended to subdue. The practice of effective history involves not only the recovery of excluded or overlooked materials but also guerrilla raids upon the dominant knowledge system; both the archive and the armory are valuable targets for the guerrilla.

M'banna Kantako is proud of his "knowledge gangsters" who "steal information from any one." In Fragments 7–15, I reproduce some of the booty brought back by one of these information guerrillas. The guerrilla in question, Zears Miles, traces his interest in U.S. Chemical and Biological warfare to his receiving a program produced by AFRTS—the Armed Forces Radio and Television Service—on his shortwave radio in November 1970.

> **Fragment 7:** *Zears Miles:* This program was a talk called "Ethnic Weapons," and you have to understand that when white people talk about ethnic weapons, they mean diseases that other people can contract but they cannot. (He quotes a military scientist.)

>> One of the basic strategies of war is to destroy members of certain nations or ethnic groups while sparing other populations; so it would be necessary to create chemical or biological agents that limit their efforts to targeted groups. Southeast Asians, for example, have a different genetic composition than do Caucasians. It is, therefore, possible that these people are susceptible to diseases Westerners are not, and we know that is true. . . .

>> Blood types that we call A, B, O, and Rh appear in different frequencies among different types of people; for example, blood type B almost never occurs in American Indians but accounts for almost 40% of certain populations in Southeast Asia. . . .

> **Fragment 8:** *Zears Miles:* In 1942, Secretary of State Stimson suggested to President Roosevelt hiding the Germ Warfare Advisory Group in the New Deal Welfare Agency called the Federal Security Agency that oversaw the Public Health Service . . . Now we all recall the Tuskegee experiment that started in 1932 and went to 1972 under the Public Health Service . . . now you have the Chemical and Biological Warfare Department and the Public Health Service sharing the same Budget.

> **Fragment 9:** *Zears Miles* (quoting from the 1970 *Congressional Record,* House Bill 15090, Part V, page 129): George McArthur of the Chemical and Biological Warfare Department of the Pentagon is recorded as saying:

>> Within a period of 5–10 years, it would be possible to produce a synthetic biological agent, an agent that does not naturally exist, and for which no natural immunity could have been acquired. . . . A research program to explore the feasibility of this could be completed in approximately 5 years at a total cost of $10 million.

Fragment 10: *Zears Miles* (quoting selections from the *Bulletin of the World Health Organization,* 1972, Vol. 47, pp. 215–438, Recommendation #3):

> An attempt should be made to ascertain whether viruses can, in fact, exercise selective effects upon immune functions, that is, say, by suppressing 7-S versus 19-S antibodies or by affecting T-cell functions as opposed to B-cell functions.

Later, Zears Miles calls this "an engineering specification for AIDS."

Fragment 11: *Zears Miles* reads selections from the *Archive Pathological Laboratory America,* Vol. 110, Aug. 1986, "OKT-4 Epitome Deficiency in Significant Proportions of the Black Population" and summarizes the paper:

> The AIDS virus is basically a T-cell destroyer. . . . Now this is the very thing that they found out in our genetic make-up that is different in us than white people, because our T-cell counts, at least those of us who have a low T-cell count, are ten times lower than those of the average white person.
>
> . . . Another effect of this [genetic difference] is that the tests for the AIDS virus are, in fact, insensitive to Black people's genetic make-up.

Fragment 12: *Zears Miles* summarizes a paper in the *Journal of the American Medical Association,* Jan. 20, 1985, Vol. 255, n. 23, called "Surveillance for AIDS in a Central African City, Kinsasha, Zaire":

> Table 2 gives the possible means of exposure to the AIDS virus of 144 men with AIDS: the highest number of the possible means of exposure is one category, OK, and for 154 women the largest number, 82, was under the same category; the category is "Medical Injection." And the next highest category, the next largest means of contracting the virus, 32 for men, 41 for women, is "Hospitalization". . . . In the full list of means of infection, neither homosexuality nor intravenous drug use occur.

Fragment 13:

Zears Miles: A front-page article in the London *Times* on May 11, 1987, headlined "Small Pox Vaccine Triggered AIDS

Virus," second paragraph "The World Health Organization . . ." is that familiar?

M'banna Kantako: Who?!

Zears Miles: The World Health Organization, you will recall I read last time I was on, how they had an engineering specification drawn up for the AIDS virus, remember that?

M'banna Kantako: Yes sir!

Zears Miles: The paragraph in the London *Times* says the same organization, the World Health Organization, which "masterminded a 13-year campaign, is studying new scientific evidence suggesting that immunization with the smallpox vaccine awakens the unsuspected dormant human immunodefense virus infection, HIV." An advisor to WHO who disclosed the problem told the *Times:* "I thought it was just coincidence, until we studied the latest findings about the reaction which can be caused by vaccinia. Now I believe the smallpox vaccination theory is the explanation of the explosion of AIDS in Africa." Now, over in the second column: "The World Health Organization information indicated that the AIDS league table of Central Africa matches the concentration of vaccinations, the largest spread of HIV infection coincides with the most intense immunization programs with the number of people immunized being as follows: Zaire—36,878,000" (that is 100% of the population), "Zambia—19,060,000 injected" (100% of the population), . . .

M'banna Kantako: We're talking about all Africa now . . .

Zears Miles: Exactly, "Tanzania—14,972,000" (75% of the population) . . .

M'banna Kantako: Brother, brother, is what you're saying to us, according to these devils writing themselves, that if you want to find out where the most number of AIDS cases will be, find out where they've given the most vaccinations?

Zears Miles: Exactly . . .

M'banna Kantako: Oh man, oh man.

Zears Miles: . . . the smallpox vaccine, the WHO's eradication campaign, and we have mentioned that it was the World Health Organization that submitted to laboratories around this country an engineering specification to make the AIDS virus.

Fragment 14:

Zears Miles: In another report, the World Health Organization has estimated that there will be 75,000,000 Africans dead of AIDS because of these vaccines by the year 1995.

M'banna Kantako: 87% of people on the planet that have AIDS are Black.

Zears Miles: Exactly.

M'banna Kantako: When they show you the TV programs they're always showing these white people, you know . . .

Zears Miles: Exactly.

M'banna Kantako: . . . because that's part of their game . . .

Zears Miles: . . . that's part of the image they're trying to paint . . .

M'banna Kantako: They're reversing, just like the crack thing, when they want to talk about cocaine, they show young black men, yet 80% of those addicted, according to the Senate Foreign Relations Committee Report, April 1989, 80% are white . . .

Zears Miles: Exactly.

M'banna Kantako: So they just flip it around. . . .

M'banna Kantako: Let me just interrupt you for a moment, brother. For the brothers and sisters here, it's 9:25 on Monday evening, if you notice a high concentration of pigs in the neighborhood, they're apparently going to create a disturbance; so that you'll stop listening to Brother Zears, they're alleging that someone was trying to shoot at them so they're crawling all over the neighborhood as an attempt to create a diversion.

Fragment 15:

Zears Miles: The base constituents of the AIDS virus are largely that of the visno virus of sheep, a pathogenic lymptovirus, and basic leucemia virus of cattle.

M'banna Kantako: Break it down here, what you're saying brother is that it is actually nothing but a cow and sheep disease brought off in us.

Zears Miles: Yes, and actually to get these cow and sheep diseases, which do not normally cross species to human beings, they took them, spliced them together through a recombinant DNA or gene splicing technology and then grew them in a human cell culture called the "hela-cell," which is short for Henrietta Lack, who was a Black woman who died of cervical cancer in 1953 out of Chicago, kept her tumor alive [sic], and now it's the standard medium for virus and bacteriological development in laboratories. So the AIDS virus itself was actually grown in a Black woman's cell culture being kept alive since 1953.

>   *M'banna Kantako:* And you know who they made it for.
>   *Zears Miles:* That's who they made it for.

I have emphasized the fragmentedness of these bits of pur-
loined information. On *Black Liberation Radio,* they are linked more
explicitly, but the links are associative rather than causal or logical.
Their power lies in the affective impact of each piece of loot and
then in the overall message of genocide. The word "genocide" is
not easily applied by whites to their own history and its strategies,
though there is a reluctant and limited acceptance that the history
of white relations with Native Americans has been and continues
to be genocidal. In contrast, the word is widely used among a significant proportion of African Americans; it appears frequently on
Black Liberation Radio, on *WLIB* in Harlem, and in the Black press.
An article in *Essence* entitled "AIDS: Is It Genocide?" (Bates) is only
one further example. I have detailed in *Power Plays* how the experience of apparently autonomous white policies adds up to a picture of genocide if one is on the suffering end of them; these include the location of toxic waste dumps and other polluters in
Black neighborhoods, the focus of tobacco and alcohol advertising
upon Blacks, the combination of drugs, guns, and the drug wars
to weaken Black communities, the systematic denial of education
and employment, and so on.

Within this Black knowledge of genocide, Zears Miles's pur-
loined fragments need only to be associated with each other, for
the connections between them preexist them in Black knowledge.
Let me just demonstrate what happens when these stolen fragments are tossed into one bag of loot: (a) The Biological and
Chemical Warfare Department has a long-standing research program for an "ethnic weapon." (b) Blacks tend to have lower T-cell
counts than whites. (c) The AIDS virus is not natural but was developed in a laboratory and relies on T-cell deficiency. (d) The WHO
is associated with both the development of the virus and its dissemination throughout Africa. (e) The WHO, like the PHS in the
Tuskegee experiment, is a white medical organization operating in
the nonwhite world.

The history at work here is a counterhistory in a number of
ways. At the macro level, the history of white genocide of non-
whites counters the white one that no such thing exists, and if it

does, it does so only as a form of black paranoia. This counterhistory challenges, too, in the sense that its writing and disseminating counter the process by which this genocide is occluded from white knowledge. Further, the process of gathering it is an antagonistic process; Zears Miles constantly recounts the difficulty he has in getting this information and often glosses his victories with comments like "the ancestors must have been working because . . ." Conversely, when the "raid" is an easy one, he will comment on the ineptitude of whites who appear to not realize the strategic value of the information he obtained so readily. Interestingly, M'banna Kantako often reads this phenomena differently; for him, whites are so arrogant in their power that they see little need to hide its oppression under benignity and little fear that it can be turned against them. "In your face, man" is a common expression of his when he meets naked power that one would normally expect to be decently covered up.

The norm is that whites guard knowledge that is strategically useful and attempt to prevent it from getting into the wrong hands and being turned against them. They also try to prevent counterknowledge from being disseminated. Such, for instance, is the claim of Barbara Justice, M.D., a Black physician in New York, who broadcasts regularly on *WLIB* in Harlem and occasionally on *Black Liberation Radio*. In her work with AIDS sufferers, she tells listeners, the white conservative medical professional does everything it can to silence her argument that the treatment of AIDS must recognize its racial dimension, the fact that statistically it is an African disease above all else. Both worldwide and in Harlem, it is the number one killer of Blacks. She argues that the accepted white treatments, of AZT and interferon, produce side effects that are as damaging as the disease itself; she also describes an African treatment developed in Kenya, called Kemron, and claims that the few Black patients she has been able to send over there have responded far better than with white treatments: so much better, indeed, that no one who was treated while the virus was in its asymptomatic stage has yet developed full-blown AIDS.

Further, she details the white medical establishment's constant attempts to suppress information about this African treatment and calls herself "a warrior queen" fighting for her people. She tells how vulnerable and lonely she felt until the Nation of

Islam came to her support. This sense of vulnerability was not a product of her imagination: her house has been broken into and her records rifled through. As Justice is a scientist, her conclusions may be limited to what she can prove, but she still concludes that AIDS is genocidal, if not in origin then certainly in the way it is being handled.

Jack Felder, a Black biochemist who has worked in U.S. Germ Warfare laboratories and who has authored and self-published a book called *AIDS: U.S. Germ Warfare At Its Best,* provided an argument similar to that of Justice. On *Black Liberation Radio,* he delivers information that supports and sometimes repeats that given by Zears Miles. As supporting evidence of the ethnic weapons program, for example, he tells of the attempt to produce a chemical gas that would bind to melanin but not to white skin and reminds listeners that white Americans gave Native Americans clothes and blankets that had been infected with smallpox. He repeats the estimate of 75,000,000 Africans killed by AIDS in this decade and refers to the disease as a strategy to depopulate Africa and U.S. ghettos. In the U.S., immunization clinics work in Black neighborhoods as WHO does in Africa and are notably absent in white neighborhoods, leading Felder to conclude that the policy is deliberate.

On another program, Bryan Harris tells of a Black worker in a vaccine laboratory in California who inadvertently switched the addresses on two parcels of the "same" vaccine: the one that had been designated for a Black clinic was sent to a white one, and vice versa. His account of the laboratory's desperate scramble to retrieve the parcels and readdress them becomes yet another "telling fragment" in the counterhistory of the recent past. This sort of counterhistory depends upon a proliferation of "telling" details whose interconnections are not explicitly traced because the tellingness of each detail reverberates with that of others, finally revealing what is already known—in this case, genocide. And this counterhistory is effective history, whose function is, in the words of Del Jones, another of the station's information guerrillas, "to help us save ourselves." Its truth is not to be measured by objectivity but by effectivity. What is true is what can be made to work, which is, in essence, how the laws of physics establish their truth—especially quantum physics: no one knows how its formulae work, they know simply that they do.

Sometimes this effectiveness is directly instrumental and results in frequent warnings to African Americans to be very wary of the white medical system. These vary from the advice of Dr. Barbara Justice, that Black patients should seek out doctors that understand them both as individuals and as Black; to M'banna Kantako's warning, that Black mothers should take afterbirths home to prevent them from being used in research hostile to Blacks and to prevent their genetic make-up from being stored as identifying information about their children; to Dr. Jack Felder's call, that African Americans will be safe only when they have developed their own health system. If some whites, with their widespread belief in the benevolence of medicine, are tempted to dismiss this Black mistrust as paranoia, they should listen to Dr. John Heller, the Director of Venereal Diseases at the Public Health Service from 1943 to 1948. Of the men in the Tuskegee study, he said, "The men's status did not warrant ethical debate. They were subjects, not patients: clinical material, not sick people" (Thomas and Quinn 1501).

Similarly, African Americans know that they must guard themselves against the white knowledge and the white history presented as truth in the education system. M'banna Kantako educates his children at home, Dr. Leonard Jeffries was demoted for refusing to conform to white educational norms in New York's City College, and Dr. Jack Felder claims simply that, "[i]f we are to survive as a race, we cannot let whites educate our children and we cannot let whites be in charge of our health" (47).

Black knowledge of white genocidal strategy does not involve only the details of its application but also encompasses its motivation. For instance, *Black Liberation Radio* reminds its listeners frequently that whites are the global minority, only 7% of its population, yet they control the majority of its wealth and its resources. One U.S. government document frequently referred to in this context is *Global 2000*, a report prepared by the Carter administration on the world's population, resources, and environment. Let M'Banna Kantako summarize what it means to him:

> *M'banna Kantako:* Brothers and sisters, in *Global 2000* what the devil said is, look, for us to continue to get the resources of the earth the way we get them—no charge, we take them—we need to make sure there aren't enough people to

pose any opposition by the year 2000. Now, they were saying that by the year 2000, there would be something like 6.3 billion people on earth, and what they said was, in order for us to stay in control, we might need to kill 2.4 billion of them. But this is something more that we need to add to this whole thing here; now they're saying that there might be 10.2 billion people on earth by the year 2000, and if they stick with the percentage, you know, they're talking about wiping off almost 5 billion people.

Jack Felder: Possibly . . . these people are serious, man.

M'banna Kantako: Another thing about it, what they might have to do to do it—wipe out about 2 million different species of plants and animals, which will cause, you know, the temperature of the planet to rise which will cause flooding, it might wipe out the planet, but they were that bent on wiping billions out that they didn't care.

Kantako and Jack Felder have just spoken of the 75 million Africans expected to die of AIDS before the year 2000 and continue reminding listeners of the almost successful genocide of Native Americans and Australian Aboriginals and the total genocide of native Tasmanians.

Global 2000 has become a cardinal document in this Black knowledge of genocide. Its argument for population control, so that the population of the world can be kept in balance with its resources, is decoded unequivocally as a policy for "controlling" or, as Kantako would put it, "wiping out" the people of the "Third World" so that its resources can continue to maintain the white world.

Other stolen fragments of knowledge are brought back into Black territory to support this truth.

Fragment 16: *Zears Miles,* reading from *Policy Planning Study 23,* Feb. 1948, labelled "Top Secret" and written by George Kinnon, a State Department Planner: "We have about 50% of the world's wealth but only 6.3% of its population. In this situation, we cannot but be the object of envy and resentment. Our real task in the coming period is to devise a pattern of relationships which will permit us to maintain this position of disparity. To do so, we will have to dispense with all sentimentality and daydreaming, and our attention will have to be concentrated everywhere on our immediate national objectives. We need not deceive ourselves that we can afford today the luxury of altruism and world benefaction. We should cease to talk about vague and unreal objectives such as" (now, pick up on this) "human rights, the raising of the living standard and democratization."

M'banna Kantako: Oh man, they don't care about no stuff like human rights, no sir.

Fragment 17: *Zears Miles,* reading from *National Security Memorandum # 200* written by Henry Kissinger: "Reduction of the population in those states"—that is, the Third World and the so-called developing countries—"is a matter of vital U.S. national security. The U.S. economy will require large and increasing amounts of material from abroad, especially from less developed countries. That fact gives the U.S. enhanced interest in the political, economic, and social stability of the supplying countries. Whenever a lessening of population can increase the prospects of such stability, population policy becomes relevant to the resources, supplies, and economic interests of the U.S."

M'banna Kantako: In plain simple language, he's saying that in order for us to take the minerals from these people, we've got to ensure that there aren't enough of them to fight us back.

Zears Miles: Exactly.

The effective history, constituted by the interplay of these fragments, has characteristics that clearly differentiate it from official history and that official history might use to discredit it. Its motivation is not objective but explicitly political. It knows that the truth that it seeks is not merely lying overlooked and unnoticed by official history, but rather that the truth has been deliberately hidden, and that hiding it is another application of the racial power that would cultivate the AIDS virus in a Black woman's body. The effectiveness of a genocidal strategy depends directly upon the success of it remaining hidden.

The stolen fragments, forming the material of this history, effectively render the hidden visible. There is no need to understand them in terms of their explicit contextual relations—the rest of the documents from which they are extracted are discarded as valueless. In fact, in general, the document as a whole is not interpreted and not included in the counterhistory. Occasionally, when the discards are "included" in the counterhistory, they are typically treated as "evidence" of a white cover-up. The London *Times* report detailing the coincidence of AIDS and the WHO's vaccination campaign in Africa pointedly includes the statement that "no blame can be attached to the WHO." When Zears Miles reads this out over the radio, Kantako's laughter is both delighted and skeptical. The lack of direct evidence of the WHO's intention to spread AIDS may indicate either that the intention did not exist or that it has been successfully hidden. *Black Liberation Radio* has no doubts about its position in this dilemma.

Interpretation depends upon the construction of relationships. Events, objects, statements do not carry their own meaning but are made to mean by the relations in which they are involved. I am here referring to the double process of articulation that Stuart Hall identifies as central to the making of meaning in "On Postmodernism . . ." The one side of articulation is a process of flexible linking while the other is that of speaking or of disseminating the meaning that is produced by the linkage. The fact that white civilian hospitals use Black bodies for research may be linked to medical science, in which case, the Blackness of the bodies does not mean anything; or, on the other hand, it may be linked to the Chemical and Biological Warfare Department's search for an "ethnic weapon," in which case, it means everything.

For instance, one of the "facts" of the Tuskegee experiment was the observation that Blacks appeared to be more susceptible than whites to syphilis, and there was interest in discovering if this was the case, and if so, why. Articulated with and in the humane discourse of medicine, this "interest" easily leads to the conclusion that such a physiological difference could be used to devise treatments for Blacks and, thus, minimize the relative difference in the health of Blacks and whites. However, when this is articulated with the facts that "health differences" between whites and Blacks are increasing, not decreasing—the differential spread of AIDS is joined, for example, by differences in life expectancy, infant mortality, and hypertension—and when these linked "facts" are articulated within a knowledge of genocidal strategy, the original "fact" means something very different.

Facts never exist independently or in isolation but rather in articulation with others. Their very facticity is a function and product of their discursive relations. Reusing them, therefore, involves disarticulating them from one set of relations and rearticulating them into another. They are never simply inert, like pebbles on a beach, waiting to be picked up by whoever finds them first. While no fact has any essential existence or meaning of its own, it always has the potential for dis- and rearticulation. Evaluating a fact's significance, which always involves assessing both how much it matters and what it means, is, thus, a matter of evaluating its potential articulations, their social location and pattern of interests, and their predicted or interpreted effectivity. The constitution of a historical fact is an articulation. Stealing facts, therefore, involves disarticulation.

Writing a history through and of stolen fragments may also be understood by de Certeau's metaphor of poaching as described in *The Practice of Everyday Life*. The terrain of knowledge is owned and controlled by the enemy; the poacher darts in and out, taking what he or she needs, extracting it not only from the physical territory of the landowner, but also from his social relations—ownership, legality, exclusivity. The researcher as poacher has to avoid being caught by the articulation or ways of knowing of the owner; he or she has to guard against being captured by the discursive and social relations within which the quarry is already held. Producing an effective history, then, is necessarily a practice of social antagonism; it is a counterpractice. Poaching information from the *Times* involves avoiding capture by the knowledge that the WHO is not to blame for the explosion of AIDS in Africa and by the knowledge that the intention of the WHO is to improve the life expectancy of Africans.

This investigation of poaching or stealing, then, leads me to a major difference between the counterhistory I have told here and Foucault's theorizings. Though he is explicit that an effective history is not objective, but affirms "knowledge as perspective" ("Nietzsche" 140), and though he hints that an effective history is about the socially subordinate, he seems not to believe that it can be produced by them. For him, effective history is produced by academics like himself who are opposed to traditional history. Indeed, he says it can only be written after "a vast accumulation of source material" and by "relentless erudition." His accounts of the events concerning Damien, the regicide (*Discipline and Punish*), and Jouy, the peasant of Lagocourt (*The History of Sexuality*), exemplify his effective history; they are events where social power is meticulously applied to the bodies of the socially subordinate. While this effective history may be *of* them, and even *for* them, it is distinctly not *by* them. Damien and Jouy do not tell their own stories or participate in the writing of their own history as do M'banna Kantako and Zears Miles. In his account of Pierre Rivière (*Power and Knowledge*), Foucault's erasure of the voice of the peasant is even more striking, because Rivière wrote his own account of his crime. Foucault, however, uses his memoir only "to render visible the medical and juridical mechanism that surround the story" (*Power and Knowledge* 49) and suggests that the other possible uses of it are those by psychoanalysts and criminologists. The words of the peasant are treated as an extended confessional that renders him a knowable object of powerful others and denies him the status of a knowledge producer. Foucault's Pierre Rivière is no Zears Miles.

Zears Miles does, however, fit Foucault's prescription for a genealogist in that he accumulates and circulates vast quantities of research material, and his erudition is totally relentless, but his history is effective only because this research is grounded in and motivated by his own lived experience of being an African American. The history of his race is written in him as well as in the documents he raids and the knowledge he helps to produce. This continuity between the body of the historian and the body of knowledge is something I recognize in *Black Liberation Radio* but not in Foucault, for its locally grounded "knowledge gangsters" are not Foucault's "specific intellectuals" though they do share some characteristics with them (*Power and Knowledge*). Foucault uses the concept of the "specific intellectual" to criticize that of the "intellectual," particularly as used by the left, as one who speaks universal justice and truth. Specific intellectuals work not universally, but within a knowledge sector, and though Foucault allows that they may thus have a more concrete awareness of struggle and may be closer to the proletariat, as he expands his account and provides examples, it becomes clear that they are typified best as discipline specific experts who contribute their "local knowledge" to the dominant regime of truth. Their specificity is "linked, in a society like ours, to the general function of an apparatus of truth" (*Power and Knowl-*

edge 132) and not to the social conditions of those whose counter-truth they are producing. "Local" thus means "limited" as opposed to "universal" and not "grounded in a particular social position"; the politics of the two meanings are diametrically opposite. While his examples are all ones of professionals working within bourgeois institutions, Foucault does allow that a specific intellectual may be "the organic intellectual of the proletariat," engaged in "a battle about the status of truth and the economic and political role it plays" (*Power and Knowledge* 132). He thus opens up a space for the likes of Zears Miles and M'banna Kantako, even if he never particularizes who might occupy it.

These Black knowledge gangsters are finally, I think, better characterized as organic, rather than specific, intellectuals. Gramsci's "organic intellectual" is one who analyzes the experience of his or her social formation from within and, thus, makes it available for forging alliances with others. Popular blocs are formed by alliances that cross class, racial, and gender lines, and they depend upon the organic intellectual to make the insider's analysis of social experience accessible to outsiders. In this model of research, the outsider—historian, sociologist, anthropologist—does not enter a subordinated social formation to dig up its truths, but rather he or she listens to the intellectuals within it. As I read Foucault, I cannot doubt that the whole of his humane sympathy, his limitless generosity of heart, lies with the victims of the power systems he analyzes so devastatingly. However, he never admits that those victims can contribute to their own analysis; he never admits that the victims of history can also be its rewriters. The guerrilla historians on *Black Liberation Radio* expose his limitations in a way that I think he would have been quick to recognize had he had the opportunity to listen to them.

So, where do I stand in all this? I have invoked Foucault, I have invoked Gramsci, and like them, obviously, I am white and an academic. I am aware of the risks involved in writing this article, but I cannot find ways of avoiding them—except by not writing, by not engaging with the issues at all. I have tried to listen to Black voices without colonizing them, without making those Black activist intellectuals into my ventriloquist's dummy. I have tried not to write an academic version of *Mississippi Burning*—I do not want to be a white gone South to help Black people solve their problems—

for African Americans know their situation within white racism far better than any white can and, thus, know the tactically appropriate moves by which to counter it.

White racial power is still a problem for whites as well as for Blacks. If we are to avoid a race war, we have to rein in white power; we have to withdraw from occupied territory to leave space wherein Americans of color can control more of the immediate conditions of their lives. And we, whites, although positioned quite differently in the struggle, must find ways of engaging in it without colonizing, disempowering, or speaking for African Americans, Native Americans, Latina/os, and everyone else except our fellow Caucasians.

This is not easy. Even finding the language with which to speak is a problem; most white discourses are, because of our history, colonizing discourses. I have set the Black voices I have listened to alongside a white theoretical discourse in an attempt to forge an alliance between the two that does not use white theory merely to colonize Black experience. I have real doubts about my achievement here, but I've learned a lot by trying.

I hope, too, that the bridge between discourses, to the extent that I have been able to build one, will help to further facilitate Black knowledge's move into white society and, perhaps, that the familiarity of theory may reduce the defensive, kneejerk reaction of many whites, particularly male ones, when faced with evidence of genocide. The respectability of theory, and poststructuralism is respectable only on the margins of academia, may serve to increase the acceptability of knowledges that might otherwise be resisted because of the otherness of both their content and their origins. Some of the comforting familiarity that theoretical discourse offers white academics may seep into the less familiar and much less comfortable discourse of Black knowledge guerrillas. If coating the pill with sugary theory makes it more ingestible, it's worth it.

If Black information guerrillas are the organic intellectuals I believe them to be, then one use of the analysis they produce must be to form alliances between those in other social formations. And "the public intellectual," to introduce another term into the paradigm, may well function best as a point where such alliances may be formed and facilitated. Foucault is persuasive in his argument that the traditional concept of "the intellectual," like that of "the author," has lost the value it once had, but the function of the public intellectual remains too important for us to dismiss it with the rest of the modern. In a postmodern society, it may help to think of her or him as a relay station, scanning the discursive resources of a society in order to bring ones originating in different social formations into pertinent conjunction and then to relay on into social circulation the resulting discursive recombination. "The public intellectual," then, is a function in a process, rather than a named individual, and "public intellectualizing" can be understood as the process of rearticulating selected knowledges—dominant, local, and counter—that constitute and contest the current regime of truth, and of relaying onward whatever newly effective, critical, and jolting knowledge may result. The teacher is, of course, one important embodiment of the public intellectual and the classroom one of the most effective relay stations. As relay, then, public intellectualizing is one stage in a process that many must join: for public articulation is a social process, within which individual discursive agency, whether exercised as author or teacher, may be necessary, but is neither sufficient nor definitive.

Articulation in the discursive realm is the equivalent of alliance building in the social. I hope, then, that this article may serve as a stage in that process around which discursive and social alliances may be extended and put into practice, and its effectivity, if any, will be judged not by what it says, but by the multiple and unpredictable repercussions of reading it. Its attempt to articulate and engage in dynamic academic and Black activist discourses may contribute to the recognition of the mutuality of social interests among social formations that occupy different positions, and, hopefully, to the activation of that recognition into further discursive and social practice. These alliances are formed among social interests rather than among individuals or social categories or groups, though, of course, interests can only become actualized in individuals and groups while never being coterminus with them. The public is the product of the alliances that are formed and discourses that are circulated. Public intellectualizing operates over only a small area of the social terrain, but the area may be extended, for each practice of public intellectuals potentially provokes more, and the public, thus constituted, may enlarge as its members engage in the process. The postmodern public, then, is a socially partial, self-constituting formation in constant process, never an entity reachable in its entirety; it is not the structurally defined public sphere of Habermasian modernity.

While the name of the author or intellectual may no longer identify an essential individual, it still serves, as Foucault reminds us, as a discursive organizer and as a point where power is both exerted and experienced. The name of this author, for example, appears not only on this and other publications but also on a university organization chart, a paycheck, an office door, and a teaching schedule. In its power relations, the name inserts "me" into an institutional system at numerous points of privilege, not least of which is a position from which to speak in public. As a result, "I" has more power than most of M'banna Kantako's listeners to rearticulate his discourse with others and to relay the result onward into different social formations. This does not make "me" into a more effective intellectual than "him"—far from it. It does, however, recognize that my position in the network of public intellectualization is a more privileged one with wider social audibility. I hope that the alliance between us provides a theoretically provocative instance of the potential relations between organic and public intellectuals, a relationship that is interdependent, ahierarchical, and, in its ideal form, mutually supportive.

The social extension of discourse is risky business, and the public intellectual must not forget that the most important function of a local knowledge, such as that of AIDS as genocide, is to defend and preserve its own community. Further, he or she must take all possible steps to ensure that any external uses of it in alliance building do not weaken that central, internal one. Even though we have to tread carefully, we must walk down the road. *Black Liberation Radio*'s knowledge of white society is a counterknowledge whose importance extends beyond its originating social formation, but in extending its circulation, the intellectual must guard against becoming a power-reversed information guerrilla; he or she must not, in the privileged position of power, steal knowledge from the "weak" and use it for interests that may oppose those of its originators. It is, therefore, very important to me that M'banna Kantako takes time out from his nonstop schedule to read what I write about his work and that he approves of my attempts to extend its reach. He is willing to run the risk that hostile readers, and there will certainly be some, may attack him with it, in the belief that sympathetic readers will support him discursively, politically, and financially. He believes not only that the extension of *Black Liberation Radio*'s knowledge into certain areas of white society take interracial relations a step in the right direction, but also that it will help to secure his position locally, for the more that the socially privileged know and approve of his work, the harder it will be for the authorities to shut him down. At the very least, if and when he is brought to trial for illegal use of the airwaves, his string of witnesses may be both lengthened and socially diversified.

A popular bloc, as Gramsci explained it, is produced by an alliance formed across the lines that divide us of race, class, gender, age, and all the other power-bearing categories of difference. Public intellectualizing plays an important role in this process. However, the alliances that hopefully result can be effective only if those of us who enter them from the side of privilege, and I assume most of the readers of *Cultural Critique* will do so, are prepared to learn from our deprivileged allies. We must take care to avoid the white liberal trip of offering *our* solutions, however benevolently, to *them*. Those whites who wish to stave off the, possibly inevitable, racial war in this country will best be able to form effective interracial alliances by trying to understand the struggle from our potential allies' points of view and not by devising tactics, however well intentioned, that make sense only from our own, much more secure, positions. M'banna Kantako believes that the social formation for, to, and about whom he speaks has something to gain from the discursive alliance this article has attempted to forge. I know that the lessons that white, privileged social formations can learn from his local knowledge are urgently necessary, and I only hope they are not too late.

Notes

A shorter version of this article was presented at the *Console-ing Passions* Conference, Tucson, April 1994.

1. The quotations from *Black Liberation Radio* are from my book *Media Matters*, but the theoretical framework within which they are discussed is original to this article. For a fuller account of *Black Liberation Radio*, see my *Power Plays Power Works*.

Works Cited

Bates, Keith. "AIDS: Is It Genocide?" *Essence* 21 (1989): 77–116.
De Certeau, Michel. *The Practice of Everyday Life*. Berkeley: U of California P, 1984.
Felder, John. *AIDS: U.S. Germ Warfare at Its Best, with Documents and Proof.* Self-published. P.O. Box 203, Springfield Gardens, NY 11413. 1989.
Fiske, John. *Media Matters*. Minneapolis: U of Minnesota P, 1994.
———. *Power Plays Power Works*. London: Verso, 1993.
Foucault, Michel. *Discipline and Punish*. London: Allen Lane, 1977.
———. *The History of Sexuality*. Vol. 1. Hammondsworth.: Penguin, 1978.
———. "Nietzsche, Genealogy, History." *Language, Counter-Memory, Practice*. Ed. D. Bouchard. Ithaca: Cornell UP, 1977. 139–164.
———. *Power/Knowledge: Selected Interviews and Other Writings 1972–1977*. Ed. Colin Gordon. New York: Pantheon, 1980.
Fry, Gladys-Marie. *Night Riders in Black Folk History*. Knoxville: U of Tennessee P, 1975.
Hall, Stuart. "On Postmodernism and Articulation." *Journal of Communication Inquiry* 10.2 (1986): 45–60.
Thomas, Stephen, and Sandra Quinn. "Public Health Then and Now: The Tuskegee Syphilis Study 1932–1972: Implications for HIV Education and AIDS Risk Education Programs in the Black Community." *American Journal of Public Health* 81.11 (1991): 1498–1505.

Strategic Credulity: *Oz* as Mass Cultural Parable

Helen M. Kim

The need to move beyond the restrictive dichotomies established by theories of the mass media is urgent. Jean Baudrillard provides the starkest characterization of this state of affairs in
the opening of his article, "The Masses: The Implosion of the Social in the Media": "Up to now there have been two great versions
of the analysis of the media (as indeed that of the masses), one
optimistic and one pessimistic" (577). While the "optimistic" side of
the debate is perhaps more easily dismissed as uncritical populism,
celebrating mass culture as "the most authentic register of popular
desires" (McCabe 7), the "pessimistic" side has generated more serious critical consequences. Chief among these is a profound nega-
tivism, precluding the possibilities of change. As Tony Bennett
points out, historically:

> [a]lthough [the Frankfurt theorists] condemned reality in
> round terms, they had no positive suggestions to make as to
> how it might be changed. Counterposing to "that which is" an
> ideal conception of "that which ought to be," but unable to
> locate any concrete social mechanisms whereby the gap be-

© 1996 by *Cultural Critique*. Spring 1996. 0882-4371/96/$5.00.

tween the two might be bridged, the result of their criticism was merely to leave everything as it is. ("Theories" 47)

Consequently, such conceptualizations of the omnipotence of the mass media have led to an alienating, and often disturbingly elitist, view of "'the people' as the innocent but also, by implication, ignorant dupes of a capitalist conspiracy":

> It's small wonder that, subjected to such a hectoring discourse, people stopped listening. It's not possible to win the hearts and minds of the people if they are conceived as so hopelessly corrupted from the outset that no discursive space is created in which—not as some ideal construct, but in their available forms, necessarily as constituted in the midst of a capitalist culture—they can be spoken both of and to as other than simply objects to be reformed. (Bennett, "Marxist" 13–14)[1]

Without resorting to the comforting banalities of populism, it has become necessary to rethink the political consequences of the contemporary mass media in order to redress this simplistic assignment of "the masses" to the status of Other—of high culture, of the critic.

Studies such as Patrick Brantlinger's *Bread and Circuses* and, more recently, Andrew Ross's *No Respect* chronicle convincingly deep-rooted tendencies in Western culture to anathematize popular entertainment as the source of social decay, contamination, and degeneration. Exposing the self-interest of those attempting to preserve the "purity" of elitist high culture provides an important impetus for reconceptualizing a popular politics of the mass media; however, such work does not go far enough in providing an alternative model.

The work of the Birmingham school, for instance, in collecting more reliable empirical "evidence" of actual patterns of media consumption has provided much needed affirmation of the vitality and creativity of popular agency and of the ways in which subordinated groups are able to appropriate and reshape the texts of consumer culture to their own ends. Yet, because they concentrate largely on working class and youth groups such studies run the risk of romanticizing "the people" as an autonomous source of political resistance as well as marginalized groups as the only ones sufficiently unincorporated in consumer culture to qualify as "the people."

Alternatively, Jean Baudrillard goes to the other extreme by valorizing the very passivity and apathy of media audiences as "an original strategy, an original response in the form of a challenge . . . [which is] ironic and antagonistic" (578). He argues that such passivity can be the only response remaining for those faced with the media's inexorable evacuation of the representational, of the political, and of public space. Self-effacement, while supposedly exerting power on behalf of the masses, however, fundamentally partakes of "radical antimetaphysics" (585), which thwarts the desires of the dominant culture by furthering the destruction of its subjects. Celebrating the negative power of refusal, however, does not so much challenge the basic parameters established by previous media criticism as invert the hierarchical valuations current in "pessimistic" circles. Rather than deploring public apathy, Baudrillard finds positive value in it, without challenging the basic notion that the masses have sunk to the level of "anesthetized zombies." This last bastion of passivity as resistance may preserve them from total colonization; however, it seems capable of little else.

Baudrillard's impulse to locate opposition to the media within its own terms, as the logical outgrowth or reaction to its own mechanisms of domination, is commendable. However, work such as that inspired by the Birmingham School presents compelling evidence that contradicts his thesis of mass refusal as the last remaining tactic open to consumers. Two factors which Baudrillard has overlooked are crucial to reforming our understanding of popular interactions with the media. The first is a recognition that the vast majority of media products market themselves as entertainment, rather than apparatuses of informational control, like the public opinion polls he cites as his example. Baudrillard's choice of this example is indicative of a widespread reluctance to theorize a politics of pleasure which must constitute the heart of commercial media studies:[2] for attempts to evade the codification or official gaze of the public opinion poll differ markedly from attempts to evade the seductive power of pleasure offered by the majority of entertainment media.

The second is a need to look beyond the abstract theorizing of the media as merely a series of negations—of the subject, of public space, of interpersonal communications, of the real, of the tangible. Rather, given the emphasis on pleasure made in my previous point, the evacuation of "all rationality of choice and [of] all exercise of will, of knowledge, and of liberty" (585), which Baudrillard ascribes to the media, may occur in exchange for greater possibilities of gratification and expanded vistas of desire. If we can identify these seductive possibilities more precisely then it might be possible to imagine the media as more than the "other" of metaphysics and, hence, requiring more productive oppositional strategies than mere derisive negation. Underlying both these points is the need to come to terms with a system of political domination which does not function according to the traditional methods of repression, codification, or, indeed, control. Instead, with the media, we are faced with the curious phenomena of a system of power which functions according to its ability to please, to gratify, to fascinate its members, hence requiring very different modes of opposition.

John Fiske strongly stresses the active role the public must play to ensure the commercial success of any commodity by citing instances in which particular marketing campaigns have failed despite strenuous efforts for success: "the people's interests are not those of the industry—as evidenced by the number of films, records, and other products (of which the Edsel is only the most famous) that the people have made into expensive failures" (23). While I, for my own purposes, would like to downplay Fiske's implicit assertion of the public's autonomous will, his remark is central to understanding the peculiar way the mass media constructs its power, which makes it unique among other structures of political domination. For, in exchange for its offer to consumers of the "freedom of choice," with all the risks to itself that entails, the media gains the tactical benefits of appearing to be "innocent" or powerless. This "innocence" is not so much a cynical ruse as the concrete result of the media's deliberately self-inflicted vulnerability to the whims and passions of the consuming public *as a means of* ingratiating itself with, and, hence, gaining a type of power over, them.

Understood in this way, the mass media cannot function as a direct form of political repression as claimed by those of the "pessimistic" school; however, neither does it simply represent a democratic consensus as claimed by those of the "optimistic" school. Rather, it incorporates its viewers into the dominant culture by its very ability to appeal to, or elicit, their desire to derive pleasure from, and mastery over, it. By presenting such a benign and attractive face, the media succeeds in saturating popular culture to a much greater extent than would be possible if it were practicing coercive or repressive measures. To assert the kind of direct control characteristic of overt systems of political domination would be disastrous, as have been attempts by critics to insist that such control actually does occur. This is not to say that, as a result, the people are unaware of the kinds of manipulations being performed on them, but rather that the different nature of those manipulations calls for a very different set of oppositional responses on their part.

Before understanding those oppositional possibilities, it is first necessary to understand more precisely the nature of the media's appeal. One of the many comparisons Baudrillard makes to the behavior of the masses when confronted by the media is that of a misbehaving child (588). In its perpetuation of common perceptions of the media as regressive and infantilizing, Baudrillard's analogy suggests a significant textual genre which informs the media's tactic of ingratiation: that of children's fantasy. Fantasy has long been considered a key component of children's literature from traditional fairy tales to contemporary cartoons. The significance of the subgenre of children's fantasy based on the fairy tale is its preoccupation with magical transformation and utopian transcendence rather than what others have theorized as the psychic "other" of rationality associated with the "darker" Gothic fantastic tradition.[3] If the latter can be considered subversive, the former is utopian and celebratory. With contemporary Western culture's construction of childhood, as a state of freedom from the normal restrictions of the adult world, come fantastic literatures, indulging in the delight and wonder of the impossible. Jack Zipes, writing on the role of the fantastic in children's literature, pinpoints the uncanny correspondences between the fantastic and the contemporary market scene:

> one can hardly walk down a street or into a building without being smacked in the eye with some artifact stamped as "fan-

tastic." . . . lurid and unimaginable book covers inviting the imagination to speculate about the fantastic stories between the covers; sensational photographs and marquees promising films to outfantasize your own fantasy; breath-taking and bizarre advertisements drawn to lure and announce fantastic images. . . . Obviously we are living in the age of fantasia. (187)

If the type of appeal the mass media uses to construct its power is, thus, closely associated with the pleasures offered by children's fantasy, then an examination of the nature of this discourse should reveal more about the way in which it is able to rouse and redirect readerly desires. For the purposes of my argument, the 1939 MGM studio's musical film *The Wizard of Oz* serves as one such exemplary text: both for its sophisticated self-reflexivity about the lures and vulnerabilities of consumer culture and its implicit allegory of American consumerism as reflected by the variegated career of L. Frank Baum, the author of the original children's books.

The spectacular success of Baum's astonishingly innovative and diverse career was due to his astute exploitation of the intersection between the fantastic and modern commodity culture.[4] Remembered today for his authorship of the *Oz* series of children's books, in his time Baum managed a theater chain, dabbled in early photography and motion pictures, excelled as a window dresser, salesman, retail merchant, magazine editor, and showman.[5] The common thread running through all these activities was an intense preoccupation with the material possibilities presented by a burgeoning consumerism for the concrete realization of utopian and fantastic visions. Already in these efforts, we can see the outlines of the paradox which will become crucial in my reconceptualization of the power of the consumer media: this perverse urge to turn into material goods that which implicitly defines itself as "otherworldly," or fantastic.

Cultural historian William Leach vividly describes the spectacles of display and decoration of the era as "surrealist because they tried to invest artificial and material things, while urban spaces, with plasticity and life, breaking down the barriers between the animate and the inanimate. . . . They strove for theatrical effects and for a new enchantment" (100). Innovations in electricity and lighting technology aided such efforts to create the "fairy-tale orientalism that overtook public dream culture" (104). As the architect of such visions, Baum assumed the role of the magician with the power to make even the most fantastic dreams come true. The key to the appeal of his many enterprises was the promise to deliver that which is desirable, precisely because it is undeliverable. Hence, the imaginary world of Oz, which he conjures up in his children's books, can be considered a direct extension of his general effort to articulate the dynamics of a fantastic spectacle that is at once elusive and readily available, in effect reworking the conventions of children's literature to create "the literary apotheosis of commodity flow" (108).

In particular, Baum's *Oz* books are concerned with the "magical" animation of material objects. One of the earliest and most enthusiastic commentators on the series, Edward Wagenknecht, cites but some of Baum's many transformations: The Gump, a machine that can fly by itself; the Sawhorse, turned magically into a living horse; as well as "rubber mountains, submarines, sinking palaces, a vegetable kingdom, a country whose inhabitants are kitchen utensils, [and] a city inhabited by various kinds of baker's products" (26). Stuart Culver makes a strong case for connecting these creations with Baum's efforts to articulate a theory of window dressing, as "unique, perhaps even bizarre, attempt[s] to explain how the manikin functions in the art of advertising by picturing the conditions under which it comes to life" (109). However, if the *Oz* books therefore concern themselves with shifting definitions of physical identity brought on by the advent of manikins and machinery, as Culver argues, then the 1939 Hollywood film *The Wizard of Oz* marks a historical and technological shift of consumer desire toward the representational, rather than the physical realization of fantasies.

Baum's career not only offers rich historical evidence of the development of American consumer culture according to the discourses of the fantastic, but the text of *The Wonderful Wizard of Oz* lends itself beautifully to adaptation into an exemplar of the spectacular, showy musicals which constituted one of the mainstays of Hollywood's popular success. One reason for its suitability is its inherent self-reflexivity over the mechanisms of consumer desire as Baum articulated them. Such strongly marked self-reflexivity is not only particularly well suited to the formal characteristics of the

Hollywood musical, but is actually constitutive of its tremendous popularity. The second aspect of the attractiveness of Baum's stories to the studio producers of the film is their overabundance of detail which is at once technological and fantastical and, hence, ideally suited to the promotion of Hollywood's unique vision of artificial happiness.

My choice of a musical film for this analysis of the media's function, then, is hardly incidental. One of the most critically neglected of film genres, the Hollywood musical traditionally takes as its subject precisely the kind of fantasy "genres [which] have persistently been marginalised, relegated to the realms of escapism and utopia (as has the musical) or classified as suitable mainly for children and adolescents" (Altman, *American Film* 21). Yet, on further inspection, a provocatively contradictory set of formal characteristics emerge: while considered at once "the most escapist of the entertainment arts," the musical also distinguishes itself as "the most reflexive, the most aware of its status and thus the most complex of all the Hollywood genres" (7). I will return to these qualities later in the specific context of my reading of *The Wizard of Oz,* but for now, it suffices to emphasize the infinite regress of a film genre most known for its popularity,[6] which has as its typical subject matter its own popularity. Such a discursive vehicle provides a crucial space in which to map out mass media's internal recognition of its manipulations of popular desire, as it wields those same manipulations to ensure its success as a popular commodity. The paradox inherent in the musical's ability to "pull the wool over its audience's eyes" by *openly demonstrating how it does so,* I would argue, is not exceptional among media texts, but characteristic of their use of the discourses of fantasy to construct their appeal. This paradox, crucially then, makes room for the reader to intervene in the signification of the text, for it opens up a permanent undecidability which requires active intervention on the reader's part, either to support or subvert the system of power the text attempts to, but can never be sure it actually does, support.

The urge to realize utopian fantasies propagated by the mass media, then, paradoxically leads to an acute state of textual self-reflexivity, therein making available unique opportunities for oppositional readings.[7] In its opening scene, *The Wizard of Oz* explicates the conditions under which consumers' desires for the fantastic can be elicited. As a self-reflexive musical, the film presents itself as a frame narrative in order to demarcate clearly the divisions, which underlie its allegorical function, between the real and the fantastic, the natural and the artificial, and the essential and the constructed. And as many commentators on hegemony have noted, one of the crucial imperatives of its successful operation lies in its ability to "naturalize" itself—to make itself seem innate, necessary, and, hence, uncontestable.

Thus, opening in rural, hard-working, plain, and virtuous Kansas, the film grounds Dorothy's magical adventures in the land of Oz firmly in the context of "real" life. The early scenes of her industrious aunt and uncle and their three farm hands, securing their animals and equipment against an approaching storm, are shot in "realistic" sepia tones. The small, bare, weather-worn Kansas farm and the aged, humble appearance of the adults evoke the harshness of midwestern rural life during the droughts and depression of the 1930s. Significantly, the characters' anxiety and haste to prepare for the storm create an atmosphere in which work, responsibility, and industry are of the utmost importance to the preservation of their frail subsistence from an unpredictably destructive nature. Such iconography in the year of the film's release, 1939, strongly enforces a sense of the harsh economic realities of "ordinary," "everyday" American life. Nature, as represented by the land and the weather, dictates the limits circumscribing human existence. The Kansas setting represents the extreme of the natural and the unmediated, against which Dorothy's "wild" flight into the fantastic, utopian, and ultimately mass cultural realm of Oz constitutes an entry into the possibilities of the artificial, mediated, or constructed—possibilities, in other words, which provide the necessary means to critique, contest, and demystify the category of "the natural," which underpins the power of hegemony.

In this scene, the figure of Dorothy stands out not only for her radiant health and youth, but also for her cheerful and playful disregard of the adults' strenuous work. She cuddles the baby chicks that her Aunt Em is frantically trying to move to shelter, balances on the pigpen fence while the farmhands try to corral the animals, and distracts the adults with her petulant and "frivolous" concerns over her pet dog, Toto. As the niece, rather than the true daughter of the two adults, as well as an idle child in their busy world, Dorothy participates in the harsh economy of the farm, yet is a liminal figure in it. In her opening song, which is the audience's first signal that this grimly "realistic" film will, in fact, become a musical, she longs to escape its hardships and go "somewhere over the rainbow" to a place in which "the dreams that you dare to dream really do come true." The American "reality" evoked in the scenes of the Kansas farm establishes the condition of the "natural" from which Dorothy, and, by extension, the viewer, whom the camera aligns with Dorothy, ardently longs to escape. Tilting her face toward the sky, "far, far away, behind the moon, beyond the rain," Dorothy yearns for a magical transcendence of the nature-bound economy of the farm, an explicit reflection of her dissatisfaction with its inability to fulfill her needs and desires. Her first steps toward the threshold of Oz come, crucially, as a reaction against the category of the "natural," not as an expression of her innate, preexisting desires. The "dreams" that she wants "to come true" emerge the moment she feels neglected and misunderstood by the intently pragmatic adults, and, thus, generally resentful of the harsh limitations of her existence. Her singing of "Over the Rainbow" demonstrates the way in which desires to escape the constrictions of the natural arise not independently of it but, instead, in opposition to it. In reference to the cinematic genre conventions, Altman explains that "[t]he escapism of the musical is accomplished only through a constant reference to the world as it is, and this reference is at the very basis of the value displacement" (141–42). Likewise, popular "[e]ntertainment offers the image of 'something better' to escape into, or something we want deeply that our day-to-day lives don't provide. Alternatives, hopes, wishes—these are the stuff of utopia . . ." (Dyer 177).

The arrival of the tornado at the farm, then, serves as the transitional mechanism which allows Dorothy to bridge the gap between "reality" and her seemingly inaccessible "fantasy." In the tornado scenes, nature violently turns the orderly domestic world "upside down": objects break up and fly through the air, Dorothy's dependable family lock themselves underground for shelter, abandoning her, and the distinction between indoors and outdoors blurs as the wind blows plants, animals, and farm equipment into the house, and plates, curtains, and furniture out of the house. In this melee, Dorothy is accidentally locked out of the site of family security and stability—the storm cellar. With literally "no place" to go, socially "dis-placed," she retreats to her bedroom where her window shutter hits her on the head and knocks her out. As the catalyst for this transitional moment in the film, the tornado facilitates the connection between mass culture and the fantastic by playing the role of the master show producer, projecting wondrous scenes for the unconscious Dorothy and, by extension, the film's audience through the window frame as the house is spun and lifted into midair. Here, the "real" slowly becomes transformed into the "unreal" through the uncontrollable violence of the storm. Farm animals float by, two men surrealistically row a boat through the air, and Dorothy's nemesis, Elvira Gulch, rides by on her bicycle only to fade into an image of a witch on a broomstick. When the storm subsides and the house lands on solid ground again, its front doorway, still shot in sepia tones, provides access to the spectacular, almost shocking irruption of the clean, bright, glowing Technicolor world of Oz with plastic flowers, mechanical birds, painted backgrounds, and ethereal, free-floating music. The film's transition to the realm of fantasy is complete once Dorothy steps through the frame, entering the sur-real vision it offers.

As an antidote to the inadequacies of "real life," Oz presents an ultimately paradoxical set of enticements. On the one hand, as is clear from the moment of its early mirage-like appearance, Oz, through its wondrous plentitude, transcends the painful restrictions of a work-based and subsistence-level Kansas economy. Its overabundant delights are freely available because they are magically self-sustaining, rather than created via human materials and labor. Hence, Oz obliterates the gap between desire and fulfillment by overriding the imperative of willful mediation. Its appeal rests in its ability to represent itself as a perfected ideal, a quality of the mass media which Richard Dyer characterizes as its

> "intensity" . . . the capacity to present either complex or unpleasant feelings . . . in a way that makes them seem uncomplicated, direct and vivid, not "qualified" or "ambiguous" as day-to-day life makes them, and without those intimations of self-deception and pretense. (182)

The infinite desirability of this prelinguistic immediacy and plenitude is due to its permanent distance from the deprivations of "real life," and hence constitutes the appeal with which the media seeks to incorporate its audience into its system of power. The childlike passivity it thus engenders comes not so much from a dulling stupor as an indulgence in the pleasures of being catered to without demands for reciprocity, a bypassing of normal economic exchanges.

Yet simultaneous with Oz's promise of a utopian escape comes an acute awareness of the impossibility of its fulfillment, for such an impossibility is the very ground on which its desirability is based. A large degree of the film's *audience's* pleasure at the spectacle of Oz is derived from their appreciation of the prodigious amounts of labor, ingenuity, money, and materials which have clearly gone into the creation of this utopia. The more perfect and convincing the vision, it would seem, the more effort and manipulation are required to achieve it. For *The Wizard of Oz*, for example, studio publicity made it widely known that the making of the film would be a monumental and unprecedentedly lavish undertaking. By May 1938 its projected budget was $3,700,000, "at that time an astounding amount" (Fordin 13), and the film eventually required over 600 actors, 1,000 costumes, 60 sets, and a grand total of 3,200 artisans, craftsmen, laborers, and technicians (Harmetz 206). Far from detracting from the audience's fascination with its vision of Oz, the film's self-conscious revelations of thoroughgoing artificiality—in the shape of its dramatic introduction of Technicolor, exaggeratedly unrealistic set designs, and so on—actually enhances it. This is precisely because an appreciation of the painstaking care required to realize such a vision pushes the finished product to the status of the inaccessible, the impossible. Only because we are aware of how Oz has been constructed can we fully realize how what it represents is radically distant from the "real." Imbedded as a character within the story, Dorothy's evident unhesitating belief in the "reality" of Oz functions for the audience as irony, but irony in the sense that it allows them to pleasurably suspend disbelief while simultaneously reinforcing the artificiality of those very pleasures. Rather than contradicting each other, both effects work hand in hand to constitute the paradoxical appeal of Oz and, hence, in the terms of my allegorical reading, the power of mass culture itself.

The drama of Dorothy's movement between "real" and "utopian" spaces, then, works itself out through the ensuing plot of the film, which immediately reverses itself in the direction of Dorothy's desire to return home. I would like to read her attempt to do so as the film working through the oppositional possibilities open to consumers: to "get out" of mass culture's system of power once they have been enticed into it. Although Dorothy arrives in Oz through violent and coercive means, the transgressive force of the tornado can be read as the strength of her own desire to escape becoming uncontrollable and literally "sweeping her away." Having been, thus, compelled to Oz, Dorothy's first thoughts upon arriving, once she has explored and digested the significance of her surroundings, revolve around finding a way home. She knows that as marvelous as Oz is, she, as a "real person," does not belong there and cannot really remain there. Through Dorothy's refunctioning of her desire, then, the plot registers the audience's own awareness that the marvels of Oz have been purchased entirely conditionally on the film maker's art and that, indeed, the pleasure of witnessing it depends on such an awareness. Thus, the typical self-reflexivity of the Hollywood musical's plot functions as a direct extension of its "simplistic" and "escapist" content, which advertises itself as nothing more than "glossy entertainment that ostensibly has no redeeming social value other than its glossiness" (Smoodin 79). Pure fantasy, which is "too good to be true," generates a backlash that propels the musical's plot toward a self-conscious exploration of the many ways in which that fantasy can be created and manipulated, a tendency, which is at once subversive and constitutive. In order to lure the consumer, mass culture must present utopian fantasies, but in order to make such fantasies appealing, it must ultimately encode a self-conscious awareness of their constructedness. This central paradox allows for oppositional readings which the film, then, chronicles Dorothy enacting.

The figure of the Wizard himself represents the type of power against which Dorothy must struggle, the *deus ex machina* of mass culture. Far from a tyrannical ruler, the Wizard derives his power over the citizens of Oz from their perception of him as "all benevolent" and capable of providing them with everything they desire. Dorothy's pilgrimage to the seat of his power, the Emerald City, represents her growing implicit involvement with the centers of mass cultural power as a necessary prerequisite to her successful escape from them. In other words, it is not "enlightened skepticism" which allows her to prevail over the Wizard but, instead, her unflagging innocence and credulity. As *The Wizard of Oz* allows its

audience to suspend disbelief, Dorothy never questions the truth-
fulness of the Wizard's promises: "Dorothy is, by virtue of her very
presence in fairyland, innocent" (Moore 153). In this sense, the
system of power the Wizard has so carefully and cynically engi-
neered (for "in reality," as we learn, he is a con man)[8] leads to his
downfall not because it fails to be convincing but rather because it
succeeds altogether too well. Petitioning the Wizard with her request to go home, Dorothy puts his "false" power to the test, for
this is the one piece of "magic" he cannot perform. His reply to
her request is, therefore, equivocal, for to admit that this feat is
beyond his powers would be tantamount to a confession that he is
a liar, while to promise something he cannot deliver would equally
run the risk of exposure. The condition which he imposes on
her—that he will deliver her request if she brings him proof that
she has killed the Wicked Witch—is an implicit denial of that request made in order to preserve the facade of his omnipotence, for
it is understood that such a feat is impossible.

Yet, Dorothy and her friends spectacularly fail to "read between the lines" of his reply, instead committing the ultimate fool-
ishness of taking his promise seriously and literally; contrary to all
expectations, they succeed in performing the impossible. Paradoxically, then, it is only because they refuse to acknowledge the limitations of his power that they are brought to light. Confronting the
Wizard with the undeniable proof of their accomplishment, Dorothy and her friends inadvertently force him into a humiliating rev-
elation of his subterfuges. As they stand solemnly before the awe-
some smoke and light display, which they believe to be his actual
presence, Dorothy's little dog Toto—the film's only character who
retains a "natural" skepticism—runs behind a curtain to reveal a
sadly unimpressive little man frantically cranking a machine and
speaking into a microphone. A full confession quickly follows: Oz
is not a "true" Wizard, but only a fast-talking carnival huckster who
happened to land in Oz in his hot air balloon and was adroit
enough to recognize a situation which could be exploited to his
own benefit. The means by which Dorothy and her friends unwittingly engineer his downfall and finally get what they want thus
employ the very mechanisms by which he has constructed his
power.[9]

As a peculiar system of power, which functions according to

its ability to incorporate its participants' desires into its own, the mass media, like the Wizard, cannot be opposed through traditional means of critique and negativity—quite unlike the Wicked Witch who functions as a more traditional villain, and, hence, can be straightforwardly defeated and disempowered. Ironically, in order to satisfy her own agenda, Dorothy must also further the Wizard's. Yet, because his powers are based on an inherent contradiction—promising to deliver what they cannot—there is room within the structures of these powers for her to subvert their intentions. By placing too great a faith in the Wizard's abilities, Dorothy simultaneously exposes their inadequacies and boldly claims for herself benefits which the Wizard cynically believes to be illusory. In this sense, the mass media similarly harnesses the discourses of fantasy to the service of the dominant culture, but because of the series of trade-offs necessary to make those discourses successful, they also offer possibilities for utopian oppositionality in which consumers can claim for themselves the power to imagine "something better," something never intended for them by the dominant culture. Simultaneously able to be popular and supportive of the dominant culture, the mass media nevertheless opens itself up to these vulnerabilities because of its very success. Like "the people," Dorothy is neither a passive victim nor the active creator of mass culture but, instead, claims the ability to intervene in its discourses through a manipulation of its dependence on her good will. Because the power of the mass media is dependent upon the people's perception of "free choice" in the matter of their participation (it must seem to be what they, and not their social superiors, "want"), this risk of inviting pleasurable subversions is always present.

Several critics of the media have convincingly identified its utopian potential as the grounds on which to locate a politics of popular pleasure able to redeem a fatalistic "pessimism." Robert Stam, for instance, declares the need to "appreciate rather than deplore the fact of mass-mediated pleasure, embracing it as a potential friend while critiquing its alienation" (238), and to that end suggests that:

> to explain the public's attraction to a medium, one must look not only for ideological manipulation but also for the kernel of utopian fantasy whereby the medium constitutes itself as a

projected fulfillment of what is desired and absent within the
status quo. (224)

Jameson offers perhaps the most well-developed theory of mass
mediated pleasure in his readings of popular films of the 1970s.
Working from the theses established by the Frankfurt School, he
nonetheless finds that:

> works of mass culture, even if their function lies in the legiti-
> mation of the existing order—or some worse one—cannot do
> their job without deflecting in the latter's service the deepest
> and most fundamental hopes and fantasies of the collectivity,
> to which they can therefore, no matter in how distorted a fash-
> ion, be found to have given voice. (144)

Yet, having significantly singled out the utopian and the fantastic
as potentially liberating aspects of mass culture, both Stam and
Jameson still treat these qualities as *exceptions* to its general rule of
"ideological manipulation," maintaining a crucial separation between this untainted "kernel" and its surroundings. Jameson, for
instance, with his heavily Marxist interpretation, defines the utopian as "genuine social and historical content" (144) indicative of
"the ineradicable drive toward collectivity" which must be "de-
tected, no matter how faintly and feebly" (148) amidst the general
repressiveness of mass culture. While concurring with my findings
in *The Wizard of Oz* that the power of the mass media depends upon
its ability to direct the desires of its audiences toward its ends,
Jameson identifies those desires as preexisting and independent
of the media itself. In this scenario, the media makes a concession
of offering "some genuine shred of content as a fantasy bribe to
the public" in order successfully to "manage anxieties about the
social order" (144) so that even in "the most degraded type of mass
culture" some version of utopian content lingers "no matter how
faintly" (144). Yet, as I have established in my allegorical reading
of *The Wizard of Oz*, locating the oppositional potential in mass culture is not so much a process of discerning what is genuinely utopian and liberating in its manifestly degrading content, as it is one
of recognizing that the very propensity of mass culture to offer
itself as a utopian alternative to "real life" generates the kinds of
paradoxes which, in turn, make available to audiences different
kinds of readings than those intended by the dominant culture. In

other words, while the findings of critics such as Jameson and Stam regarding the politics of popular pleasure in general support my own, their formulations still maintain a separation between that which is utopian and that which is manipulative. To the contrary, as Dorothy's experiences with the Wizard reveal, within the general economy of the mass media, these two forces are *the same thing*, and so the media makes itself permanently vulnerable to exposure, even as self-exposure is its very means of survival.

As a result of this permanent paradox, then, in the same moment that Dorothy and her friends shatter the illusion of the Wizard's power, they also transform his lies to truths. For, if it is undeniable that they expose him as a fraud, then it is equally undeniable that their actions *confirm* his power because when all is said and done they have gotten what they have been promised even if not by the means promised. Dorothy goes home, due to the "real" magic of the red shoes, which she has had all along, and the Scarecrow, Tin Man, and Cowardly Lion each receive what they have been seeking in the shape of "material objects that symbolize the spiritual qualities" they feel they lack (Culver 97). This "false magic" may serve as an occasion for the film to moralize "that all such immaterial values are essentially unpurchasable" (97); however, in another sense, it is perfectly satisfying, for it is an empty fulfillment of a lack which was never really there in the first place. Through the course of their adventures, each character is given the opportunity to prove amply his possession of that which he is purportedly missing and, thus, seeking. The Wizard's superficial tokens provide the Scarecrow, Tin Man, and Cowardly Lion with all they ever really needed, which was the confidence to believe in themselves; in this sense the illusory "commodities" are not incidental but rather key to conferring that confidence even though, or more precisely because, they are not "real." As Stuart Culver asserts in his reading of the original book, the ending of the film also demonstrates that the Wizard's power "is perfected and not compromised by the scene of exposure and enlightenment" (104). This effect serves as a pointed reminder of the irresolvability of the mass media's system of power, for if it is vulnerable, it can always turn that vulnerability into a strength: in this case, the formidable ability to continue to appeal to its consumers even after, and sometimes as a result of, being exposed as a fraud.

Having arrived at this "perfect" Hollywood resolution in

which the characters all come together to celebrate the fact that they have gotten what they want, the Wizard departs in his balloon amid a sentimental send-off by his subjects, who reassure him that they still love him. With this shift in the governing power of Oz—the scarecrow with his "false" brains takes over—comes the moment of Dorothy's departure as well. Just as Oz's position has been altered due to Dorothy's interference, so too has Dorothy's status in the "real world" been significantly altered due to her adventures in Oz. Her return to Kansas is, thus, by no means a return to the status quo or a choice of the stable "real" over the paradoxical "fantastic." Waking up in her bed surrounded by concerned friends and family after the Good Witch sends her home, she immediately notices that each character in Oz has been strikingly reincarnated into a familiar face. Hunk resembles the Scarecrow, Hickory the Tin Man, and Zeke the Lion. Even the Wizard, in the shape of Professor Marvel, stops by the house to inquire after her health. Able to win the hearts and minds of the citizens of Oz, who adore her superior attributes as a human being, much as they adore the bogus Wizard, Dorothy is able to capture the attention and concern of those who so frustratingly ignored her at the beginning of the film. In other words, the drama enacted in Oz symbolically and materially resolves the drama which initiated her flight away from home. Indeed, the film's central conflict in which the evil, greedy, landowning spinster Elvira Gulch calls for the destruction of Toto is also resolved when Dorothy destroys her symbolic equivalent, the Wicked Witch. Upon her return to Kansas Dorothy's heroism in Oz translates into a reprieve for Toto in real life; her adventures act not merely as escapism from her problems but a way in which to resolve those problems. The roles Dorothy plays in Oz have direct applicability to the events in her "real" world because of their open demonstration of their constructedness. Even though a wide-eyed innocent while in Oz, the lessons she has been taught about the mediated nature of the Wizard's power leave her in good stead when she returns. The kind of self-reflexivity engendered by mass culture's invocation of an impossible utopian makes it possible for her to understand that the power at work in the "real world" is similarly constructed, opposable, and not natural. In this sense, consumers learn to subvert the "givenness" of the discourses which control their own lives as a result of their involvement in the constantly self-undermining discourses which constitute the media.

Discovering how, in specific contexts, consumers translate these opportunities for oppositional readings of the mass media into significant interventions in the structures of dominant power is an important subject for future research. My reading of *The Wizard of Oz* has uncovered two of the internal mechanisms of the mass media's function which provide these opportunities not despite, but rather *because* of, the way they construct its enormous popularity. In order to be properly legible to its audiences, *The Wizard of Oz* demonstrates that the media must also offer them the room to establish significant popular agency in the face of ideological manipulation: if manipulation is to succeed, then it must provide the means of its own subversion. By reforming our understanding of the mass media as a system of power which operates according to the kinds of pleasures it can provide, we avoid the danger of stigmatizing "the masses" for their ill-formed tastes, their ignorance, their victimization, and, hence, rethink the role of the critic as social reformer. As Colin Mercer insists, "an engagement of politics and cultural analysis with pleasure does not only challenge the complicity of popular forms, it also dissolves the certainties and authority of the theorist. No longer can the contradictory play of ideology be reduced to questions of meaning and truth" ("A Poverty of Desire" 85). A clearer conceptualization of the type of power by which the mass media operates necessarily leads to a greater appreciation of "the people's" own understanding of and active interventions in its workings. While opposing the pleasurable, the utopian or the fantastic may strike one as an oxymoron: it is possible to imagine once we recognize oppositional behavior as more than a straightforward refusal to participate in the system. Just as power based on pleasure is still power, oppositions based on the use of the mass media to "make one's dreams come true" or "escape from the real world" can still succeed as disruptions of that power.

Notes

1. For a thorough treatment of the issue of conservative backlash in the 1980s, see Bennett's "Marxist Cultural Politics: In Search of 'The Popular,'" which openly declares at one point that in "the struggle for a national-popular, the right in Britain has won" (4).
2. As Fiske insists, the "left has generally failed to win the support (or the

votes) of the people whose interests they support, and with whom they wish to be aligned" because "[w]ith few exceptions, left-wing theorists have failed to produce a positive theory of popular pleasure" (162).

3. See, for example, Tzvetan Todorov's *The Fantastic* for one of the foundational theories of this view of the fantastic. In contrast, Ernst Bloch's *The Utopian Function of Art and Literature* provides the classic treatise characterizing the utopian.

4. The years in which Baum's career flourished were a time of extraordinary growth for American consumerism: "In the short space of just thirty years (1890–1920) American society had established the institutional basis for a consumer society. Where once large retail businesses clustered in only a few urban centers, now, in cities across the country, a whole spectrum of stores . . . had come into being. What was remarkable about this pattern was that, almost uniformly, it far outpaced the needs of the population" (Leach 100).

5. Not only did Baum participate in these activities, he was a genuine innovator, founding *Show Window,* the first magazine wholly dedicated to the arrangement of show window displays, creating the first National Association of Window Displays, and writing *The Art of Decorating Show Windows and Dry Goods* (Leach 109–10). In addition, Tik-Tok, his fictional clockwork man, is considered the first "genuine robot to be found in imaginative literature" (143).

6. For instance, "[f]or three decades more money was poured into the musical than any other genre (the average musical made by MGM's Freed Unit coming in at well over two million dollars). For musicals Hollywood recruited the country's most talented performers. . . . Technically, the musical has also been in the vanguard" (Altman, *Genre* 1).

7. In contrast to that practiced in avant-garde texts, this type of popular, or more accurately, commercial self-reflexivity arises inadvertently out of the pressures exerted by media texts to attain impossibly utopian states. Rather than overt self-disclosure and challenging of conventions, this type of self-reflexivity paradoxically achieves similar effects in its overwhelming desire to conceal, conform, and please.

8. His precedessor in the books, likewise, is associated with a long American tradition of hucksterism, "connected with Barnum and Bailey's consolidated shows, and his magic was, all of it, pure fake" (Wagenknecht 28).

9. I am deeply indebted to the insights of Ross Chambers about the interdependence of power and oppositionality in formulating this conclusion: "At every stage, then, one encounters the law of oppositionality, which is that change of an oppositional kind is generated *within* a system of power even as it works against it" (xvii). And, also: "It is not easy to grasp the idea that the role of power, while it is inescapable and limiting, is also—as Foucault taught—enabling. The condition of there being change is also the condition that constrains the nature of change" (xviii). For the application of these principles to everyday life, see Michel de Certeau's *The Practice of Everyday Life.*

Works Cited

Altman, Rich, ed. *Genre: The Musical: A Reader.* London: Routledge, 1981.
———. *The American Film Musical.* Bloomington: Indiana UP, 1987.

Baudrillard, Jean. "The Masses: The Implosion of the Social in the Media." *New Literary History: A Journal of Theory and Interpretation* 16.3 (1985): 577–89.

Bennett, Tony. "Marxist Cultural Politics: In Search of "The Popular"." *Australian Journal of Cultural Studies* 1.2 (1983): 2–28.

———. "Theories of the Media, Theories of Society." *Culture, Society, and the Media.* Ed. Michael Gurevich. London: Methuen, 1982. 30–55.

———, Colin Mercer, and Janet Woollacott (eds). *Popular Culture and Social Relations.* Milton Keynes: Open UP, 1986.

Bloch, Ernst. *The Utopian Function of Art and Literature: Selected Essays.* Trans. Jack Zipes and Frank Mecklenburg. Cambridge: MIT P, 1988.

Brantlinger, Patrick. *Bread and Circuses: Theories of Mass Culture as Social Decay.* Ithaca: Cornell UP, 1983.

Chambers, Ross. *Room for Maneuver: Reading (the) Oppositional (in) Narrative.* Chicago: U of Chicago P, 1991.

Culver, Stuart. "What Manikins Want: *The Wonderful Wizard of Oz* and *The Art of Decorating Dry Goods Windows*." *Representations* 21 (1988): 97–116.

De Certeau, Michel. *The Practice of Everyday Life.* Trans. Steven F. Rendall. Berkeley: U of California P, 1984.

Fiske, John. *Understanding Popular Culture.* Boston: Unwin Hyman, 1989.

Fordin, Hugh. *The Movies' Greatest Musicals: Produced in Hollywood USA by the Freed Unit.* New York: Ungar, 1984.

Harmetz, Aljean. *The Making of the Wizard of Oz.* New York: Knopf, 1977.

Jameson, Frederic. "Reification and Utopia in Mass Culture." *Social Text* 1.1 (1979): 130–48.

Leach, William. "Strategists of Display and the Production of Desire." *Consuming Visions: Accumulation and Display of Goods in America, 1880–1920.* Ed. Simon J. Bronner. New York: Norton, 1989. 23–36.

McCabe, Colin. "Defining Popular Culture." *High Theory/Low Culture: Analysing Popular Television and Film.* Manchester : Manchester UP, 1986. 1–10.

Mercer, Colin. "Complicit Pleasures." *Popular Culture and Social Relations.* Ed. Tony Bennett, Colin Mercer, and Janet Woollacott. Milton Keynes: Open UP, 1986. 50–68.

———. "A Poverty of Desire: Pleasure and Popular Politics." *Formations of Pleasure.* Ed. Tony Bennett. London: Routledge and Kegan Paul, 1983.

Moore, Raylyn. *Wonderful Wizard, Marvelous Land.* Bowling Green: Bowling Green U Popular P, 1974.

Ross, Andrew. *No Respect: Intellectuals and Popular Culture.* London: Routledge, 1989.

Smoodin, Eric. "Art/Work: Capitalism and Creativity in the Hollywood Musical." *New Orleans Review* 16.1 (1989): 79–87.

Stam, Robert. *Subversive Pleasures: Bakhtin, Cultural Criticism and Film.* Baltimore: Johns Hopkins UP, 1989.

Todorov, Tzvetan. *The Fantastic: A Structural Approach to a Literary Genre.* Trans. Richard Howard. Ithaca: Cornell UP, 1975.

Wagenknecht, Edward. *Utopia Americana.* Ed. Glenn Hughes. Seattle: U of Washington Chapbooks, 1929.

The Wizard of Oz. Dir. Victor Fleming. MGM, 1939.

Zipes, Jack. "The Age of Commodified Fantasticism: Reflections of Children's Literature and the Fantastic." *Children's Literature Association Quarterly* 9.4 (1984–85): 187–90.

CONTRIBUTORS

Tom Cohen teaches literary theory and American studies at the University of North Carolina at Chapel Hill. He has published on literary theory, modernism, and film in a variety of critical journals and collections, and is the author of a book on the materiality of language as cultural intervention, *Anti-Mimesis from Plato to Hitchcock* (Cambridge UP). He is currently working on books on black figuration in Faulkner and the role of language in Hitchcock.

Samir Dayal taught in the English Department at Franklin College and is an assistant professor of English at Bentley College. His primary interests are in non-Western literatures and contemporary and postcolonial literary and cultural theory. Most recently, he has published on the work of figures associated with the Indian subcontinent such as Salman Rushdie, Bharati Mukherjee, Sara Suleri, and filmmaker Mira Nair. Other essays, focusing on theoretical issues in postcolonial studies, are forthcoming in several collections of essays. He is completing a book on Rushdie and is editing another entitled *Postcolonial Diasporas*.

John Fiske is a professor of Communication Arts at the University of Wisconsin, Madison. He has published widely on the media and popular culture. His latest book is *Media Matters* (University of Minnesota).

Helen M. Kim is a graduate student in English at the University of Michigan, Ann Arbor. Her research interests include postmodernism and popular culture. She is currently completing a dissertation on the oppositional potential of the mass media as it emerges in postcolonial contexts.

Peter McLaren is an associate professor in the Graduate School of Education and Information Studies, University of California, Los Angeles. He is the author of numerous books and articles on critical pedagogy, cultural studies, and the politics of liberation. His most recent book is *Critical Pedagogy and Predatory Culture* (Routledge, 1995). He lectures widely throughout the United States, Europe, and Latin America.

Robert Miklitsch teaches critical theory in the English Department at Ohio University. His work has appeared most recently in *Camera Obscura, Cultural Materialism* (Minnesota), *Minnesota Review,* and *Social Text;* his work on Slavoj Žižek and *Melrose Place* is forthcoming.

Mario Moussa received his Ph.D. from the University of Chicago's Committee on Social Thought and his MBA from the Wharton School of the University of Pennsylvania. He is currently an associate at the Center for Applied Research in Philadelphia.

Ron Scapp is director of the Graduate Program in Urban and Multicultural Education at the College of Saint Vincent, where he also teaches education and philosophy. He has published on a range of topics from homelessness to education. He is the co-editor of the forthcoming cultural studies volume *Eating Culture* (SUNY Press) and is currently completing a book on the issue of philosophical legitimacy and voice.

REVIEW

FERNAND BRAUDEL CENTER